4 NOV 2021

To Helen

Seeking Common Ground

Seeking Common Ground

A Theist/Atheist Dialogue

Andrew Fiala & Peter Admirand

Foreword by Jack Moline

CASCADE *Books* • Eugene, Oregon

SEEKING COMMON GROUND
A Theist/Atheist Dialogue

Cascade Books
An Imprint of Wipf and Stock Publishers
199 W. 8th Ave., Suite 3
Eugene, OR 97401

www.wipfandstock.com

PAPERBACK ISBN: 978-1-7252-7529-4
HARDCOVER ISBN: 978-1-7252-7530-0
EBOOK ISBN: 978-1-7252-7531-7

Cataloguing-in-Publication data:

Names: Fiala, Andrew, 1966–, author. | Admirand, Peter, author. | Moline, Jack, foreword.

Title: Seeking common ground : a theist/atheist dialogue / by Andrew Fiala and Peter Admirand ; foreword by Jack Moline.

Description: Eugene, OR : Cascade Books, 2021 | Includes bibliographical references and index.

Identifiers: ISBN 978-1-7252-7529-4 (paperback) | ISBN 978-1-7252-7530-0 (hardcover) | ISBN 978-1-7252-7531-7 (ebook)

Subjects: LCSH: Religion—Philosophy. | Philosophy. | Ethics. | Atheism.

Classification: BL51 .S38 2021 (print) | BL51 .S38 (ebook)

08/23/21

For my Aunt: "The Laughing Lady," Sister Maryellen Ryan. You have always shown me the way with your dedication to the poor and belief that change in the Church comes from our work within and in dialogue with others.

—Peter Admirand

With thanks to my friends in the interfaith community, who demonstrate the value of hospitality.

—Andrew Fiala

Contents

Foreword

The conversations between believers and nonbelievers, between the faithful and the faithless, are always plagued by the same disadvantage. Even in describing the participants, the default position is presumed to be the religious perspective, leaving the dissenter to "play defense." Even the description "atheist" begins with a rejection of the divine.

As a result, there is an unspoken contest in so many dialogues. Each side dares the other to disprove the deeply held convictions that inform their worldview. Too often, each participant walks away feeling smug—or injured.

Rarely do these exchanges take place on an equal footing, presuming that each participant brings a perspective that reinforces what members of society hold mutually. In the conversations here in *Seeking Common Ground*, Peter Admirand and Andrew Fiala plumb their convictions without the suspicions and resentments that have typified so many other discussions. The result, detailed in the pages ahead, enlightens both positions.

This volume appears at a moment in human history that is difficult even to describe. The isolation most people are experiencing during the global pandemic makes us yearn for the give-and-take of meaningful conversation. At the same time, the divisiveness of the American political season (and its parallels around the world), with a particular abuse of religious language and values, has created barriers to the very notion of respectful disagreement.

My work with Interfaith Alliance is devoted to protecting faith and freedom. As an organization, we position ourselves in that space that honors both the Constitution and the personal convictions that it safeguards. As a matter of fidelity to the law of the land, we seek to ensure that no person will be denied the right to their convictions of conscience and that neither a religion nor religion itself will be deemed favored by the government. As a matter of our faith convictions, collectively and diversely, we affirm that the law of the land is the law, never superseded as a matter of policy by the individual or collective beliefs or practices of any person or group of people.

For most of my adult life, I served in the Jewish community as the rabbi of a synagogue. In that capacity, I mostly promoted and defended the tenets of my tradition. When I transitioned into the world of advocacy, I was forced to ask myself about my responsibilities not only to Jewish tradition, not only to Abrahamic religions, not only to the many communities of faith in the mosaic of American life, but also to the growing population of Americans who profess no particular faith, whether out of uncertainty about their religious identity or out of deep certainty of their secular values.

My encounters and conversations with highly principled adherents of different philosophies and faiths convinced me that, our name notwithstanding, it was insufficient to set religious faith as the default in considering the civil rights guaranteed by the free exercise clause. Aside from the respect due to those whose worldview is secular, careful consideration of the presumptiveness of religious accommodations is necessary to ensure equal protection for all. A secular friend asked me, tongue in cheek, why a Jewish sabbath-observer should have Saturday off of work, therefore preventing him from subscribing to season tickets for his favorite college football team.

The essence of meaningful and respectful interfaith conversation is a willingness to affirm each partner's truth. Ironically, most people of conviction (and this is truer of those with deepest conviction) reject the notion of relativism in morality and belief. If you believe that only belief in Jesus as son of God and savior can rescue your mortal soul from eternal purgation, then the similarly exclusive claims of submission to the will of Allah and practice of the Five Pillars is a cause for sadness rather than celebration. If you believe in the one-ness of God and the singularity of the revelation at Sinai, the thirty-three expressions of divinity are a cause for polite (or not so polite) disdain. So much of interfaith discourse involves the comparison of my faith's ideals with your faith's inadequacies. Instead, people of goodwill try to retreat into identifying similarities in practices or traditions to find places of common ground.

But the workaround is dysfunctional when participants include those who do not subscribe to an external theistic (or cosmological) source for their worldview. The presence of an atheist in interfaith dialogue may be the most unifying element for adherents of established faiths!

That is why the decision to affirm seven virtues that frame these dialogues in both substance and kind is so important—almost as important as the extraordinary content of the conversations themselves. The virtues themselves are building blocks of a pluralistic society, one that is embedded in the ethos of the United States and has become increasingly presumed as other societies affirm the inherency of human differences. Admirand and Fiala have hit on the basis for careful reflection on how people of devotion to their own perspective can live together, not merely as neighbors (albeit halfway around the world), but as friends and full participants in the Beloved Community.

And more so, this dialogue is not simply a feel-good exercise in how two academics can arrive at similar destinations along separate paths. Instead, it is a critical look at their own deepest convictions (and, with respect, at teachings of different faiths and philosophies) as well as each other's. In the end, it is what this divided world needs—a way to agree on how we live together for each other's betterment.

In the end, modeling for other educators how to teach a generation of students to think critically while holding to their (eventual) convictions is the largest contribution of this volume. It is particularly satisfying to me in my mission of protecting faith and freedom, and it makes me hopeful that the next generation of academics, clergy, philosophers, and intellectuals—and the students they raise up—will secure these virtues for all people with integrity.

—Rabbi Jack Moline, September 2020

Acknowledgments

I thank Andy for being such a generous, open, and intellectually stimulating writing partner. I also (again) thank Dr. Charlie Collier for his ongoing support and acceptance of my work at Wipf and Stock. This is now book three at Cascade Books, which is becoming a positive pattern in my life. As always, I thank my wife, Kelly, for making life interesting and seemingly always knowing more than me (which can be really annoying, but adds to the interesting bit). I also thank my five fun, irrepressible kids, whom I especially like right now as they are all sleeping, so it's momentarily quiet.

—Peter

Peter invited this dialogue. He took a risk in reaching out to me. I took a risk in responding. Sometimes it pays to open those uninvited emails! Thanks, Peter, for the opportunity to learn, think, and grow.

—Andy

Peter and Andy also want to thank Emily Callihan for her sound copyediting, Calvin Jaffarian for typesetting, and Elizabeth Walker for the index. This book received financial support from the Faculty of Humanities and Social Sciences Book Publication Scheme at Dublin City University.

Part 1

On Virtue and Dialogue

Personal Stories and Academic Contexts

Prologue

Narratives of Faith, Doubt, and Unbelief

Dialogue and Lived Experience

Is it possible for atheists and theists to talk to one another? What would such a dialogue look like? This book attempts to demonstrate such a dialogue is possible and to show we each have something to learn from each other. Too often, religious institutions, cultures, the media, and publishers pit atheists and theists against each other, like cock fights, or a matador and the bull, with interchangeable roles. A red cape flutters—some argument about God existing or not existing—and one or the other charges or feints. Theists and atheists end up on opposing sides as a result of propaganda, rumor, slander, misunderstanding, and fear. We too often fail to look in and through another's eyes, to sense their worries and motivations, weaknesses, and all-too-human dreams and loves. The other was "the Jew" or "the Bosniak," "the woman" or "the homosexual," or damnably: vermin, cockroach, heretic, Christ-killer, infidel—so many words to distance and remove possible connection, empathy, overlap, reflection. Theists and atheists have also participated in such name-calling—and they too have committed violence against one another.

Often, face-to-face, personal interactions can stem the ignorance and hatred that divide us—a shedding of the impersonal. In academic circles, however, often under the banner and guise of objectivity, some scholars scoff or delete the turn to the personal and subjective, deeming the autobiographical thrust as self-serving, unnecessary, common, an intrusion; shadowboxing. Not really knowing the other, of course, makes the dissection and pummeling so much easier. The focus can be on the knockdown argument; the knockout question, perhaps converting in some evangelical context, or just jockeying for any claimed victory.

When that "other" is actually Andrew or Peter, Mustafa or Maria, one's neighbor, son-in-law, doctor, or car mechanic, the call for combat, for walls and slurs, for vanquishing and outlasting, rings hollow. There can still be pointed questions and challenges, a call for clarification and deeper explanation, but always in the context of mutual respect, hospitality, and humility.

Effective dialogue must be grounded in the lived reality of its participants. Discussions of ideas that are abstracted from the lived context of thinking and being quickly become debates. A debate, in this sense, is not a dialogue. A debate aims at victory: debaters seek to score points and defeat their opponents. But a dialogue is governed by a different set of norms. Dialogues aim at understanding. There are no victors in a dialogue; instead there are human beings who seek to understand themselves and the mystery of being human.

So, we begin our dialogue with a biographical prologue. What has led, inspired, or drawn the authors of this book down a path of theist-atheist dialogue and partnership? Let's hear from Andrew first, and then Peter.

Andrew's Path to the Dialogue

"When did you become an atheist?" My adult son asked me this question recently on a long car trip. It just so happened that Peter Admirand and I had been exchanging emails about the possibility of co-authoring a dialogue between a theist and an atheist. So my son and I spent an hour or so talking about my journey to atheism. I am thankful that my son took the time to talk with me, just as I am grateful for Peter's interest in this project. As I hope to explain here, one does not simply become an atheist. Rather, there is a journey and a path. We are always underway and in the middle of becoming. And our beliefs and commitments arise out of our interactions with friends, family, texts, and traditions.

I have always enjoyed getting into these kinds of discussions with my kids and my friends. I am fortunate that I have had many productive and interesting conversations about religion and other topics with close friends and family. I am a philosophy professor. I have the privilege of talking about this kind of stuff for a living. Dialogue has always been part of what I do and who I am. My whole life has been, in a sense, one long conversation and inquiry. It is difficult to imagine living any other way. So as I think about my path to the present dialogue with Peter Admirand, I want to assert that from my point of view dialogue is natural and normal. I realize that there are lots of people who do not feel comfortable talking about what they believe and what they don't believe. But for me, dialogue is a way of being. It is an existential anchor. I find meaning in thinking. I enjoy learning new things. And I like to be challenged to think about new ideas and defend my beliefs.

But my son's question left me with a furrowed brow and momentarily speechless. When did I become an atheist? I scratched my head. The honest answer is that I don't exactly know. So I had to think it over before responding. And as I thought, I also realized that I had a paternal obligation to answer this question with care. The context of my son's question was a longer conversation about religion and social relationship. We were talking about how difficult it can be to be nonreligious. My son was raised without any religion, as was his younger brother. This made our family a bit odd, living as we do in Fresno, California, in the heart of the Bible belt that is California's Central Valley. We have evangelical megachurches here, as well as a strong Catholic diocese. Many of the kids in my children's peer group are engaged in religious youth groups of various sorts. Around here the kids huddle together before school events to pray. But my older son and his younger brother were raised by me, a philosophy professor, whose work focuses upon religion, ethics, and politics. My sons are both independent thinkers with a strong sense of personal integrity. This often left them feeling excluded during student prayer circles or when the other kids went to church dances together. The other kids were not mean—far from it. But atheist kids simply don't have a place in a circle of prayer. Despite this, I think my wife and I have done a good job raising our children. They care about virtue and reason. They are kind, compassionate, and actively engaged in the world.

We never had our children baptized. Nor did we ever attend church or any other religious ceremony, with the exception of a few Christmases, a wedding or two, and some touristic visits to temples and cathedrals in far-flung places. We raised our sons with love and encouraged them to understand the importance of honesty, integrity, and hard work. We also encouraged them to learn about religious diversity and to respect the diverse people who live in our community, including people from a growing number of Jewish, Muslim, Sikh, and other religious communities. Our sons have turned out to be fine and decent human beings, who are open-minded and inclusive. And although we never viewed what we were doing with our children as a kind of experiment in atheistic child-rearing, in retrospect our children provide some anecdotal evidence for the claim that religion is not needed as a means of moral education and spiritual health. Furthermore, it is the experience of being excluded—including seeing the ways that my children were subtly and unintentionally excluded by the religious majority—that has led me to be deeply committed to the idea of religious liberty and the importance of secularism. Atheists in unfree societies are censored and even killed. It is much easier to be an atheist in a society that values freedom of conscience and religious toleration. The good news is that in my part of the world there is a growing number of nonreligious people who are finally coming out of the closet. The Pew Center and others report that nearly a quarter of Americans now admit that they are not religious.[1] And even though atheism remains in the shadows, the nonreligious are being invited into dialogue with our religious neighbors.

At any rate, I had a difficult time answering my son's very direct and simple question because that question is connected to so many more ideas and issues. And given the difficulty of being an atheist in a world that assumes that everyone is religious, I wanted to be clear about all of this. So when did I finally become an atheist? Well, the answer is that it is a long story that is still underway. I'm not sure, in fact, what it might mean to "finally" become an atheist. And what I have learned about religion and spirituality is that narrative and process are more important than any final statement of belief. Our beliefs are not merely stated as abstract propositions. Rather, they are embedded in narratives that involve biographical details and our relationships within communities of meaning and inquiry. So to answer his question, I had to tell my son some of the story of my own journey to atheism.

Unfortunately, this journey is not a dramatic story. There was no moment of conversion on the road to Damascus. Rather, there was a slow unfolding of a long conversation between myself and the world around me, which eventually led me away from religious faith. I suspect that this is similar to the experience of many of the growing number of nonreligious people. Phil Zuckerman has offered an analysis of how people end up as nonreligious.[2] He notes that in European contexts, there are fewer dramatic stories of radical conversion to atheism. In the countries he studied, it just seems natural not to have any religion. But he argues that loss of faith is more significant in American contexts. I suppose much of this depends upon the religiosity of one's community and peer group. If you grow up in a very religious community, it might be traumatic to break with the group. But if your friends are not religious, then it is no big deal to be nonreligious.

In my own story, I can only recall one moment that seemed traumatic—and it was very minor. One day, when it was clear that I was already not religious, a younger cousin outed me to my grandmother and the rest of the family. He said something like " . . . but Andy does not believe in God" as we sat down to pray before a meal. I kept my head bowed. I recall being nervous that someone would do or say something. But nobody said anything. My pious grandmother didn't flinch. We ate our meal and the subject never came up. Maybe they thought it was a prank. Or, as is more likely, it was

1. See Pew Research Center, "America's Changing Religious Landscape." For more recent data, see a report about a study that puts the number of nonreligious at 23 percent: Jenkins, "'Nones' as Big as Evangelicals."

2. Zuckerman, *Faith No More*.

just inconceivable to my devout grandmother that someone in her family might be an atheist. This is not "denial"—but more like lacking a category for thinking such a thing: for the religious people of my youth (at least in my retrospective imagination), it seemed that everyone was religious and that there simply was no such thing as atheism.

I don't blame my cousin for this, by the way. We were kids. I was probably sixteen and he was twelve or thirteen. My cousin was, like me when I was his age, active in his church. He sang in the choir and went on a tour of the Holy Land. And today, he does not go to church or send his kids to church—and likely identifies himself as one of the growing number of nonreligious people. I've talked about religion with him now that we are adults. He does not recall the episode when he outed me. Like me, he is no longer moved by religion. And he finds meaning in work, family, and enjoying the wonders of the natural world.

So as this anecdote indicates, I was raised in a religious home where religiosity was simply taken for granted. We prayed over dinner. We said our prayers at night before bed. We went to Sunday school. My grandparents on both sides were deeply involved in religious life. Well, mostly my grandmothers. The grandfathers seemed to find ways to skip church, even though they were bastions of the community who of course were members of the church and led the family prayers at dinner time. But despite the patriarchal dinner table, on both sides of the family religiosity seemed more deeply connected to the matriarchal side of life. My grandmothers usually sent me cards and gifts for birthdays and holidays that included Bible verses and had religious messages. My parents took me to Sunday school, which I mostly liked. They forced me to go to religious youth groups on weeknights, which I mostly did not like. We even went to church-related weekend camps and summer Bible camps. Of course, we celebrated the rituals of Christmas and Easter. And when the time came, I studied the creeds, read the Bible, took communion and was confirmed in the First Presbyterian Church.

But at some point, I decided that I didn't really believe in all of that. It is difficult to say when that happened. As I concluded my first stab at explaining my story to my son, I could see that he was not satisfied. I had not really answered the question after all. I explained the background religiosity of my childhood without explaining what led me to reject all of that.

The Lack of a Spectacular Conversion

It would make for a better story if there were some radical moment of conversion or loss of faith. Perhaps the story would be something like we find in

Dostoevsky, where an encounter with the problem of evil makes it suddenly obvious that a good and omnipotent God does not exist. Or perhaps the story would be more dramatic if one were raped by a priest; or if your church were destroyed by a tornado; or if you stumbled upon a secret Gnostic text that suddenly opened your eyes. But faith and loss of faith mostly don't work like that. Even people who are abused by the church remain in the church. Evils can be explained away. There must be very few miraculous conversions—faith takes sustained practice. And there must be very few episodes of what we might call radical de-conversion—loss of faith also develops over time and through sustained reflection.

Now it just so happens that we know more about conversion than we do about de-conversion. A central moment in Christianity is Paul's vision on the road to Damascus. This story and others like it, recounted by saints and mystics, provide a kind of script for thinking about religion, especially among those who emphasize rebirth and testimony. I recall being invited at one point early in my academic career to give a lecture on Kierkegaard to a group of Christian students. I had expected merely to give my lecture. But the event had me speaking after students came forward and offered their testimony—accounts of how they had encountered God and how God had entered into their lives. When my turn came, the students seemed to want me to offer a similar testimony. They thought that since I was willing to speak about Kierkegaard, I must be a Christian. But even though I understand what Kierkegaard says about faith, I did not have faith or a testimony to share (and if you know anything about Kierkegaard, it is not clear on his account that he himself had the kind of faith he discussed). Nor do I have a testimony to give about my loss of faith.

One problem is that we know less about atheistic de-conversion than we do about religious conversion. In our culture, despite the growing numbers of nonreligious people, atheism is one of the few remaining taboos. Atheists learn to keep quiet in mixed company. We don't brag about our atheism or publicly recount episodes of de-conversion. Nor, for the most part, do we want to convert others to atheism. We are on the outside of the various circles of prayers and community groups that form around the core of religion. There are some outspoken atheists—Richard Dawkins, Sam Harris, and the like. But they want the attention that their blunt and blustery nonbelief attracts. The majority of nonbelievers are probably like me: we prefer to not get into it with our pious friends and family members. We bow our heads along with others who are praying at public events or at our grandmother's table. We say "under God" when we pledge allegiance. We go through the motions of public religion and generally keep a low profile

and the biblical traditions taught about issues in applied ethics. I concluded in that book that we often do not know: the Bible is a text addressed to an ancient audience who did not know anything about medical abortion, social security, nuclear weapons, or gender equality. But that implicit critique of our tendency to fetishize the Bible was part of my own early experience of the text. I read the Bible as a child—in Sunday school and in confirmation class. I seem to recall that when I read the Bible, I was not overly impressed. I may be projecting this memory from my own present vantage point, but I seem to recall leafing through the onionskin paper pages of my Bible and thinking how silly it was that this book was supposed to contain the truth of religion. I have the copy of the Bible that was given to me upon my confirmation here in front of me as I write these words. This Bible was given to me on June 7, 1981 when I was confirmed into the First Presbyterian Church in Racine, Wisconsin. As I thumb through it today, I seem to recall that one of the oddest things that struck me about the Bible was all of the long lists of weird and foreign names—both of people and of places. What did (or does) any of that have to do with life lived in the 1980s in Wisconsin? It seemed harder and harder to believe that God—if there was a God—was somehow located in and concerned with some corner of the desert on the other side of the world in the ancient past. I may be projecting this into the past, but when I first read Rousseau's "Confessions of a Savoyard Vicar"—long after my teenage years—I recall thinking that I had independently discovered what Rousseau was talking about. The religion I had settled upon was a kind of a combination of deism, agnosticism, and Stoicism. It amounted to the idea that we should be good, do good things, and not get overly worked up about religion. At any rate, even as a teenager reading the Bible for confirmation class, it seemed difficult to believe that those obscure words were somehow more important than the other books I was reading, including the books of science and history that I read for school.

And then there are all of the religious people I have known. And this is where my interest in dialogue dovetails with my atheism. I have been living with and working with religious people my whole life. Nearly everyone I know is religious—even those who do not regularly attend a religious service. There are very few atheists in the world. Even the growing number of nonreligious people do not self-identify as atheists (only about 3 percent of Americans identify as atheist). Most people have some religious commitment, even if they do not regularly attend church or subscribe to all of the tenets of a particular faith. But what is important for me is that there is a diversity of these people. Some of my earliest memories of religion come from my early childhood, when we lived in a suburb of New York City. In elementary school I realized that our family was not Jewish because I did not get to do what my Jewish friends did. My best friend, Stephen Miller, was a Jew. He went to Hebrew School and Jewish summer camp along with lots of the other kids in the neighborhood. I did not get to go. At one point, I remember wanting to be Jewish because the Jewish kids seemed to have more fun—and they got to go to camp. It is difference that helps make us aware of our identity and our idiosyncratic beliefs. But this also leads to curiosity. I wanted to know what the Jewish kids were up to. Curiosity is the psychological and intellectual root of dialogue.

In retrospect, I'm pretty sure that my early exposure to religious diversity was an important factor in my eventual atheism, even though I don't recall ever meeting someone who identified as an atheist until I was in college. I feel that I've always known that there was more than one religion. Another relevant biographical detail has to do with the way that my mother's family (who was Methodist) and my father's family (who was Lutheran) did holidays. My mother's family—and ours—enjoyed gifts from Santa Claus on Christmas morning; but my father's family shared gifts on Christmas Eve. And in fact, since I grew up as a Presbyterian, I was aware that my family's religion was different from that of either set of grandparents. As a child, it seemed to be a given fact that there were different Christianities. This sense of diversity also included a sense that the Catholics among us were different from the Protestants. They had a catechism class (on Wednesdays, I recall) that was not open to the rest of the kids in the neighborhood. As I grew older, I met Mormons and Muslims, Buddhists and Hindus, and a variety of others (and again, very few atheists). My experience of diversity grew as we moved and traveled. I have lived in Tennessee, New Jersey, New York, Wisconsin, and California. Growing up in the midst of this diverse hodgepodge of a country, it seemed impossible to derive a true religion. During high school some of my best friends were Mormon. They had cool stuff—including the "mission" they all dreamed about going on and seminary class before school. But their faith was not for me. A friend shared the Book of Mormon with me—I also have that here on my desk as I write. Again, I'm left with the question of why these words matter so much that one would go on a mission to spread them. There are so many different books that it seems odd to simply pick one and remain wedded to it for eternity.

What I learned in all of this was that people believe all kinds of things—and that we could be friends, despite these differences. I also liked reading about these differences and talking with people who believed different stuff. But the more you talk and read and learn about religious diversity, the harder it is to believe in your own faith. I know that this is not always the case. Some religious people become convinced that their faith is the right one when they compare their faith to others. And a few religious people believe that they must convert people to the one true faith. But what I seemed to learn from my early experiences with religious diversity was that the religious differences seemed less important than whether someone was honest, kind, smart, witty, and fun.

Dialogue and Critical Thinking

Finally, in reflecting upon my path to atheism and returning to my understanding of the importance of dialogue, I also believe it is crucial to acknowledge that my parents and my teachers were committed to open inquiry and critical thinking. They were not philosophers. Nor were they radicals. I went to ordinary schools. My parents are college educated. But they are not revolutionaries. Rather, my family and the schools that I attended embraced the spirit of open inquiry that is part of the American tradition. To my knowledge, my parents never read Dewey; nor were my teachers engaged in projects of experimental education. But they taught by example. My own parents discussed ideas around the dinner table. They taught Sunday school and were interested in questions—such as whether Noah really fit all of the animals on the ark. And my teachers exposed me to a variety of literature and sources that made it easy to think openly and ask questions. I remember in the second and third grade reading texts that talked about Greek mythology. I loved the stories about Zeus and the rest of the Olympians. Those texts left an important impression. When I studied more deeply the Christian religion of my family, I was interested in how Christianity contrasted with the Greek myths. That contrasting set of narratives sparks reflection and philosophical questioning. In my case, it led to a lifelong philosophical quest, which has brought me into contact with a wide variety of people and ideas. I am an atheist who is involved in interfaith work. For several years, I sat zazen with a Buddhist community. I've traveled widely and visited a number of holy places. I speak regularly to religious communities and to atheist and humanist groups. I have attended the Parliament of the World's Religions, where I spoke about the Global Ethic and represented the need for humanism and atheism to be included in this work. And I have been vocal about defending religious liberty. My atheism developed slowly. But at every stage, this development involved dialogue. I want to continue to engage in dialogue with my religious friends. I still have much to learn—about myself and about what others think. And that is why I look forward to what I hope to learn from Peter Admirand and our dialogue.

And so, in answer to my son's question of when I became an atheist, I would like to say that I never *became* an atheist. I am not an atheist pure and simple. I am a human being who is in the process of learning and thinking. The supposition of the question "when did you become an atheist" is that one arrives at a foundation and stakes a claim. But my path is one of becoming through questioning and dialogue. From what I have learned about religion, I suspect that this is true for theists as well. One is never finally at the destination. Instead, we live in the middle of time, engaged in a process of becoming who we are. This existential quest involves a lifelong conversation with family, friends, texts, and traditions.

Peter's Path

"But faith, like a jackal, feeds among the tombs, and even from these dead doubts she gathers her most vital hope."[3]

When I was a child,[4] I thought I had to be a Catholic priest. This notion didn't spring from my parents, though my mother had once been in the novitiate. When she told Mother Joseph Dolores, her novice mistress, she couldn't take her final vows, she was "compassionately" admonished for putting her soul in jeopardy. My generally reserved father, unless ranting about Hilary Clinton and Barack Obama, did once mumble something about "it's not natural," when a discussion of priesthood arose (long after I was already married with kids). Devoutly loyal, he attends the same 11 AM Mass every Sunday, even as he finds the priest's homily grating and the singing awful. We can blame our parents for many things, but I can't blame them for the priest idea.

Somewhere along the way, I heard about vocations and God calling you. As the athletic son my dad yearned for, I presumed I had some kind of spiritual significance. And if God so called, all was decided—even if you had other ideas. Weren't we all Abrahams, told to respond "Here I am, Lord,"[5] if and when such a "voice" or face whispered? I knew I wanted to be

3. Melville, *Moby-Dick*, 32.

4. First Corinthians 13:1. Paul here dismissed his childish thoughts. It is an interesting passage to play off of Jesus' words calling for adults to be childlike, or welcoming the child. For an examination of children in the Gospels, see Admirand, "Millstones, Stumbling Blocks, and Dog Scraps." While this section is not full of "All that David Copperfield kind of crap," as Holden Caulfield moans, our childhood biographies have much to speak on our adult desires and hopes (Sallinger, *Catcher in the Rye*, 1).

5. Genesis 22:1. This "here I am" response—*hineni*—is of crucial importance to much of Emmanuel Levinas's work. See, for example, Levinas, *Ethics and Infinity*, 109–10; and Putnam, "Levinas and Judaism," 37–39.

a father, though, and foolishly, such an option (along with women priests) is not viable along the traditional path of Catholic priestly ordination. I'd like to end the story here, but as usual, my wife bore the brunt of my own stumbles and confusion.

She sometimes reminds me (she has a talent for this) that I once gave her a Valentine's Day card when we were dating in college saying I loved her, but then adding that I think I might want to be a priest! Talk about a mixed message and thinking primarily of myself. As James Baldwin wrote: "It is the innocence which constitutes the crime."[6] I couldn't have waited for a different moment, especially as such an idea came and went, like the moon behind clouds?

"Battling with God, is now my prayer."[7]

My remnant of religious faith is held aloft by doubt and questioning, my own caryatids, along with that childish voice, or the voice in childhood, telling me about priesthood. It's a strange mix: pious and sentimental, still borne by innocence and naiveté while reverently critical, too.[8] It sometimes feels like I'm a compass with a needle broken or a weather vane or sail when there is either no wind or a torrent of bluster, sending me spinning and seemingly going nowhere. I act like all is okay, not so much feigning wholeness (isn't it evident I'm broken?), but because a part of me believes this is how it should be. Don't we all grope for definitive direction, amidst life's outer and inner darkness, seeking any light, when some beams are false, an illumination-mirage, and others so faint you can squint until your eyes ache? The dark, meanwhile, encroaches and thickens.

Sometimes, maybe dreamlike, you feel yourself in a presence of a light so warm and tender, or big-bang intense, you want to linger forever. Such energizing moments and encounters, often personal, usually involve a shared space with those we love. Sometimes, you glimpse a flash of someone or something with a boundless supply of laughter, wisdom, compassion, joy. You are blessed when in their midst. Nietzsche lamented that he was "girt with light" which so many craved, while no one offered

6. Baldwin, *Fire Next Time*, 6. He is speaking, of course, on so-called white "innocence" in the context of white racism against Black Americans.

7. Hopkins, "My Prayers."

8. For a great example of a biblical scholar drawing on his academic expertise and personal piety, see Kugel, *How to Read the Bible*.

such light to him.[9] Some are drained by our needs; but others sustain and nurture us without depletion.

And maybe, a few of us, are even lucky, delusional, or attuned enough to feel something even more. This "more" is beyond the material, beyond words, tests, rationality, statistics, quantification, and brainwave scans, even more than what the atheist Loren Eiseley penned as "beyond Darwin's entangled bank of unceasing struggle, selfishness, and death."[10] It whispers and graces the divine.

In the context of the next, mostly faith-damning section—where faith better resembles Swiss cheese or a ship hopelessly scuppered, easy to sink—these thoughts are anchor-like, or resemble the loaves and fishes offered on a Galilean hillside two millennia ago.

Neither saint nor mystic, I am just another humbled being who once thought he knew so much, the right way to live, the right way of relationships or of faith, the right path for happiness. With each calendar year, I only seem to learn how misdirected and self-righteous I am. Is this a healthy or self-defeating development, a painful truth about the Delphic maxim?[11]

My religious faith can seem like a collapsing star in space, ever dwindling. Yet, while pulled towards atheism, too many odd feelings and coincidences offer resistance, a type of celestial counter-pull, a gravitational force pushing me towards some orbit of theism. Part of me would rather entomb these "truths," but exposure and honesty are demanded in the journey before us. Some of my later words may seem to seamlessly blend with much of Andrew's critiques and doubts of religious faith, but like a rubber band stretched almost to its limit, here is what ricochets me back to God, to faith, to something "more." It is also why, for me, the atheist-theist dialogue is indispensable for any religious faith operating in a world of too many unanswered prayers.

While I was in the Jesuit Volunteer Corp in Santa Rosa, California, we were scheduled for a silent retreat. A new experience, I was scared both that I would or would not hear anything. Weren't you supposed to encounter an inner voice, God "speaking" to you somehow?[12] I was desirous, even ambitious, that it would go well, whatever well meant. I still battle trying always to succeed, the need for others' acclaim; fearing waste and

9. Nietzsche, *Thus Spoke Zarathustra*, 105.

10. Eiseley, *Star Thrower*, 184. For Eiseley, compassion and love are what is beyond mere survival—especially in our connection to all life.

11. "To know thyself." Socrates's comments: "The unexamined life is not worth living" (Plato, *Apology*, 38a5–6). No doubt true, but much depends on what is examined and uncovered.

12. Above, Andy noted how he came to realize this "voice" was just his own, interior one—nothing more, nothing less.

the failures littered within and around me. But getting more anxious as the retreat approached, I tried to reassure myself: "Stop pressuring yourself. Don't worry if nothing happens. Don't even try for something to happen." At the time, I still strove to be a famous novelist. Kelly, the college girl, now wife of twenty-plus years, who had to deal with that stupid note on her Valentine's Day card, supported my need to get away for the year and head West to volunteer. She was still in Washington, DC, where we met at college, but then getting a MA in applied anthropology while on archaeology digs, slashing Virginia tree branches, tick-covered.

During the retreat, I was relaxed and sought nothing. Sure enough, I "heard" an inner voice, whatever you want to call it, unprompted: You should be a theologian. Immediate peace poured over me. When Augustine heard those repeated words, "Pick up and read,"[13] it still took a while before everything sunk in. While I first did a MA in literature after my volunteer year (so I could be closer to Kelly in DC), the formal theological path consciously began after that moment.

Some really strange coincidences also filtered into my hope and plan to move to Ireland. Kelly wanted to stay in New York, where we were then living in my Irish grandparent's ground floor apartment. My Uncle Jackie, though, was selling the house, so we had to move, but where? We had one child then and I was an adjunct English lecturer at four or five New York City colleges, still deciding PhD programs after finishing another MA, this one in theology at Boston College. I was leaning toward doing the PhD in Boston, but neither of us wanted to live so close, yet so far, from New York. "What about Trinity College Dublin?" I asked, my eyes widening. Kelly and I had both visited together in 1997 when I was on study abroad at Oxford. I had been looking for any excuse to return to Europe. She said, "Go and apply," and hoped it would end there.

Eventually, I was offered full scholarships at BC and Trinity. Kelly (to repeat) preferred we stay in New York, and no one in the States wanted us to go to Dublin. Only me. As a joke, I played a Boston versus Ireland game while running or walking about New York City or Long Island. I would scour for Massachusetts license plates, Boston Red Sox shirts, Boston University jumpers—anything linked to Boston was 1 point. And If I saw a shamrock or Irish flag, that was 1 point for Ireland. If I saw a Boston Celtic shirt with shamrocks, it was a wash. Anyway, I played the game numerous times, and yes, deep down I wanted Ireland to win, so maybe I was searching more than usual, but the way Ireland would "triumph" every time was eerie. Boston would be winning as I was about to reach my agreed endpoint on a run, and

13. Augustine, *Confessions*, VIII.29 (152).

then I'd see a random Irish flag outside some front porch and then a van would drive by advertising "Luck of the Irish Plumbing."

Living in our Irish grandparents' house, there was a part of me that felt they were watching over us—including Jack, who would have been their first great grandchild, living in their former house. When we moved in, I found my grandpa's old shillelagh hidden behind a couch. Okay, so we (and that shillelagh) ended up in Ireland; call it reverse emigration. What does it prove beyond my desire to be here?

It was not easy at first: Kelly, pregnant with our second child, hated Dublin that first year. We were economically strapped because I wasn't allowed to work full-time while doing the PhD and we had high student loans and credit card debt from various car and health bill charges from the States. But oddly, on numerous occasions, I would find money on the ground in the middle of nowhere, not just a coin, but bills. At least three times, 50 Euro notes (then almost 80 US dollars) seemed waiting for me in a deserted place. I don't find such bills anymore; maybe the Irish are getting better at not dropping their money or maybe it's also because we're more settled (Kelly loves Dublin now).

Another example: studying theology is one thing, but actually getting a decent academic job in theology is another; and Ireland is a small country where academic positions are held for life. As I was finishing my PhD, I did not want to leave Ireland, but you (usually) go where the job is, especially with a growing family and only debt. In retrospect, what I'm about to say is even more odd because Irish people do not usually share or talk about their accomplishments or work life. You could be in a running club and log miles with people for months and not know they're a chemist or lawyer or car salesman. A close friend only told me years after we met about the various languages he knew or books he wrote. There just isn't this desperate need to sell yourself that way. So, it's the first day of Jack's Junior Infant class, of about thirty kids. Kelly and I are standing in line in the schoolyard, holding little Jack's hand, more nervous than he was. In talking to whoever was near us, probably being asked why we were in Ireland, my studying theology came up. It just so happened that right behind me was Andrew Pierce, a theologian at the Irish School of Ecumenics at Trinity College Dublin. He heard me talking, spoke about his own role as a theologian, and also thought: "Hmmmm." He had just gotten a grant which included a salary for a full-time post to replace him for a year. When you live in a foreign country, you often are at a disadvantage because you don't know the system and you don't have the connections that are sometimes needed. Well, I fortuitously got my connection in Andrew (now a friend). Though I later ended up moving from Trinity to Dublin City University, I now have a lifetime contract until I have to retire at sixty-five.

A few lucky breaks and eerie premonitions, so what? Perseverance may be my greatest strength, with any success heaped around ample failures. Yet, there's still more: sometimes, something strange can seem to happen when I pray. To be clear, there is obviously so much diabolically wrong in the world, and I feel as helpless as anyone else amidst the sobering reality of senseless suffering and atrocity. But when I do pray in the presence of another—let's say an arguing couple on the street, a young homeless kid shouting at someone—I can't really describe it, but I feel this bond, a serenity. And this calm seems to manifest outward somehow. The couple stops yelling, the homeless kid lowers his tone. It's not a magical power, but there seems to be something there. "You just prayed for me didn't you?" my wife once asked, while we were in bed at night, and she was feeling waves of anxiety. She had her body turned away, facing the wall, crying. I just extended my hand over her, not touching, not saying anything aloud. Well, maybe it's a card trick, a one trick pony, but she immediately felt a sense of peace.

One more example, something I mentioned in *Humbling Faith*, but not this part. I wrote, or at least hinted, that I battle depression, but this period was a sullen, bitter implosion. I had just finished my PhD but dreams of a permanent job fizzled when the Celtic Tiger and the Great Recession crashed. A government hiring freeze meant even if a department wanted to hire me, they had their hands tied. My ego, my fragility, I just couldn't handle all the welfare forms, the waiting, the begging, the depressing scenes in various welfare offices; the heavy stress on people's faces; the kids who got the brunt of their parents' anger and helplessness. It wore away at me: think water on rocks; warming temperatures and icebergs. I tried to fake it with the best of them, but probably because I'm on the Autism spectrum, I couldn't hide it—even as Kelly likes to joke that my happy, sad, mad, and surprised face can be the same. She's mostly right, so I can laugh about it—especially as her outward emotions can sizzle, crash, burn, and glimmer within minutes (much like the Irish weather gives you four seasons in one day).

I couldn't laugh, though, when my then four-year-old daughter drew a happy smiling family picture, except for me. My oval face, with two dots for eyes and a squiggly line for a nose, had an upside down "u" for my mouth. Something had to change.

During that time, despite my best intentions, I was often a killjoy, a happiness-sucking vacuum, my own private black hole. Not exactly traditionally pious, one day I went to the Carmelite church on Aungier Street in Dublin, where the remains of St. Valentine are alleged to be. The last and only other time I remember specifically prayer-dialing a saint was St. Patrick through the "whither Boston or Dublin" episode.

I sometimes went to the Carmelite church (which incidentally I'm looking at now as I head home on the 16 Bus, typing away) because it's peaceful and pretty, and, perhaps as a romantic, I was drawn to the saint.

In a shrine, there's a painted statue of St. Valentine on a small altar, below which is a casket, said to contain reliquaries. You can light a candle nearby, and there's a spiral notebook where people write their prayers and intentions. Adrift and steeped in gloom, I scribbled, doctor-like, embarrassed, a few lines about needing help, that I wasn't looking for a job or anything tangible, just help to get me, for my wife's and kids' sakes, through this despondency, the inner-clawing, to try to be more grateful, not bitter and gloomy. After I arrived home, my wife immediately asked what had changed or happened. Attuned like an instrument of godlike precision, she said she felt a sense of peace from me. I smiled and smile now, even as I remain and will always remain humbled by that period. I must accept how a dark, depressed, bitter version, a Jekyll, exists within. I can't forget that I did, and likely will, need help, natural or supernatural, to keep aflame an inner joy.

"Then one by one they turned and blinked in the pitiful light.
'Help us,' they whispered. 'Please help us.'"[14]

There are celestial and earthly reasons to render the stuff above circumstantial coincidence and narcissistic fodder. When I academically pivoted towards theology, I decided to immerse myself in the problem of evil if my theological words and standing were to have any credibility. As I argued in my first book, there can be no viable theism without a viable theodicy. Turning in sustained depth to the memoirs and witnesses of the Shoah, gulags, genocides, and dirty wars, the theological landscapes and structures became rutted and enfeebled—rubble in my language. As theists could not credibly bypass theodicy, the result (if not atheism or agnosticism) was a fractured theology built upon a fractured theodicy. Doubt, humility, unanswerable questions, protest, and (perhaps unrealistic) hope need to be embraced if any religious faith can be maintained.

There are many reasons for any surviving faith to be fractured, and there are numerous reasons to no longer profess any religious faith. What this path signaled were two main follow-ups:

14. McCarthy, *Road*, 110. Such a horrific scene, here in post-apocalyptic fiction, has played out too many times in concentration camps, prisons, gulags, and slums. See, for example, Langer, *Using and Abusing the Holocaust*, 1–15.

1. I was exposed to the rich atheist response of many Jews towards the Shoah (along with the practice of theological protest among Jews who maintained some kind of religious faith despite the Shoah). I was also deeply challenged by Buddhist (and so nontheistic) interpretations and responses to real suffering (especially among Engaged Buddhists).
2. Because of the extent of (useless) evil, especially caused or sustained by religious texts, doctrines, and practitioners, I became more attuned to the need for interreligious theology and interfaith dialogue. *Loss and Hope*, my edited collection of essays by survivors of atrocity, interreligious practitioners, and peace studies experts, expanded many of these ideas. A robust but principled religious pluralism was the way forward—a pluralism that included atheist, agnostic, and nontheist accounts. *Humbling Faith* was my major follow-up, emphasizing the brokenness of all theistic and moral systems and so the need for deeper partnership, dialogue, and engagement.

I cannot quite sing with Wordsworth that "the things which I have seen I now can see no more."[15] I certainly see differently, and hopefully more compassionately and truthfully. Again, it is a swirl and barrage of faith and doubt.[16]

Is there a thread, a seamless path through and among these jottings; a cohesive unity of some kind? That would be deceitful. What I wanted here was transparency and exposure, even if that meant positioning myself on the verge of embarrassment, easily dismissible. There have already been too many clashes between atheists and theists, or maybe a detached, professional, soul-covering, nothing but harmless, polite discussion. Such "polite discussion" has its place, but I won't pretend or hide here. Too many atheist-theist discussions have been replete with feints and concealment, often claiming a crystalline certitude. Following Montaigne, "I speak the truth, not my fill of it, but as much as I dare speak; and I dare to do so a little more as I grow old."[17]

In the following chapters, I may try to justify belief in God. I will sometimes sing of my deep love (can I still use that word, with meaning?) for Christ. I will celebrate religious diversity and religious pluralism (unlike Andrew, I see the breadth and diversity of religious expression as a boon to religious faith).[18] I may have deep doubts about claims of uniqueness from

15. Wordsworth, "Ode [Intimations of Immortality]," 434.

16. For a moving account of a humanist's search for meaning, see Ozment, *Grace without God*.

17. Montaigne, *Complete Essays*. The essay is "Of Repentance" (610–21).

18. Religious pluralism is an important topic we will return to, as it certainly

any faith position (especially those of my Roman Catholic Church), but I cannot fathom a world coalesced from chemical happenstance, a vast, interstellar universe bereft of ultimate meaning or purpose, embedded in only what can be quantified and numbered, tested with microscopes, telescopes, video recorders, and MRI scanners. Such seems as naïve and confused as a boy thinking he had to be a priest, a young man feeling his ancestors were guiding him to Dublin, and a father believing a Christian Roman martyr helped restore his broken, enfeebled soul, so that a little girl never, ever again drew a family picture with her daddy having an upside down "u" for a mouth.

challenges, and in some cases seems to undermine, many tenets of religious belief, especially exclusivist ones. See, for example, Race and Knitter, *Schmidt-Leukel's Fractal Interpretation*.

Chapter 1

Dialogue: Virtues and Contexts

Andrew Fiala and Peter Admirand

In this chapter, we consider the context for our dialogue, outline shared principles of dialogue, and explain the framework of key virtues that guides the structure of this book. The general context for our discussion is the growth of secularism, theology's maturation, and the difficulty of the atheist-theist divide. In the background of our dialogue lie several decades of serious work on ecumenical, interfaith, interreligious, and inter-ideological dialogue—both our own work in this area and work done by a growing number of people who are interested in dialogue, in finding common ground, and who are challenging us to be more inclusive. The goal of this book is to explore how these ideas can be applied in a dialogue between an atheist and a theist, which is one of the final frontiers of the project of inclusive dialogue.

Dialogue, Atheism, and Inclusivity

Andrew Fiala

Dialogue has existed as long as thinking and speech have existed. Plato provides an obvious source, showing us that thinking involves an exchange between partners. Ideas and identities are created, developed, and understood through a dialectical interchange. The dialogue form was adopted by a range of thinkers from Cicero to Hume. We also see it in Thomas Aquinas's dialectical approach, where objections are raised and replies are offered. In the nineteenth century, Hegel, Marx, Kierkegaard, and Nietzsche contributed to a dialectical and dialogical conception of the movement of ideas. In the nineteenth and twentieth centuries, scholars have confronted the problem of shifting identities, conflicting vantage points, and the difficulty of discovering a universal, monological theory of everything. In the twenty-first century, the need for inclusive dialogue has become more obvious. We have become increasingly aware of diversity, pluralism, and intersectional identities. At the same time, the idea of dialogue has been analyzed, celebrated, and criticized in a number of ways.

A whole philosophy of dialogue has emerged and a "dialogical philosophy" has developed—associated especially with the work of Martin Buber. The ideal for Buber is for people to encounter one another in the I-Thou relationship. That is a dialogical relationship, which Buber also describes in terms of communion and community. Buber was actively involved in interreligious dialogue. Some of his thinking about dialogue comes from his experience as a Jewish "other" in dialogue with the dominant Christian majority. In his essay "Dialogue" (1929), after recounting a difficult situation between himself and a Christian (that was resolved amicably through dialogue), Buber explains what he has in mind in terms of dialogue, communion, and community:

> Each must expose himself wholly, in a real way, in his humanly unavoidable partiality, and thereby experience himself in a real way as limited by the other, so that the two suffer together the destiny of our conditioned nature and meet one another in it.[1]

Buber explains that the basis of dialogue is a "turning toward the other."[2] He contrasts this with monologue, which Buber describes as turning away from the other and toward the ego/self in what Buber calls "reflexion." Buberian dialogue has been developed and explained by Bergman, Friedman, and others: Bergman suggests at one point that reality is conceived in terms of dialogue—as the result of an ongoing dialogue "between God and man, between man and man, and between man and nature."[3] This way of characterizing things, of course, begs the question for atheists, who simply do not conceive the I-Thou relationship in theological terms. Indeed, Buber seems to imply that even when we deny God, we affirm him insofar as we relate to the world, to others, or to ourselves as a Thou. Buber says, "But when he, too, who abhors the name, and believes himself to be godless, gives his whole being to addressing the Thou of his life, as a Thou that cannot be limited by another, he addresses God."[4] But such a description seems to disrespect the atheist. The atheist denies that there is a God—but in dialogue

1. Buber, *Between Man and Man*, 7.
2. Buber, *Between Man and Man*, 25.
3. Bergman, *Dialogical Philosophy*, 2. Also see Friedman, *Martin Buber*.
4. Buber, *I and Thou*, 76. See Kovacs, "Atheism and the Ultimate Thou."

with the atheist, Buber suggests that in his denial, the atheist affirms God. And already here we see one of the significant challenges for this work: Can we have a dialogue across the religious/nonreligious divide if dialogue itself is understood in religious terms?

Of course, one need not be religious to think that dialogue is important. From a quite different perspective, the physicist David Bohm has pointed to the power of dialogue as a kind of group thinking, what he calls "thinking together" and participating (or "partaking") in "creating a common meaning."[5] He describes dialogue as "a stream of meaning flowing among and through us and between us."[6] But Bohm recognizes that there are serious difficulties for obtaining consensus. Religious people disagree with each other. Scientists disagree with each other. And, of course, religious people disagree with scientists. And so on. Bohm's ideal dialogue is an "empty space" with no rules, where there is no presumed object, agenda, or program. The idea is for meaning to emerge. But this ideal dialogical space is an ideal such as the physicists' ideal of a vacuum or a frictionless plane. In the real world, it rarely works this way. The question for the present dialogue between an atheist and a theist is whether there is an ideal dialogical space in which nothing is presupposed and no point of view is privileged. This seems unlikely, of course. Bohm reminds us that friction remains between people who would seemingly have much in common. He recounts the animosity and lack of dialogue between Albert Einstein and Niels Bohr, two physicists who would presumably be able to work in dialogue with one another—but couldn't.

Another example of a nonreligious approach to dialogue can be found in the work of American pragmatists, such as John Dewey, who emphasized the need for public deliberation and communities of inquiry, while also recognizing the social nature of the self. Dewey stresses that deep community requires "face to face intercourse"; and he worried about threats to community that occur in mass society, collectivism, and under the pressure of what he calls "the machine age."[7] Dewey argued that the "final actuality" of genuine communication "is accomplished in face-to-face relationships by means of direct give and take." He continued:

> Logic in its fulfillment recurs to the primitive sense of the word: dialogue. Ideas which are not communicated, shared, and reborn in expression are but soliloquy, and soliloquy is but broken and imperfect thought.[8]

5. Bohm, *On Dialogue*, 27.
6. Bohm, *On Dialogue*, 5.
7. Dewey, *Public and Its Problems*, 211, 217.
8. Dewey, *Public and Its Problems*, 218.

Dewey's warning against the imperfect and broken thinking that occurs in the monologue or soliloquy has much in common with Buber's similar warning. But where Buber waxes theological, Dewey reminds us that this process of dialogue and communication is central to the idea of democracy—and that the dialogue must be open and inclusive. Dewey explains that in despotic communities this does not happen. In despotic communities, people are isolated, excluded, and afraid to express themselves. Dewey explains that in a democratic community things ought to be different:

> In order to have a large number of values in common, all the members of the group must have an equable opportunity to receive and to take from others. There must be a large variety of shared undertakings and experiences. Otherwise the influences which educate some into masters, educate others into slaves. And the experience of each party loses in meaning, when the free interchange of varying modes of life-experience is arrested.[9]

We will return to the need for equity and inclusivity of the sort Dewey describes in a moment. But let's also consider a few other inspirations of the importance of dialogue. In Russia, Mikhail Bakhtin offered a similar assessment of the social and dialogical nature of the self. Bakhtin claimed, for example, that life and consciousness are inherently dialogical. He explains, "The single adequate form for verbally expressing authentic human life is the open-ended dialogue. Life by its very nature is dialogical. To live means to participate in dialogue: to ask questions, to heed, to respond, to agree, and so forth. . . . A reified model of the world is now being replaced by a dialogical model. Every thought and every life merges in the open-ended dialogue."[10] Bakhtin is a literary theorist. He discovers this principle of dialogical identity in his analysis of literature, suggesting that identity and life itself are expressed dialogically. In a different context, Gadamer has suggested that what happens in hermeneutics, dialogue, and conversation is the creation (or discovery) of a common language and a community of inquiry and interpretation. Gadamer says, "In a successful conversation they [the dialogue partners] both come under the influence of the truth of the object and are thus bound to one another in a new community. To reach an understanding in a dialogue is not merely a matter of putting oneself forward and successfully asserting one's own point of view, but being transformed into a communion in which we do not remain what we were."[11] Gadamer reminds us that when there is a genuine dialogue, the partners discover something in

9. Dewey, *Democracy and Education*, 98.

10. Bakhtin, *Problem of Dostoevsky's Poetics*, 293.

11. Gadamer, *Truth and Method*, 371.

common—and are themselves transformed by this process. While Gadamer develops his own thinking against the background of Heideggerian atheism, Gadamer remains more open to dialogue within and between religion and philosophy, theism and atheism—and he went on to inspire a generation of authors (such as Rorty and Vattimo) who attempted to move beyond the dichotomy between religion and nonreligion, beyond atheism and theism.[12] Of course, as our present dialogue demonstrates, religion has not faded away as a topic of discussion; nor have we moved beyond the need for dialogue between atheists and theists.

Indeed, in the twenty-first century, things have become more interesting and complex. This complexity was always there—even if unnoticed because of the blinders of traditional notions about race, class, gender, and religion. But today, the traditional account of dialogical theory must include the insights of feminists, queer theorists, and critical race theorists, who remind us that the dialogical situation often contains structural violence, inequities, and exclusions. This is true in the context of interfaith and interreligious dialogue. A "dialogue" between Jews and Christians will contain structural inequities, for example, tied to the long history of anti-Semitism. The same is true of other interfaith dyads: Muslim-Jew; Muslim-Christian; Hindu-Sikh; Buddhist-Christian; etc. These structural problems and inequities also afflict any atheist-theist dialogue. There is no frictionless plane or empty space in which dialogue occurs: dialogue emerges out of the background of history, injustice, and exclusion.

The problems of exclusion, oppression, and inequity have been brought to the fore by feminists, race theorists, and decolonizing theory, who provide us with critical insight into interfaith and interreligious dialogue—and by extension into similar problems in a dialogue between theists and atheists. Male dominance in religion and in interfaith dialogue has been called out, for example, by Catherine Cornille and her colleagues in a volume on *Women and Interreligious Dialogue*. Cornille puts it bluntly: "By all appearances, dialogue between religions is conducted mainly by and between men. . . . The majority of the scholars working on topics in the area of interreligious dialogue are men."[13] Similar points can be made from the standpoint of race: white religion excludes Black experience. Frantz Fanon put it this way: "The Church in the colonies is a white man's Church, a foreigners' Church. It does not call the colonized to the ways of God, but to the ways

12. See the dialogue between Richard Rorty and Gianni Vattimo, in *Future of Religion*.

13. Cornille, "On Women and Interreligious Dialogue," 1–2.

of the white man, to the ways of the master, the ways of the oppressor."[14] Fanon also points out that when there is dialogue between the colonized and the colonizer, this dialogue usually operates among and for the elites. Such a dialogue does nothing to decolonize the minds of those who have been colonized; nor does it include those who are most in need of being heard. This point has been made in a different way by John McClendon, who has critically examined Black American theology in his recent book, *Black Christology and the Quest for Authenticity*.[15] Drawing on ideas found in the work of James Cone and other defenders of Black Christianity, McClendon reminds us that Black Christianity develops as a response to white, racist Christianity. This suggests the need for ongoing dialogue (and decolonization)—for inclusive and liberatory dialogue that is aware of the history of oppression—*within* the Christian church. It also reminds us that there is no such thing as a simple dialogue between religions—or between theists and atheists. Which Christianity—white or Black—would be represented in a dialogue between a theist and an atheist? James Cone once said, "Black theology refuses to accept a God who is not identified totally with the goals of the black community. If God is not for us, if God is not against white racists, then God is a murderer, and we had better kill God. The task of black theology is to kill gods that do not belong to the black community."[16] Now, Cone is not an atheist, even though he provides the outline of a uniquely African American atheist argument, perhaps something like what Finley and Gray call "immanent atheism" or what William Jones calls "humanocentric theism."[17] But—and here is the point with regard to the complexity of inclusive dialogue—this conversation makes one wonder: "Why aren't there more African American atheists?" which is in fact a question asked by a prominent African American atheist (or "non-theist"), Anthony Pinn, in the first line of a recent book.[18] Would a dialogue between an atheist and a theist look different if both (or one) of the partners were Black? If both (or one) were female, queer, poor, a refugee, etc.? The answer here is obviously: yes. Our embodied reality matters—as does the set of meanings and traditional practices in which we were raised, as does the structurally advantaged or disadvantaged viewpoint from which we speak.

14. Fanon, *Wretched of the Earth*, 7.

15. McClendon, *Black Christology*.

16. Cone, *Black Theology of Liberation*, 28. See also: Jones, *Is God a White Racist?*

17. Finley and Gray, "God Is a White Racist." See also Jones, *Is God A White Racist?*

18. Pinn, *Writing God's Obituary*. Pinn explains his non-theism, what he calls "African American nontheistic humanism," in Pinn, *End of God-Talk*. For another discussion of African American atheism, see McClendon, *Philosophy of Religion*.

Before concluding this discussion of the challenges of dialogue, let's return for a moment to a real world example found in Buber's work. At one point, Buber engaged in a failed "dialogue" with Gandhi regarding Nazi atrocities and Zionism. Actually this "dialogue" was basically a couple of open letters that Buber wrote in response to Gandhi's public suggestions about the Jews of Europe—letters that Gandhi never responded to.[19] As Buber pointed out in response to Gandhi's call for Jews to adopt Gandhi's model of satyagraha, Gandhi's advice ignored the reality of the suffering of Jews under Hitler. Gandhi gave advice without entering into dialogue with those Jews he offered his advice to—without attending to their suffering or to their unique historical reality. Buber suggested that Gandhi merely offered general principles that were not thoughtfully applied to the real circumstance. Buber says, "The listener is aware that the speaker has not cast a single glance at the situation of him who he is addressing, that he neither sees him nor knows him and the straits under which he labors."[20] To have an inclusive dialogue, one must really listen to the other. This means that in light of the challenges of diversity and inclusivity mentioned above, the task of dialogue becomes quite difficult. A genuine dialogue must endeavor to listen to and include as many voices as possible.

But this is very difficult in a dialogue between atheism and theism. This dialogue has often simply reiterated the problem that Buber points out: it is typically monological, with each side presuming much about the other, while also failing to listen. We saw above how Buber himself stumbles upon this issue with regard to his suggestion that a godless person is still addressing God. Gandhi—who despite his conflict with Buber was also a proponent of dialogue and inclusivity—also seems to disrespect atheism in his attempt to include atheism in his point of view. Gandhi once said,

> To me God is truth and love; God is ethics and morality; God is fearlessness. God is the source of Light and Life and yet He is above and beyond all these. God is conscience. He is even the atheism of the atheist. For in His boundless love God permits the atheist to live.[21]

In the same discussion Gandhi also denies that Jains and Buddhists are atheists. His effort here is to be inclusive—and to reinterpret all traditions, including atheism, as having something in common. But to suggest that Jains, Buddhists, and atheists (!) are not atheists is to beg a number of

19. See Crane, "Faltering Dialogue?"

20. Buber, "Martin Buber to Mohandas K. Gandhi."

21. Gandhi, *Collected Works*, 334.

important questions. Atheists have also been poor listeners, often simply lumping all religious believers into a single category to be rejected. As Sam Harris once said, "It is time we recognized that all reasonable men and women have a common enemy. It is an enemy so near to us, and so deceptive, that we keep its counsel even as it threatens to destroy the very possibility of human happiness. Our enemy is nothing other than faith itself."[22] Harris is primarily aiming his attack at Muslim fundamentalists, with whom he claims it would be impossible to have a dialogue. However, if the more general claim is true—that faith and reason, religion and atheism, are enemies—then there can be no dialogue.

Already, it is easy to see that the question of whom to include in a dialogue and how to include them is complicated. Should atheistic Buddhists or fundamentalist Muslims be invited to the dialogue? Should militant atheists such as Harris be invited—or only inclusivist pluralists like Gandhi? And what about the marginalized and excluded of all traditions and faiths? One solution is to take care to create what might be called "socially engaged dialogue" or a "dialogue of social action" that calls into question hermeneutical privilege.[23] The point here is that the privileged must take care to listen to and include the voices of the marginalized and oppressed. Admittedly the present effort lacks the kind of diversity discussed here: we are white male academics. Our goal is less grandiose than the idea of developing a genuine dialogue that includes all voices. We are offering a dialogue that occurs from our own vantage points—one that we do not presume to be all-inclusive. We will do our best to acknowledge the need for socially engaged dialogue as we proceed, making a special effort to include voices other than our own who speak from vantage points different from our own. But—and here is another point derived from the general philosophy of dialogue—while the task of creating an inclusive dialogue is infinite, dialogue begins with an I-Thou pair.

A Model for a Religious/Nonreligious Dialogue

PETER ADMIRAND AND ANDREW FIALA

With this brief overview of some of the background and some of the challenges for thinking about dialogue, let's consider some models for framing effective dialogue. These framing models are useful, as is the general effort to construct models for dialogue. However, our contribution to this effort grows

22. Harris, *End of Faith*, 131.

23. Knitter, "Inter-Religious Dialogue and Social Action."

from a recognition that these models have usually been construed as models for interfaith or interreligious dialogue, which do not include atheists or aim to cultivate dialogue across the religious/nonreligious divide.[24]

In 1978 Leonard Swidler proposed ten basic principles ("the dialogue decalogue") for interreligious and inter-ideological dialogue.[25] We take this as a jumping-off point, summarizing these ten principles as follows:

1. **Learn and Grow.** Change will occur through dialogue. My understanding of the other will change as well as my understanding of myself.
2. **Across and Within.** Dialogue occurs between (across) different communities. But it also must occur within communities.
3. **Honesty and Sincerity.** Each participant must be honest and sincere. And each must assume honesty and sincerity on the part of the other.
4. **Compare Ideals AND Practices.** Fairly compare virtues with virtues, and vices with vices.
5. **Self-Identification and Self-Definition.** Each participant is entitled to define his/her own beliefs and identities. We should avoid imposing a definition on the other.
6. **No Preconceptions but Sympathy and Openness.** The goal is self-discovery as well as learning. And we should strive to find points of agreement.
7. **Equality of Participants.** Each comes to learn. Dialogue is not a one-way communication but a meeting of equals.
8. **Trust Must Be Established among Persons.** Trust is based upon common ground that depends upon what we share as persons—and not merely as representatives of a tradition.
9. **Self-Criticism Is Assumed.** The participants should not merely be defensive and assume that their tradition is infallible and has all the answers.

24. For example, Cornille's edited volume, *The Wiley-Blackwell Companion to Inter-Religious Dialogue*, does not include any discussion of atheism or of nonreligion.

25. Swidler, "Dialogue Decalogue ; and expanded to "Dialogue Decalogue: Ground Rules for Interreligious Dialogue." Also see Swidler, "Deep-Dialogue/Critical-Thinking/Competitive-Cooperation." The title was changed to "Dialogue Decalogue: Ground Rules for Interreligious, Interideological Dialogue" after 1984. Leonard Swidler was born in 1929. He is professor of Catholic thought and interreligious dialogue at Temple University and a founding figure in ecumenical, interreligious, and interideological dialogue (and cofounder of the journal, *Ecumenical Studies*). In the forty-plus years since the Dialogue Decalogue's initial publication, there have been various modifications and expansions.

10. **Put Oneself in the Place of the Other.** The goal of understanding includes experiencing the other's ideas "from within" through emotional and affective experience.

Swidler's principles are useful and important. But Swidler's own efforts have been explicitly focused on interfaith or interreligious dialogue—and more generally on what Swidler calls inter-ideological dialogue. In *The Age of Global Dialogue*, Swidler explains a significant problem for trying to expand the idea of dialogue in a way that includes nonreligion. He says, for example, that his idea of "dialogue on a religious subject [involves] persons who understand themselves to be in different religious traditions and communities."[26] He allows that this could include "ideologies" such as "atheistic Humanism and Marxism." But—and here is a crucial point—dialogues of the sort he has in mind are communal affairs, with the dialogue partners understanding themselves as members of a community/tradition and representing that membership or identity in the dialogue. Swidler concludes:

> There is clearly a fundamental communal aspect to such dialogue. For example, if a person is neither a Lutheran nor a Jew, she or he could not engage in a specifically Lutheran-Jewish dialogue. Likewise, persons not belonging to any religious or ideological community could not engage in interreligious, interideological dialogue. They might of course engage in meaningful religious, ideological dialogue, but it simply would not be interreligious, interideological—between religions or ideologies.[27]

This, of course, begs a significant question with regard to a dialogue for an atheist, who simply does not view himself as a member of a community and who does not enter the dialogue as a member of a tradition who is representing the views of that tradition or community. As we will have occasion to note in what follows, atheists do not often view themselves as representing an ideology (and there is an open question about whether there is any such thing as an atheist community)—even though, as often occurs in conversation with theists, there is an attempt to categorize atheism in this way. Of course, Swidler's point is that interreligious or inter-ideological dialogue must include some expertise and knowledge of the tradition that is in dialogue with another tradition. But again, there is an open question here about what the atheist is supposed to have knowledge and expertise about.

Nonetheless, Swidler's early model of dialogue remains useful. In our effort, we have however also found it useful to formulate another heuristic

26. Swidler, *Age of Global Dialogue*, 13.

27. Swidler, *Age of Global Dialogue*, 13.

or model—one that focuses on virtue. Building on several decades of combined experience in working on dialogue, we have discovered a number of key values, virtues, or commitments that are necessary for effective dialogue. We have settled on seven key commitments or virtues. There are other proposals for key values guiding dialogue. But we have concluded that an effective dialogue should be:

1. Harmonious
2. Courageous
3. Humble
4. Curious
5. Honest
6. Compassionate
7. Honorable.

These values form a useful heuristic that guides the structure of this book. This is a practical set of rules of thumb for effective dialogue. The list is not intended to be complete or definitive. Rather, it is offered as a pragmatic attempt to summarize our shared values, including what we have learned from our experience in working in concrete dialogical situations. Other lists of "virtues for dialogues" have been proposed. Swidler himself offers an approach that points in the direction of virtue. He suggests that dialogue is a "cosmic dance"—indeed suggesting that the universe itself is dialogical. He explains, "Dialogue—in its broadest, deepest understanding, the mutually beneficial interaction of differing components—is at the very heart of the universe."[28] He then suggests that there are four registers of dialogue, corresponding to four aspects of our humanness: dialogue of the head, the hands, the heart, and the holy. This corresponds to the intellectual, the ethical, the aesthetic, and the religious dimensions of human life. Of course, we see again a difficulty posed by this schema for the atheist—who may agree that life has intellectual, ethical, and aesthetic components, but who may disagree with the conception of the holy.

Our own approach does not begin with a conception of a human being that postulates something like these four essential features of human experience. Rather, our heuristic is constructed inductively, based upon our experience of what works in concrete dialogue. A similar approach has been offered by Catherine Cornille, for example, who offers us five virtues for interreligious dialogue: humility, commitment, interconnection,

28. Swidler, *Age of Global Dialogue*, 7–8.

empathy, and hospitality.[29] Building on Cornille's work, Knitter offers five principles or "movements" of socially engaged dialogue: compassion, conversion, collaboration, comprehension, and communion.[30] It is no surprise that there is much in common here. In a sense, it does not require much thought to understand that dialogue should be hospitable, collaborative, and so on. And there is a common effort here to settle upon a manageable number of principles or virtues, which is an obvious part of the effort to come up with a useful heuristic.

In our case, we have settled on seven virtues, organized and described in terminology that has appeals to an alliterative mnemonic that weaves among the concepts identified by some of the authors mentioned above. While Swidler gives us four Hs (head, hands, heart, and holy) and Knitter presents five Cs (compassion, conversion, collaboration, comprehension, and communion), we alternate Hs and Cs. There is nothing magical about this choice of words, letters, or the number itself—the point is to provide a memorable way to organize our thinking. Of course, there is something significant about the number seven, which corresponds with traditional notions of the seven deadly sins and the corresponding seven virtues of the Western Christian tradition. But the number seven has no mystical power here. There are various ways these ideas can be fleshed out and enumerated. Swidler's appeal to a decalogue reflects the Abrahamic tradition's Ten Commandments. A different approach might hone in on what the ancient Greeks saw as the four primary or cardinal virtues. But the number seven corresponds with the Christian tradition's attempt to build upon the Greek tradition, focusing on the four cardinal virtues—prudence, justice, temperance, and courage—and three theological virtues—faith, hope, and love. There is some overlap here in terms of the seven traditional virtues and our seven virtues for effective dialogue. But the lists are not identical. And as should be obvious, in a dialogue between a theist and an atheist, there will be an open discussion of the value of the seven traditional virtues. The virtues of faith, hope, and love would have to be reinterpreted in a non-theistic fashion for an atheist to affirm them, for example. It is possible to achieve some kind of consensus about a list of key virtues for human flourishing.[31] But such a consensus will

29. Cornille, *Im-Possibility of Inter-Religious Dialogue*.

30. Knitter, "Inter-Religious Dialogue and Social Action."

31. Some attempts to find a consensus about virtue have been found in the popular press, for example, in Brooks, *Road to Character*. A deeper approach can be found in Michael Ignatieff, *Ordinary Virtues*. In the background here is extensive work in virtue ethics from Aristotle through modern reappropriations of virtue. We should note that there is some skepticism in modern virtue ethics about the viability of a consensus approach. Alasdair MacIntyre has pointed out, for example, that virtues are

not be "metaphysical," i.e., based upon an account of fundamental human nature.[32] Rather, any list of key values will be built up inductively, will be incomplete, and will be open to revision.

Thus, the list of values identified here is not simply a list of virtues for individuals that postulates an account of human nature. Rather, it is a set of values that makes for a virtuous dialogical situation. These are thus not virtues in the traditional sense. Rather, they are key values that have proved to be effective in dialogue.

We will use the language of virtue in what follows. But we must be careful with this conceptual framework. Virtues are typically defined in terms of purposes and functions. A virtuous pencil is one that stays sharp and writes well. A virtuous dialogue is one that is: harmonious, courageous, humble, curious, honest, compassionate, and honorable. In order to make sense of this, it is important to provide a basic concept of the purpose and function of dialogue. A virtue is a characteristic that makes something excellent at doing what it is supposed to be doing or that helps a thing fulfill its purpose or function. A virtuous pencil stays sharp and writes well because that is what pencils are supposed to do. So what is dialogue for? What is it supposed to do? We propose that dialogue ought to aim at understanding. Dialogue is not debate. The point is not to defeat one's opponent or to establish epistemological supremacy. It is true that at issue in any dialogue are metaphysical and epistemological issues. But dialogue as we conceive it here is not intended to resolve metaphysical or epistemological questions. Rather, the goal of dialogue as we understand it is both less definitive and more down to earth. The point is to listen and learn from the other, while also representing and defending one's own point of view. Dialogue should bring people together despite their differences, rather than creating further difference and division. But the lingering presence of difference means that metaphysical and epistemological issues will remain unresolved. Indeed, one of the things that remains unresolved is the basic distinction between faith and reason. Notice that we have refrained from including "reasonable" as one of our key values—as this is one of the values that is most vigorously

tradition-bound and that it may not be possible to find a pluralistic convergence about virtue. See MacIntyre, *After Virtue*; and MacIntyre, *Whose Justice? Which Rationality?* We do not pretend to resolve the challenge of difference and diversity in virtue traditions here. Rather, our goal is to map out some consensus values that we have seen as being effective in dialogical encounters.

32. See Rawls on overlapping consensus. The point here aims at something less expansive than what Rawls aims at. We are not seeking to establish a set of procedures for liberal democracy. Rather, we are seeking to outline some key values for dialogue. In this sense, we are closer to Habermas than to Rawls. See Rawls, *Theory of Justice*, and *Political Liberalism*.

contested in a dialogue between theists and atheists. This is not to say that such a dialogue is irrational or that it does not require that we give reasons and offer logical explanations. Rather, the point is that what counts as "reasonable" in a dialogue may fail to pass muster with what is reasonable within a specific tradition or discourse.

To be blunt here, we must admit that there remain a few fundamental elephants in the room when it comes to dialogue between believers and nonbelievers. The biggest elephant is God. The believer affirms the existence of God; the atheist denies this. The believer also believes that there is some epistemic access to God—whether through direct experience, theological speculation, or faith itself. The believer thinks that his or her religious epistemology is reasonable enough—and that faith may in fact supplement reason. The nonbeliever is not persuaded by such knowledge claims. Moreover, the believer affirms that some specific set of revelations, narratives, and texts contain truths about God, about salvation, and about the meaning of life. The nonbeliever does not believe that such texts, narratives, and revelations contain metaphysical truth. And the nonbeliever may well believe that the believer's appeal to faith is irrational.

It is easy to see that a dialogue between believers and nonbelievers, theists and atheists, will be much more difficult than dialogues between believers. In ecumenical, interfaith, and interreligious dialogue, there is some presumption of a common epistemological framework (say that takes ancient texts as revelatory or that is willing to admit that faith is welcome alongside of reason) and some shared metaphysical notions (say that there is a reality that transcends the material world or that there is something important about the concept of the holy). In such dialogues, it is possible to agree to disagree about the details of a more general epistemological and metaphysical source of agreement. But in a dialogue between a believer and a nonbeliever, there will even be disagreement about the generalities of such a larger epistemological and metaphysical frame of reference.

Nonetheless, despite such fundamental differences, dialogue is possible. But for dialogue to begin, there must be some basic commitment to an overarching value that guides dialogue. We might begin from a basic commitment to harmony, balance, and reciprocity. This helps us imagine procedural constraints in dialogue. For example, in order to achieve harmony in a dialogue: one person cannot use up all of the time; there should be equal amounts and opportunities for talking, listening, and thinking. We might explain this in terms of reciprocity and respect. Or we might ground this in something like the "golden rule" that should guide a harmonious dialogue: each party must do unto the other as he or she would like the other to do for him/her. This also means that something like the silver rule applies: to avoid doing to others what we would not want them to do to us. But the grounding for the value of harmony is not to be located in some abstract and fundamental claim about what counts as reasonable dialogue. Rather, the value of harmony is grounded in a basic ethical sense of fairness and in a vision of dialogue as a process of give and take that depends upon reciprocity and balance.

Once the principle of harmony establishes basic ground rules for dialogue, there are pairs of values that guide behavior and attitudes in the dialogue. The participants should be courageous but also humble. This means participants should be free and feel empowered to express their point of view (which is part of what we mean by courage). At the same time, participants should be humble and moderate enough to make room for the other and learn to remain silent, to listen, and to admit ignorance or uncertainty.

The participants should also be curious and honest. This means that each participant should seek to learn something from the other, rather than seeking only to impose an idea upon the other or aiming to refute what the other is saying. But curiosity must be paired with honesty insofar as differences should be expressed and explored. The point of curiosity is not to convert oneself to the other's point of view or to refrain from critical thinking. Rather, we must be honest about our differences and critical of one another (and ourselves) even while we remain curious about the other and about those very differences.

Finally, the last pair of opposed values is compassion and honorableness. Compassion means that we care about the other and are willing to put ourselves in the place of the other, to the extent that this is possible. This value gets paired with honorableness because a sense of honor means that we keep our own commitments, even while we care about the well-being of the other. Compassion does not mean we give everything away to the other. There is still room for disagreement in dialogue, especially when such disagreement is grounded in the need to honor one's own commitments, values, and beliefs—and in the basic idea that we honor the rationality, goodwill, and sincerity of our dialogue partner.

These seven values will guide our discussion in what follows in this volume. In the next two sections, we outline the contexts of our dialogue. Andrew offers an account of the growth of secularism in the contemporary world; and Peter offers an account of the present situation in theology.

Contexts: The Growth of Secularism

ANDREW FIALA

The growth of secularism in the past few decades has been astounding. There are more nonreligious people now than at any time in history.[33] There is also growing interest in secularism among scholars and the punditocracy. For example, in 2008, the Nonreligion and Secularity Research Network was formed along with a scholarly journal devoted to this, the journal *Secularism and Nonreligion*.[34] At around that time there was substantial news reporting about the growing number of nonreligious people, prompted by research done by the Pew Institute and in response to the new wave of atheism associated with Richard Dawkins, Sam Harris, Daniel Dennett, and other so-called "new atheists." More recently, the number of nonreligious people has grown. According to a recent analysis by US political scientist Ryan Burge, about 30 percent of Americans are "nones"—those who say "none of the above" or "nothing in particular" when asked about their religious affiliation. This group has grown quickly in the United States. There are more nones now in the US than there are Catholics, Evangelicals, or any other single faith group. And the nones are growing fast, while other affiliations are declining. A similar story is occurring across the Western world.

At the same time, confidence in organized religion is at an all-time low. The Gallup poll reported in 2019 that only 36 percent of Americans have "a great deal" or "quite a lot" of confidence in "the church or organized religion." The causal story here is complicated. Scandals in churches prompt people to leave them; but at the same time, a general decline in religiosity precedes this, making faith more susceptible to the negative impact of such scandals. At any rate, the decline of trust in religious organizations and institutions parallels the growth of nonreligion.

This does not mean that the "nones" are atheists or even agnostics. Among the nonreligious there are those who describe themselves, for example, as "spiritual but not religious." Many terms must be defined here, which we will do in the next section. But let's get the term "secularism" on the table, since we are discussing it here. Secularism is a form of political organization in which church and state are kept separate. Political

33. Information in this section follows some of the following sources: Burge, "Growth and Decline"; McCarthy, "U.S. Confidence in Organized Religion"; Pew Research Center, "2. Young Adults around the World"; Pew Research Center, "Generational Cohort." Also see Sherkat, *Changing Faith*; Zuckerman, *Faith No More*; and Zuckerman and Shook, *Oxford Handbook of Secularism*.

34. See https://nsrn.net/; https://secularismandnonreligion.org/.

secularism takes different forms in different countries. But the term "secular" is also applied to a worldview, personal philosophy, or way of life that is nonreligious. Some religious people see secularism as anti-religious. However, the political structure of secularism can be pluralistic and inclusive, encouraging diversity along with religious liberty. And those who describe themselves as "secular" can also still identify themselves with religious terminology—as, for example, among so-called "secular Jews," who identify with Jewish culture and ethnicity but who are not religious. We will have to be careful as we proceed in using terms like "secularism" (along with the term "religion" itself).

At any rate, political secularism emerged historically as an attempt to find ways to deal with political power under conditions of religious pluralism. Oppressive and theocratic regimes attempt to enforce religious conformity. This oppressive structure can include totalitarian regimes that are secular, such as in China or the former Soviet Union. But liberally-minded, democratic secular regimes allow different religions to exist out of respect for religious liberty or out of a desire to establish a religiously neutral political sphere. Secular pluralism can create a system of separate communities who do their best to exist side-by-side under a regime of toleration. Toleration is often a kind of grudging acquiescence to the fact of diversity. But a more robust and hopeful effort occurs when diverse faith traditions encounter each other in their difference through interfaith and interreligious dialogue. But—and here is the important point—some kind of secular political structure is essential for genuine dialogue, if such dialogue is to include free and open discussions that are to occur without threat of political oppression.

I (Andrew Fiala) have written quite a bit about the need for secularism. I have also had the good fortune to work with interfaith and interreligious efforts in the US—both at the local level and in interactions with scholars and activists working nationally, for example through the Interfaith Alliance (presently led by Rabbi Jack Moline, whom I got to know when he visited our local interfaith community). At the local level, I have worked with school leaders dealing with religious diversity in the classroom, with local religious leaders who are engaged in defending the rights of diverse religious communities against hate crimes and in other difficult situations, and with scientists who struggle to work with religious believers. Essential in all of this is a basic commitment to secularism. I have also worked with Charles Haynes and the First Amendment Center, where I learned about the idea of finding what Haynes calls "common ground." For Haynes, the First Amendment's focus on free exercise of religion and its non-establishment clause provide a substantial kind of common ground that must underlie discussions of religion. Similar ideas developed out of my work with Dr.

Vincent Biondo and colleagues from across California, including Bruce Grelle from California State University, Chico's Religion and Public Education Program, who worked with me on a two-year project focused on "ethics, religion, and civil discourse": civil discourse occurs within free spaces of discussion provided by secular social and political life. I have also had the opportunity to interact with scholars in Europe, Israel, and Asia—from whom I have learned quite a bit about the diverse forms of secularism and the challenges facing religious communities around the world. Recently, I have become involved in the Parliament of the World's Religions, which was founded a hundred years ago as a place that diverse faith practitioners can come together to find common ground.

What has been remarkable to me in my interactions with hundreds of scholars and religious practitioners is that nearly all of these interactions have been peaceful and productive. This is remarkable because I am an atheist. But I have been welcomed by religious communities, fed by them, and have become friends with a wide range of people who see the world in ways quite different from the way I see things. I know that there are religiously intolerant people in the world. I know that people kill each other over religious difference. I also know that atheists have been executed. But there is a kind of common kindness, hospitality, and generosity of spirit that one finds among those who engage in interfaith and interreligious work. This is accompanied by a desire to understand and to be understood. Dialogical interaction among religious practitioners provides a chance for different people to explain to one another what they believe. These discussions are not focused on conversion or comeuppance. The goal of dialogue is not to defeat one's opponents and prove that the other person is wrong. Rather, dialogue is about self-exposure without self-righteousness.

This process is, however, more difficult when we encounter the religious-nonreligious divide. Among religious people there is a kind of shared sense that the discussion points toward mysteries that go beyond the ken of mere mortals. Serious differences exist between Christians, Jews, Muslims, Hindus, Sikhs, and Buddhists. These diverse faiths will never agree about the specifics of theology, spirituality, tradition, ritual, and community. But they agree that there is something larger and more mysterious than what the rational human mind can grasp. It is possible for these diverse faiths to agree that we can remain respectfully silent before those mysteries. And there are at least a few religious people who believe that there is a common core of the world's religions and that all religions are pointing toward the same thing. This is typical of the effort of the Parliament of the World's Religions and of efforts at interreligious dialogue that grow out of the spirit of Gandhi, who once said, "The soul of religions is one but it is encased in a multitude of forms."[35] Before Gandhi, Swami Vivekananda espoused this sort of idea in his speech at the first meeting of the World's Parliament of Religions in 1893, where he quoted a hymn: "As the different streams having their sources in different paths which men take through different tendencies, various though they appear, crooked or straight, all lead to Thee." Vivekananda continued, "We believe not only in universal toleration, but we accept all religions as true."[36] He concluded the first Parliament meeting saying this: "The Christian is not to become a Hindu or a Buddhist, nor a Hindu or a Buddhist to become a Christian. But each must assimilate the spirit of the others and yet preserve his individuality and grow according to his own law of growth."[37] This idea of assimilation and mutual growth through dialogue is inspiring. However, it is problematic for a number of reasons, most importantly because most religious people will refuse the idea that all religions are true. We can call the idea of assimilation and shared truth "reductive pluralism," as I have explained elsewhere.[38] Reductive pluralism informs the approach of a number of scholars of religion, such as John Hick, who wrote a book whose title makes the idea clear: *God Has Many Names*. In my own work on this issue, I have called for a different idea—that of "nonreductive robust pluralism."[39] We need to admit that there are deep differences among religions and not pretend that they all agree.

This is especially true when atheism is thrown into the mix. A significant problem for reductive pluralism occurs when religious mystery or the supposed one truth underlying all religions is presented to nonreligious people. Nonreligious people—and atheists in particular—operate in a different epistemological and metaphysical field. For atheists, these mysteries appear as superstition, humbug, or nonsense. It is quite difficult to engage in meaningful dialogue when one partner in the dialogue views the other as bewildered by bullshit. While the atheist often points this out with regard to religion, a similar problem occurs from the opposite direction, whereby the theist or religious believer in general thinks that the atheist's beliefs are demonic, nihilistic, or willfully ignorant. Again, it is quite difficult to engage in a meaningful dialogue when one partner views the other's soul as lost to a Satanic impulse. It is also difficult to have a meaningful dialogue when one partner believes that he knows better than his partner what his partner is "really" talking about. When Gandhi said, as quoted above, that God is

35. Gandhi, "Young India."

36. Vivekenanda, *Swami Vivekenanda*, 3.

37. Vivekenanda, *Swami Vivekenanda*, 19.

38. Fiala, *Secular Cosmopolitanism*, chapter 2.

39. Fiala, *Secular Cosmopolitanism*, chapter 2.

even "in the atheism of the atheist" it is easy to understand that this claim will seem insulting to many atheists. Atheism develops out of and against the theistic attempt to include and justify everything under the name of religion. One of the things that atheists rally against is the patronizing claim that they are really Christians or believers in disguise.[40]

The good news, however, is that it is even possible for theists and atheists to find common ground. One simple way that this happens is for the conversation to skirt and avoid epistemological and metaphysical issues. Much common ground can be found in discussing food, education, sports, art, and other issues of common human concern. This may seem like a weak strategy of avoidance. But human beings need to understand that they share a common humanity—and develop trusting relationships—before they can dive into the depths of epistemology and metaphysics. And even then, it is possible to find common ground. The Western humanistic philosophical tradition, for example, contains mysteries of its own. Wittgenstein reminded us that there are things we cannot say that must be passed over in silence. Consciousness remains mysterious as does the source of normativity (in ethics and politics). This remains true, even though we have developed an elaborate neuroscience and complex theories of metaethics and political philosophy. Culture, language, nature, and poetry provide sources of meaning that mysteriously transcend the confines of our individual brains. A place for common ground among theists and atheists can be found in reflecting on the value of love, beauty, justice, and other meaning-filled concepts.

I (Andrew Fiala) have had many fruitful discussions with religious believers at the venues I've mentioned above. But—and here is a criticism of some of my atheist friends—I have also seen a kind of small-mindedness on display in conversations with humanists, philosophers, and atheists. One example that is worth considering occurred when I was giving a lecture on religion and ethics to a fairly large audience of atheists in Southern California. My slides included a picture of Pope Francis. The audience booed and hissed when the image appeared. I was surprised and made a joke about this. And to be honest the audience was primed to have a bit of fun during my lecture. But—and here is the problem—there is a tendency among some atheists to be mean. They enjoy attacking religious figures and mocking religious believers. We can understand this aggressive anti-religious approach given the fact that atheists have often been marginalized and maligned. But aggressive atheists will generally not be invited to engage in dialogue with religious believers. And this is in fact a strategic political problem, given the fact that atheists can benefit from cooperation with religious believers in

40. See Nielsen, *Atheism and Philosophy*, 148.

activism that aims to support and expand secularism. Atheists and theists both benefit from religious liberty and need to work cooperatively in efforts to protect religious (and nonreligious) minorities. Such a practical alliance may make for strange-bedfellows. And there may be reasons for atheists and theists to part ways in some political circumstances. But the secular idea is in general a place of common ground and shared interest.

Context 2: Theological Resources for Theist-Atheist Dialogue

Peter Admirand

At the Second Vatican Council (1962–65), Pope John XXIII (and later Pope Paul VI) steered the Roman Catholic Church towards deeper engagement and dialogue with the modern world. This turn has had major significance for not only the world's billion Catholics, but in Catholic understanding, interaction, and living with non-Catholics, and in our context, atheists. While the work of the World Council of Christian Churches (and other Christian bodies) also deserves mention,[41] the depth and scale of the Catholic Church in the Western world meant their (late) participation in interfaith dialogue had wide consequences within and beyond the church. The landmark document in this regard was "*Nostra Aetate*: The Relation of the Church with Non-Christian Religions," which had a long, and somewhat windy journey before finally being promulgated by the bishops on October 28, 1965 after a final count of 2,221 for and 88 votes against.[42]

The document was originally envisioned to focus on the church's historic and troubled relationship with the Jewish people, but based on a number of concerns and reservations, it was broadened to include the church's relationship to all non-Christian religions. Some of the initial reservations were political: bishops based in Muslim-dominant lands feared a pro-Jewish document could signal a pro-Israel stance and place Christians in danger. As Christian life has sharply dwindled in the Middle East, many of these fears were not unfounded.[43] (Note that the Catholic Church did not officially establish diplomatic ties with the State of Israel until 1985.)[44] Less credible

41. See, for example, Pratt, *Church and Other Faiths.*

42. See, for example, Cohen et al., *Future of Interreligious Dialogue*; and Latinovic et al., *Catholicism Engaging Other Faiths.*

43. See Dalyrimple, *From the Holy Mountain*; and Jenkins, *Lost History of Christianity.*

44. See, for example, de Souza, "Israel and the Holy See."

reservations were also rooted in still-unaddressed anti-Judaic and supersessionist views.[45] Only two decades after the Shoah, and with the role of Catholic Christians and Christian institutions unaddressed in that genocide, *Nostra Aetate* was an important, but still only a first, "stepping stone" to address these major issues.[46] The Catholic Church, it should be noted, would not explicitly confront the role of Christians in the Shoah until the 1998 document "We Remember: A Reflection on the Shoah," written (with John Paul II's approval) by the Commission for Religious Relations with the Jews.

As a tentative first step in reforming (some would say reinventing) the church's views toward non-Christian religions, *Nostra Aetate* is rightfully lauded. From our atheist-theist dialogue perspective, the document is not without limitations and weaknesses, but all the major Catholic interfaith initiatives, meetings, books, and groups in the decades since have sprung from this core document. Bear in mind that the declaration never addresses atheists as a separate group. The point here is that this document inspired and guided the deeper interfaith dialogue, partnership, and interactions we see today, which includes atheist-theist relations. The omission of atheists and humanists in *Nostra Aetate*, however, remains troubling, and is not without negative consequences (confer, for example, the rejection of the phrase "a human right to freedom from religion" by the Vatican Observer to the UN in 2018).[47] While the post-Vatican II response to atheism and salvation, especially as embodied by Pope Francis,[48] stresses a God of Love, beyond our human understanding (so that we cannot know who is or is not "saved"), church proclamations like *The Catechism of the Catholic Church* seem to imply otherwise.[49] We will return to this essential issue in later chapters.

A very brief summary of *Nostra Aetate* is pertinent here. It opens stressing how "mankind" (sic!) is united in their search and seeking for ultimate meaning and purpose in our world. Today, we rightly challenge the patriarchal language, and atheists would also counter the document's structure as it moves from this broad universal aspect to brief sections on ancient peoples, Hindus, Buddhists, Muslims, and then the Jewish people. The implication is a movement towards those most near the ambit of the

45. For a helpful overview, see Cunningham, *Seeking Shalom*.

46. Lane, *Stepping Stones to Other Religions*.

47. Atheist Ireland, "Catholic Church at UN." The church contended that this position was meant as a defense of minority religions and the spread of religious pluralism. See Catholic News Service, "Vatican Official Warns."

48. Bentz, "Was Pope Francis Right."

49. See the troubling comments about atheism in *The Catechism of the Catholic Church*, 2123–27, 2140. http://www.vatican.va/archive/ccc_css/archive/catechism/p3s2c1a1.htm.

church (and so closest to the truth). Atheists would occupy a very marginal (at best) position.

The declaration's most important quotation (outside the ones on the Jewish people) is the following: "The Catholic Church rejects nothing that is true and holy in these religions. She regards with sincere reverence those ways of conduct and of life, those precepts and teachings which, though differing in many aspects from the ones she holds and sets forth, nonetheless often reflect a ray of that Truth which enlightens all men."[50] While proclaiming Christ "as the way, the truth, and the life" follows this expansive statement, the preceding words are nevertheless revolutionary in its context. Most Catholics would have been taught that outside their faith tradition, there was mostly (or only!) darkness and sin, yet here the church admits its deep respect to what is holy in other faiths. Not surprisingly, these words have been variously interpreted. The phrase "reflect a ray of Truth" has particularly divided Catholics. Some read the phrase to mean salvation is possible in other faiths and ways (and so is a major doctrinal change or points in that direction). Others contend the declaration does not advocate a pluralist stance, but does move away from an exclusivist stance and towards an inclusivist one. Thus, salvation is still through the life, death, and resurrection of Jesus and in the sacramental life of the church (established by Jesus and passed on through the apostles). But other faiths, (unknowingly) guided and led by the Spirit, can reflect the ultimate and complete truth of Christ. The foundational source, though, is not in the Vedas, Qur'an, or Buddha, but in the Trinitarian God. Such ways have often been called *evangelium preparatio*—preparation for the Gospels. In 2000, the Congregation for the Doctrine of the Faith (led by Cardinal Ratzinger, future Pope Benedict XVI), and with the approval of John Paul II, issued the controversial Declaration "*Dominus Iesus*: On the Unicity and Salvific Universality of Jesus Christ and the Church," which clearly rebuked more liberal interpretations of *Nostra Aetate*.[51]

For our purposes here, the essential idea is *Nostra Aetate's* call for Catholics to dialogue and collaborate with non-Christians, even as it seems to undermine such dialogue in a concomitant call to evangelize.[52]

50. "*Nostra Aetate*," §2.

51. See, Congregation for the Doctrine of the Faith, "*Dominus Iesus*." For commentary on the document, see Pope and Hefling, *Sic et Non*. During Francis's papacy, the church seems to have abandoned the strident and defensive tone of *Dominus Iesus*.

52. The question of dialogue and evangelization remains a fraught issue in many church circles, where evangelization is often included in the process of dialogue. See, for example, the 1991 document by the Pontifical Council for Inter-Religious Dialogue, "Dialogue and Proclamation." The document contends that a Catholic must always

While the declaration does not mention the Buddha, Muhammad, the Qur'an, or the Vedas, it praises religious followers of Hinduism, Buddhism, and Islam—a rare, even if all-too-brief moment. Hindus are lauded for their deep philosophical inquiries (and myths), and Buddhists for seeking a path to "perfect liberation," while "the Church regards with esteem also the Muslims."[53] Considering the fraught history of Muslim-Catholic relations, amidst wars and crusades, this is a subtly revolutionary statement. It praises Muslims for their commitment to belief in one God, their respect for Jesus (as a prophet) and his mother, Mary, and so calls for more dialogue and discernment. The statements on Judaism and the Jewish people are the longest in the document and, in many ways, form the bedrock for all Catholic interfaith engagement. The church stresses "her special" relationship with the Jewish people, springing from the *Tanakh* (the Old Testament). Jesus, the document stresses, was Jewish, as were his parents, the apostles, and earliest followers. In Nazi Germany, for example, it was common (and expected) to deny the Jewishness of Jesus. Jews today, *Nostra Aetate* also intones, are not to be blamed for the death of Christ (a common occurrence throughout the centuries). It also rebuked any form of anti-Semitism or anti-Judaism. Sadly, this language should not only have been stronger, but was especially needed from 1933–45. Note also that many in the US Civil Rights movement were dismayed that the document made no explicit comment regarding their just struggles against segregation and racism.

Theologically rich, the document also acknowledges what John Paul II later proclaimed as God's unrevoked covenant with the Jewish people. In an oft-cited talk in Mainz in 1980, the pope drew upon Paul's Letter to the Romans to highlight how God is still in covenant (in relationship) with the Jewish people. While this has since raised questions of whether there is a single, dual, or manifold covenant,[54] previously the general belief had been that the Jewish religion was now dead, especially after the coming of Christ. The Jews were deemed a stubborn people for holding on to their outdated faith. Again, this is no longer maintained by the Catholic

---

witness his faith, and so evangelization is also included in the process of dialogue. See also the more troubling and assertive text from the Committee on Doctrine and Committee on Ecumenical and Interreligious Affairs: "A Note on Ambiguities Contained in 'Reflections on Covenant and Mission.'" As noted by Swidler above, though, attempts to convert another (whether explicitly or implicitly) would seem to undermine the requisite trust needed in the dialogue.

53. "*Nostra Aetate*," §3.

54. See, for example, Kogan, *Opening the Covenant*; and Korn and Pawlikowski, *Two Faiths, One Covenant?*

Church, which most recently decreed that institutional attempts to convert Jews are no longer supported.[55]

As I was born eleven years after the close of Vatican II, many of *Nostra Aetate*'s revolutionary steps now seem either obvious or needing further development and growth. But on reflection, I benefited from being raised in a church where we needed to study, learn, partner, and dialogue with those of other faiths. Mine is the generation where "hell" and "purgatory" have virtually disappeared in the classroom and church, rarely heard in sermons. Jesus is the merciful and good shepherd, the friend, and the supporter. Especially growing up as an American (and a New Yorker), the reality of religious pluralism (in my case, mostly a strong Jewish presence in my Long Island town) heightened a dialogical faith. Claims about who was or who was not saved—rooted in the pompous statement: "outside the church there is no salvation"—were discomfiting, if not laughable. Such sentiments not only problematized original sin, but any claims on who (perhaps outside of a Hitler) would be in hell—certainly not the nice Jewish neighbors or Jewish friends on my soccer team. While childhood encounters with Muslims and Buddhists—let alone outright atheists—were then rare, interreligious exposure encouraged more theological openness. The ethical framework that mattered was whether you were kind to others. While raised in a fairly devout Catholic family, as noted previously, it was clearly a post-Vatican II, American Catholic family.

Context 3: Interfaith Locations and Initiatives

PETER ADMIRAND

Recent decades have seen a flowering of interfaith books, institutes, centers, journals, documents, conferences, and other initiatives. There seems no strong reason to expect this development to grow. In addition to listing a sample of global examples, I (Peter) will highlight some of my own links.

At Dublin City University, I am the director of the Centre for Interreligious Dialogue (CIRD). DCU, at present, is the only public university in Ireland that offers theology as a degree (which is taught in the School of Theology, Philosophy, and Music, in the School of Humanities and Social Sciences). CIRD, as our website notes, "is an academic centre committed to the study and practice of interreligious dialogue. The Centre seeks to promote research, teaching, and public engagement in the area

55. Commission for Religions Relations with the Jews, "Reflection on Theological Questions."

of interreligious dialogue in Ireland and beyond, including the religious-secular dialogue today."[56] It thus seeks to further the role of interreligious dialogue and engagement in the classroom and in broader social, religious, and political contexts. A key part is through interreligious learning and cooperation, serving as an academic platform through public events (seminars, symposia, lectures) and publications. The focus is deeply interdisciplinary. For example, in a 2018 symposium on climate change, CIRD gathered experts in various religious traditions on climate change (like Michael Northcott, Hilary Marlow, and Azizan Baharuddin, along with scientists, journalists, and other climate change experts). The symposium examined the impact, historical role, ethical positions, and value of studying climate change from an interreligious perspective.

Some recent events include a talk on Jewish ethics and climate change; a seminar dedicated to the 550th anniversary of Guru Nanak Dev Ji (co-organized with Dr. Jasbir Singh Puri and the Irish Sikh community); a co-organized event on Muslim-Christian dialogue with the members of TIECS (Turkish Irish Educational and Cultural Society); and a talk on human-elephant "dialogue" with Gerry Creighton, Dublin Zoo operations manager and an expert on Asian elephants.

The CIRD website also is useful for links to other interfaith organizations, initiatives, and centers. Such a list (by no means authoritative) includes: the Oxford Centre for Muslim-Christian Studies, the Woolf Institute, Humanists International (the International Humanist and Ethical Union, or IHEU), the Centre for Religion, Conflict and the Public Domain (University of Groningen), Berkley Center for Religion, Peace & World Affairs, Hickey Center for Interfaith Studies & Dialogue, Center for Interfaith Projects, Eastern Mennonite University Centre for Interfaith Engagements, Centre for Interfaith and Cultural Dialogue (Griffith University), Interreligious Dialogue Network (Australian Catholic University), the Centre for Christianity & Interreligious Dialogue, the Cambridge Inter-faith Programme, European Intercultural Dialogue Organizations, Three Faiths Forum, Unesco Forum for Interreligious Dialogue, Institute for Jewish-Catholic Relations (Saint Joseph's University), KAICIID Dialogue Centre, the Council of Centers on Jewish-Christian Relations, the World Council of Churches, Ontario Consultants on Religious Tolerance, the Pluralism Project (at Harvard), the Pontifical Council for Inter-religious Dialogue, the World Congress of Faiths, the Interfaith Peace Project, the Center for Muslim-Jewish Engagement, Interfaith Encounter Association, the Jordanian Interfaith Coexistence Research Center, and Bridging Spiritual Cultures.

56. See CIRD's homepage: https://www.dcu.ie/cird.

Unless a hybrid element in a novel of Joyce or Melville, such lists can seem anodyne. But in thinking how such a list is barely the tip of the clichéd iceberg, we can see how vast and pervasive the field has become. Note, though, that the inclusion of atheists and humanists in interfaith bodies still remains under-resourced and underrepresented. Hopefully this will change, both on account of the growing number of nones in the West (as Andrew highlighted above), and a vastly changed pluralist context. Going forward, interfaith bodies (especially sponsored by governments and not focused on specific groups—Muslim-Jewish initiatives, for example) should always include humanist and atheist voices and representatives.

In terms of a focused interfaith group, I am the Christian co-chair of the Irish Council of Christians and Jews, established in 1981, comprised of members of the various Christian and Jewish religious groups in Ireland, with the aims of promoting Jewish-Christian dialogue and partnership and working towards the elimination of any anti-Judaic or anti-Semitic language or prejudice, especially in judicial and legal acts. Principally, the council organizes public lectures in Jewish-Christian relations. In recent years, for example, we had Debbie Weissman lead sessions on the Talmud, while Dominican sister Sabine Schratz spoke on Pope Emeritus Benedict XVI's confusing (and seemingly unhelpful) comments on Christian-Jewish relations. Our local council is affiliated with the International Council of Christians and Jews, founded in Germany in 1947, with groups now in thirty-two countries. While engaged in interfaith work year-long, the highlight is the summer international conference. The conference of 2019, held in Lund, Sweden, had the theme "Transformations within and Between: How Does Our New Relationship Affect Christian and Jewish Self-Understandings?"

The yearly conference also has links to a young adult interfaith group, the Youth Interfaith Council, which also includes Muslims in representation and dialogue. There are also close links with the Abrahamic Forum, which specializes in dialogue among the three main Abrahamic faiths. While participation and attendance at an ICCJ event does not require Jewish or Christian (or Muslim) affiliation, most participants would identify as Christian and/or Jewish.

Finally, I will mention the Dublin City Interfaith Forum, of which I am an external stakeholder. DCIF was envisioned and founded by Adrian Cristea in 2012. It serves as an interfaith body of new and established religious groups in Dublin with close links to political, business, and social justice organizations. Most impressively, through the support of the Lord Mayor of Dublin, the forum produced the Dublin City Interfaith Charter, inaugurated at Mansion House in Dublin in December 2016. The Interfaith Charter, the first ever such charter proclaimed by a city, has since become copied and adapted around the world. As the forum notes, "The Charter has been agreed and signed by representatives of the Dublin City Interfaith Forum and deals with issues including religious freedom, inter-faith dialogue and the promotion of religious diversity in the city."[57]

Again, the range and scope of interfaith initiatives are impressive, but as discussed, more still needs to be done to integrate and include atheists and humanists in the conversation. One way of increasing such awareness is to highlight overlapping and mutual principles for theist-atheist dialogue.

Context 4: The Atheist-Theist Divide

ANDREW FIALA

As Peter mentions, there has been a substantial growth in interfaith initiatives. I have participated in some of this in my own part of the world. In Central California, I have been involved in our local interfaith community. One focus of these efforts has been to prevent hate crimes—and so our work has been supported by the law enforcement community. I have also been involved with the Parliament of the World's Religions and the national Interfaith Alliance. But, as has also been mentioned, the concept of "interfaith" implies that these discussions occur within and between religious people of different faith traditions. Atheists have often been left out of these discussions.

One reason for this is that there is still substantial work to be done between and among faith traditions. But another difficulty has to do with what often seems like a fundamental divergence and unbridgeable gap between atheism and faith. The atheist-theist divide has been created by long-standing and mutual hostility. For many long centuries, atheists were actively persecuted. Socrates was suspected of being an atheist. He denied the charges. But he was sentenced to death for not believing in the gods of Athens and for corrupting the youth. Atheists continue to be threatened with legal execution in some countries—and by extra-judicial killing by religious fundamentalists in other places. In return, atheists have railed against religion. In recent decades, a group of so-called militant atheists has appeared in the headlines, among them: Sam Harris, Daniel Dennett, Christopher Hitchens, and Richard Dawkins.[58] Some of the language used

57. Dublin City Interfaith Forum: https://www.dublincityinterfaithforum.org/resources/.

58. I discuss this in Fiala, "Militant Atheism, Pragmatism, and the God-Shaped Hole"; also see Fiala, *Against Religions, Wars, and States*.

by the militant atheists is hyperbolic: Dawkins has claimed that belief in God is a delusion; and Hitchens has said that religion poisons everything.[59] Such claims are not exactly new: a similar critique can be found in nineteenth- and twentieth-century authors such as Feuerbach, Schopenhauer, Bakunin, Marx, Nietzsche, Freud, Camus, and Bertrand Russell. Atheists in this lineage have argued that the Christian god is a silly myth based upon a false metaphysics and cosmology. They have also argued that Christians are fools to believe these things. Bertrand Russell argued in his widely read essay "Why I Am Not a Christian" that one of the reasons he rejects Christianity is because Jesus threatens people with eternal damnation in hell. A similar argument is made by David Lewis in an essay called "Divine Evil." Lewis sees eternal damnation for non-belief as exorbitant, excessive, and unjust. He says that a God who punishes nonbelievers eternally is more evil than good. And he suggests that Christians who believe this are also evil and lacking in compassion.

It is easy to see that the divide between theists and atheists can be quite wide. Of course, the same is true of the divide between Christians and Jews, Jews and Muslims, Christians and Muslims, and so on. The Abrahamic religions alone have engaged in crusades, anti-Semitic pogroms including the Holocaust, terrorism, war, and on and on. When we bring in the history of colonialism and the confrontation between Christendom and the rest of the world, we discover a similarly unhappy history. But—and here is the point—Christians, Jews, Muslims, and the non-Abrahamic religions are trying to find ways to build common ground and heal some of these past harms. Atheists and theists should learn from this and see if it is possible to engage in dialogue and find common ground.

But a significant problem remains for the atheist-theist dialogue, which makes it substantially different from other efforts at interfaith and interreligious dialogue. And this is the fact that atheists do not think of themselves as having a faith or as being religious. In a dialogue between Muslims, Jews, and Christians there is at least the assumption of the Abrahamic tradition and a common set of texts, heroes, and history. In dialogues between Abrahamic faiths and Asian traditions or Indigenous traditions, the issues are more complicated. But there remains some assumption of common ground found in the importance of ritual practice, inspired textual traditions, enlightened gurus/prophets, nonmaterialistic metaphysics, and the experience of transcendence in prayer and meditation. But atheists remain, for the most part, materialists. They tend to see ancient texts as having merely historical interest. They do not believe that there are gurus

59. Hitchens, *God Is Not Great.*

or prophets who have transcendental insight. And they tend to think that prayer and meditation have merely psychological (and not spiritual) significance. Sam Harris said, for example, in his "Atheist Manifesto" that atheism is merely a name for the "noises that reasonable people make when in the presence of religious Dogma."[60] Atheism is not a "faith" with the same kind of content that other faith traditions have. Christopher Hitchens put it this way in describing what he and other "infidels" believe: "Our belief is not a belief. Our principles are not a faith."[61]

The effort of the present book is to try to see whether we can make any headway in finding common ground between atheism and theism. As we can see, this will not be easy. There will remain substantial differences, especially when it comes to epistemology (how we know things and why we believe them) and metaphysics (what we think about the ultimate structure of reality, including the existence of God and the soul). In the present effort, we cannot deny those differences. But we might employ the virtues we outline above in an effort to engage in dialogue about our differences.

60. Harris, "Atheist Manifesto."

61. Hitchens, *God Is Not Great*, 5.

Part 2

Seven Virtues in Dialogue

Chapter 2

Harmony and the Global Ecosystem of Belief

PETER ADMIRAND, PRIMARY AUTHOR

AS I WRITE, so much of the world is burning.[1] Fires, like vengeful gods, rage across Australia, unleashing untoward destruction.[2] In California, summer fires in 2019 and 2020 leave a landscape resembling something out of World War I. The cover of the July 31, 2019 magazine of *The New York Times* proclaimed this smoldering, desolate landscape was not an outlier but part of our future and the horrific effects of human-orchestrated climate change.[3] In the Amazon rain forest, trees and wildlife continue to be scorched and leveled, especially with the election of Brazilian president Jair Bolsonaro. "It's worse," David Wallace-Wells writes regarding climate change and our ecological crisis, "much worse, than you think."[4]

"The world is in agony," begins the 1993 "Declaration towards a Global Ethic," the movement to bring together the world's faiths to unite for positive change around key moral principles and agendas. The declaration continues: "The agony is so pervasive and urgent that we are compelled to name its manifestations so that the depth of this pain may be made clear. Peace eludes us—the planet is being destroyed—neighbors live in fear—women and men are estranged from each other—children die! This is abhorrent. We condemn the abuses of Earth's ecosystems."[5] The condemnation of injustice, poverty,

1. Orphan, "As the World Burns."

2. "Australia Fires." See also Flanagan, "Australia Is Committing Climate Suicide."

3. Mooallem, "'We Have Fires Everywhere.'" See also Rich, *Losing Earth*; and McKibben, "Very Grim Forecast."

4. Wallace-Wells, *Uninhabitable Earth*.

5. See Parliament of the World's Religions website: https://parliamentofreligions.org/new-publications/towards-global-ethic-initial-declaration-fifth-directive. The idea was initiated by Hans Kung. See also Kung and Kuschel, *Global Ethic*, 13–16.

and global abuse continues in the "Declaration," which then expresses a hope and a plan that the world's faiths can put aside historical wrongs, misgivings, and distrust, and work together to heal the many agonies of our world. The call may seem as utopian as the eradication of rain forests, the melting of icebergs, and the desiccation of the Great Barrier Reef is dystopian, but then the stakes and the context can seem, and are, extreme.

While reflecting on global sea level rise, as depicted in recent non-fiction and sci-fi accounts (where the division between them is diminishing),[6] I then googled the phrase "the world is drowning." The search engine inundated me with even more depressing links, focusing on how we are drowned in trash and plastic. Such reality is especially evident in impoverished places, sometimes desperate to accept (or unable to refuse) endless mounds of other people's garbage. Think also of what is illegally dumped or ends up in our oceans and other bodies of water.[7]

Yet, as I write, sitting comfortably on my couch at home, looking out the window to a lush, emerald Irish field (which locals call "The Green"), these problems can seem a world apart. Distant. So, too, the wars and fighting in Syria or Yemen; the inner-city spirals of neglect and daily violence, whether in the slums of Haiti or Chicago, or perhaps nearby in Dublin Council Estates, but still, so far away. Somebody else's problem. Is the world really burning and in agony and drowning, or only for them, the unfortunate and unlucky? Is not the world actually getting less violent, as works from Steven Pinker's *The Better Angels of Our Nature* to Hans Rosling's *Factfulness* show with detailed studies and graphs? Aren't there always naysayers and doomsayers? Wouldn't we all be rich if we got a dollar every time someone proclaimed the end of the world?

In the Gospels, Jesus, or at least his early followers, genuinely believed the end of the world was nigh.[8] Portents were evidenced with the usual clichés of wars and famines, so banal and destructive that you can't blame many for later thinking, "This really is the end." Think of plague-strewn Europe in the Middle Ages or victims of genocide and slaughter. Who could imagine life after experiencing an earthquake that levels a city, let alone the cold stares and brutality of a Nazi towards one's fellow Jews; machete-wielding Hutus storming the church you and your family were praying in for shelter and protection; or the trauma of family members eating the corpses of freshly

6. Nonfiction accounts include: Rush, *Rising*; and Goodell, *Water Will Come*; while sci-fi and fictional accounts include: Robinson: *New York 2140*; Barnes, *City Where We Once Lived*; Lanchester, *Wall*; and Charnock, *Bridge 108*.

7. See, for example, O'Neill, "World Is Drowning in Rubbish"; "World Is Drowning in Plastic," para. 18; and Sieff, "World Is Drowning."

8. For analysis and commentary, see Fredrickson, *When Christians Were Jews*.

dead townspeople, as in China's Great Famine of 1959–61, perpetrated with seeming indifference by the Communist elite and their lackeys?

Yet, the world goes on. Some believe the same about the perils of climate change, or dismiss it with a shrug or skepticism (even as wealthy naysayers perhaps also keep an eye on developments of space colonization on the Moon or Europa). Let me leave aside ecological hypocrisy (confer the Hindu reverence for the river Ganges and its grossly polluted reality,[9] or the majority of us, believers or nonbelievers, who accept the reality of climate change but act otherwise in our daily lives). Of climate change deniers or those most opposed to drastic counter-action, the overwhelming majority profess religious belief, with conservative white Christian evangelicals a prominent subgroup.[10] Atheists have been at the forefront of climate change advocacy and so the onus in this chapter could be why so many religious people and traditions are ignoring, or worse, perpetrating the ecological crisis by a failure to make it a priority. Pope Francis's *Laudato Si'*, which I'll discuss at the end of this chapter, has been a sea change in this regard—at least from a doctrinal and church policy standpoint. But before seeking any call for harmony in that 2015 document, I will delve further into the meaning, challenges, and limitations of this foundational virtue, especially in the context of atheist-theist dialogue.

I first examine the Confucian sense of creative tension in harmony and then harmony as the mean or middle way. While praising such a path, I then grapple with the question of Jesus and moderation—is not his path radical? After touching on arguments against harmony as passive, I raise the issue of whether agnosticism should serve as a middle way between atheism and theism and whether it makes sense to speak of a mean between faith and doubt. I close with how Indigenous faiths can help serve as a guide to harmony, especially in the area of ecological harmony.

Harmony's Creative Tensions

Harmony, often linked with the great Eastern religious systems of Confucianism, Taoism, and Buddhism, seeks a space or position that achieves equilibrium and stability, often at some midway point between polar opposites. The Chinese symbol of the yin and yang best represents this conversion of apparent opposites (or dualistic thinking). We all know the image of a circle divided in half by a swirly line, one part white, the other black, with

9. See Mallet, *River of Life*.

10. See Veldman, *Gospel of Climate Skepticism*. See also the call by Islamic Relief Worldwide, "Muslims Must Take Action."

each often containing a smaller circle of the opposite color. Such an image challenges the notion of a bifurcated or Manichaean world of opposition and clashing, but shows that so-called opposites are often contained within one another and are actually interconnected, interdependent, and ultimately one. As the Taoist master Chuang-Tzu proclaims, "To be in harmony with all people is called human happiness; to be in harmony with heaven, this is called heavenly happiness."[11] Such heavenly happiness is an integration of all with the cosmos, uniting sentient and non-sentient life.[12]

In Confucianism, societal peace and functioning revolve around the principles of compassion (*ren*) grounded in the notion of practicing propriety and respect (*li*) between various strands and strata in society: ruler/citizen; husband/wife; father/son; older brother/younger brother, among friends, and so on. Not eliding difference or claims of superiority, such harmony should radiate from above through actions of the Ruler of Heaven and the sages (or wise men). All individuals, through *ren*, should respect their roles and status towards others in various relationships. As Roger T. Aims writes, "Indeed, it is only when tension that emerges from the real differences that obtain among things truly make a difference for each other that an ideal of a complex, diverse, and inclusive Confucian harmony can be attained."[13] This "creative tension," as Chenyang Li argues, is necessary for any lasting harmony to occur.[14]

Highlighting the need for creative tension, in the hopes of harmony, is another solid starting point for our atheist-theist dialogue, for if there are any polar opposites in the history of intellectual and spiritual thought and practice (at least in the West), it is the atheist-theist divide. Historically, there has been little evidence of harmony between atheist and theist adherents. Distrust, bias, persecution, flogging, burning—the drive to remove, convert, privatize, or conquer, have been the usual aims and rituals. A word like "harmony," however, can seem to imply the erasure of distinction and boundaries, as if terms like "theist" or "atheist" melt away.

Perhaps in some Taoist or Meister Eckhart(ian) "beyond," individuals may feel they have transcended all linguistic, terrestrial binaries, or think of Nietzche's transvaluation of values, sometimes correctly showing that what is deemed "good," "proper," or "right" is not, or should not be so. Recall, moreover, how the early Christians of the Roman Empire were deemed atheists, as were other theists who challenged or critiqued the

11. Chuang Tzu, *Book of Chuang Tzu*, 107.

12. For more on harmony in Taoism see, Deng, *Everyday Tao*.

13. Ames, "Foreword," xi–xii.

14. Li, *Confucian Philosophy of Harmony*, 1.

dominant religious understanding of their times, like Spinoza, Hobbes, Newton, or Locke. Atheists like Chris Stedman have even been derided as faitheists for their opposition to New Atheist invective and willingness to partner with and highlight what is good and valuable in some theist positions and religions.[15]

While a case can be made for transcending or blending terms like "atheist" or "theist," here I want to highlight how Li's interpretation of Confucian harmony is particularly helpful in the context of atheist-theist dialogue and relations for maintaining difference and highlighting the value and role of tension.

As a theist, my hope here is that this dialogue of creative tensions can help foster a greater harmony both within myself as a theist and Andy as an atheist and so serve as a model for harmonious interactions between theists and atheists. This harmony, or better, harmonies, is present and nudging all the virtues highlighted in this work, while also challenging itself (harmony as and within harmony). Let's remember that seeking some kinds of harmony can have the sniff of totalitarianism and Orwellian doublespeak. Harmony is not universal sameness. To repeat: we seek a harmony that thrives and celebrates diversity and maintains unique identities. Such identities often include myopic, subjective, and contradictory views. Ours is a harmony sought amidst a seemingly unbridgeable gap.

As a theist, what of my views or relationship with God? Here, creative tension as conducive to harmony is also pertinent. This is especially the case when I reflect and grapple with the problem of useless, extensive agony and suffering in our world and any claim of a loving, omnipotent God (the problem of theodicy) which I'll return to later in this book. There, too, I will argue for a healthy tension, a kind of harmony of doubt and faith.

Harmony as the Mean or Middle Way

In Aristotle's *The Nicomachean Ethics*, the fourth-century BCE philosopher advocates a life of virtue, inculcated and taught, through habit, coalescing in one's character as virtuous. One aims, so he contends, for the mean, the point midway between too extremes, and so absorbing what is good and best in each. The courageous man, then (and Aristotle would have in mind a male, property-owning citizen of the polis), would avoid the extremes of recklessness and cowardice, and so live and embody a courage that is grounded in reality but still aware of the risks and demands of the brave.

15. Stedman, *Faitheist*, 1.

For Buddhists, the Middle Way is espoused as the path to forge and follow for enlightenment. The historical Buddha, Siddhartha Gautama, born a prince, had lived a life of pleasure and self-contentment until realizing the world he inhabited was false and manufactured. Seeking meaning, he then practiced an extreme form of asceticism, deteriorating to mere skin and bones. One day, he realized such an extreme path was not the way either, and to the dismay of his followers, he took some sustenance. They abandoned him, thinking he was a fraud. Undeterred, he meditated under the Bodhi tree, saw visions of all his previous lives, and reached liberation (moksha). After some prodding, he then shared the Four Noble Truths and especially the eightfold path as the Middle Way between the unhealthy extremes he had previously lived. Comprising such practices as right judgment and right mindfulness, it is built on the notion that everything comes from everything, so there is no isolated, self-referential being, no real you or me. We are interdependent (resembling, in many ways, the *ubuntu* saying,"I am because we are").

For many Muslims, Islam is also deemed a Middle Way that practices and promotes moderation.[16] As the last of the Abrahamic faiths, it corrects and moderates where earlier paths went astray or fell into unhealthy or extreme practices or beliefs. In Judaism, Maimonides, the great thirteenth-century sage and lawgiver, advocated a middle way in which one is "neither . . . easily angered" nor, like the dead, "does not feel." As Rabbi Edythe Held Mencher notes, Maimonides "taught that through study and cultivation of new actions and ways of thinking, each of us can be elevated to 'walk in God's ways.'"[17] The key, though, is to make sure even one's pursuit of moderation is also in moderation. No one way or path can be universally suitable, and even seeking and practicing moderation or striving for some perfect pitch or gradient of harmony can be unwarranted, unhealthy, or perhaps boring. Think of the scattershot beauty of a painting by Jackson Pollock, or the odd and fanciful architectural flourishing of Antoni Gaudí. Palladian proportion and balance have their merits, but would we want every building to mirror one another this way?

Jesus and Harmony

While Christianity remains a minority religion in most of Asia, Asian Christian theologians and churches weave and examine the role and importance

16. See, for example, Kamali, *Middle Path of Moderation in Islam*.

17. Mencher, "Everything in Moderation." See also Maimonides, *Book of Knowledge*, 29–33.

of harmony in church documents. In 1998 the Federation of Asian Bishops Conferences (FABC), for example, highlighted the importance of harmony or balance in promoting and studying ecology and stressed four interlocking aspects of harmony: towards God, oneself, one another, and Nature.[18] In their document "Asian Christian Perspectives on Harmony," they refer to the "Jesus of harmony." Theologian Peter Phan, moreover, has written how the Asian Catholic bishops encourage the use of symbols and tropes like the Enlightened One (the Buddha) or Spiritual Guide (Guru), when introducing Jesus to the people of Asia.[19]

Like the bishops, Phan does not advocate the blending or total appropriation of such terms from non-Christian Asian religions. Seeking spiritual and intellectual balance, he promotes what he calls an "interfaith Christology," the study of Jesus through and by different religious and faith systems.[20] He believes Christians, in particular, have much to learn from the study of other faiths, including the quest to understand and follow Jesus. He contends pluralism can be celebrated. Historically, the Vatican sought to graft European ideas and ways of life into contexts where church terms or phrases were often deemed foreign, hostile, or simply unintelligible. Uniqueness, for example, so often cherished in the West (and thus stressing Jesus' salvific and universal uniqueness), is often a value of minimal importance in the East, where community integration is vital.

Traditionally in Christian thought, Jesus' death and resurrection is said to have restored harmony and healing to our world after the ravages of original sin.[21] This harmony is best expressed in the trope of the reign of God, instituted and fulfilled by Christ, as one of peace, forgiveness, and love. Was such a call radical or extreme? Rabbi Jacob Neusner, when hypothesizing whether, as a Jew, he would have followed Jesus in the first century, concluded that even the most challenging of Jesus' moral exhortations (like love your neighbor) still fit in the ambit of Jewish ethics. It was common for each sage or rabbi to push such boundaries for social justice, and he found Jesus no different in this regard than his predecessors or those that succeeded him. Where Neusner could not follow Jesus was when that Nazarene seemed to promote following him over God's call to "be fruitful and multiply" (having a family) or unnecessarily encouraging

18. See Eilers, *For All the Peoples of Asia*, 229–98. See also Phan, *Asian Christianities*; and the United States Conference of Catholic Bishops, "Encountering Christ in Harmony."

19. Phan, *Being Religious Interreligiously*, 119. See also Sugirtharajah, *Jesus in Asia*.

20. Phan, *Joy of Religious Pluralism*.

21. FABC, "Asian Christian Perspectives on Harmony," 3.3.2 [37].

the breaking of Sabbath (something instituted by God) because Jesus was greater than the Sabbath.[22]

As preached (and sometimes lived) by many Christians, it can seem following Jesus allows few compromises. Echoing the old refrain "Outside the church there is no salvation," recall the more recent (and I would add infamous) opening words to the "Declaration," *Dominus Iesus*, published in the year 2000 by the Congregation for the Doctrine of the Faith (then led by Cardinal Ratzinger, future Pope Benedict XVI, with the approval of Pope John Paul II):

> The Lord Jesus, before ascending into heaven, commanded his disciples to proclaim the Gospel to the whole world and to baptize all nations: "Go into the whole world and proclaim the Gospel to every creature. He who believes and is baptized will be saved; he who does not believe will be condemned" (Mk 16:15–16).

The argument is that Jesus commanded his disciples to preach this good news and so the church was only echoing, and thus faithfully carrying out, Jesus' commandment. Fortunately, the church under Pope Francis mostly avoids such strident claims, most evident in the recent church proclamation that systemic attempts to evangelize the Jewish people are no longer supported.[23]

The question remains: Does Jesus promote harmony and moderation? While studying abroad in Oxford (Keble College), I met fellow Christians convinced I was going to hell because I was Catholic. A few were Nazarenes adamant that drinking alcohol was expressly forbidden. Leaving aside how some of those same students later enjoyed their pints in the Eagle and Child pub that Michaelmas term, was not Jesus also called "a glutton and a drunkard" (Matt 11:19)? Did he not perform his first miracle turning water into wine at Cana (John 2:1–12) and use wine in what Christians call the Last Supper, now commemorated and enacted in the Eucharist at Mass (Matt 26:17–30; Mark 14:12–26; Luke 22:7–39; and John 13:1—17:26)?

On reflection, I don't usually connect Jesus with moderation. His call to "deny yourself, take up your cross, and follow me" (Matt 16:24) often haunts me, as do his words to the rich man who told Jesus he kept all the commandments but wanted to do more. Jesus challenged him, "Go sell everything you have and give to the poor" (Mark 10:21). Such a call is shocking, seemingly

22. Neusner, *Rabbi Talks with Jesus*. Note that in rabbinic Judaism, Jews were expected to break the Sabbath to save a life, unless such entailed idolatry, murder, or sexual sin.

23. See, for example, Commission for Religious Relations with the Jews, "Gifts and the Calling of God."

unfair, utopian (especially for those of us with a family), and demoralizing. Who can reach such a state, outside a Francis, Ignatius, or Aquinas who responded to those words with literal effect: Francis stripping down naked, Ignatius exchanging clothes with a beggar, and Aquinas, later locked up in a basement by his upset family who even sent in a prostitute to try to get him to reconsider. "Surely, not I, Lord" (Matt 26:22).[24]

The apostles, initially dismayed by Jesus' words to the rich man (who walked away), had Peter say, "Look, we have left everything and followed you. What then will we have?" (Matt 19:27). It's a fair and very pragmatic question, but where one finds the moderation is challenging. Think also of Jesus' total commitment to nonviolence (I take no stock in claims of violence to the money lenders at the temple).[25] Such remains a needed and enduring legacy, coupled with his challenging, if not extreme, view of forgiveness and love, carried also towards his enemies.[26]

Even for non-Christians, Jesus' life can be celebrated for the stark and seemingly uncompromising choices he made to live in solidarity with the broken and marginalized, and to do so nonviolently, amidst threats of harm and rancor, which culminated in his crucifixion. How can such a life, if meant as a model or guide, though, be called moderate, of living a middle way, reflecting harmony? Does Jesus signal for us a higher moral calling, seemingly extreme, but where true harmony ultimately, and most meaningfully, rests? Perhaps such a question, because of my own failures, will always haunt me.

Harmony and Its Discontents

Are there not cases and contexts, then, where moderation is too weak, not reaching or extending far enough? Don't we praise those who take their gifts, talents, and vision to extremes, whether saintly reformers and social justice advocates (some seeking to emulate Jesus) like Dorothy Day, Martin Luther King Jr., or the great Hindu reformer Gandhi? Day, King, and Gandhi lived their principles of radical nonviolence and promotion of the dignity of the poor and oppressed with little regard for their own well-being or life. Indeed, beatings, imprisonment, torture, and sometimes murder followed. Archbishop Oscar Romero of El Salvador knew he might pay with his life if

24. The disciples mutter such words after Jesus says one of them will betray him (Matt 26:21).

25. For commentary, see Myers, *Binding the Strong Man.*

26. Oddly, the one sin deemed unforgivable is blasphemy against the Holy Spirit (Matt 3:28–29), which remains mysterious and underdeveloped.

he continued to challenge the military junta who were kidnapping and killing his fellow Salvadorians, and yet he believed in "the violence of love" that would not shirk from responsibility. He reached out to those forsaken—and even extended hope and forgiveness to the perpetrators.

So, too, think of the Benedictine monks of Tibhirine, Algeria. Despite likely persecution during the Algerian Civil War, the monks believed remaining and facing their perpetrators in peace and forgiveness was the best witness both to their love of Christ and to the many kind and generous Muslim townspeople they knew. The abbot Charles-Marie Christian de Chergé even hoped to greet his expected perpetrator with love while being slain. De Chergé did not seek "martyrdom," knowing the cost to the slayer. Instead, he prayed to God—in advance!—for the grace to forgive his likely and unknown murderer. After a litany of gratitude to God and all those in his life, Brother Christian writes in his "Testament" of the one who may kill him:

> And also you, my last-minute friend, who will not have known what you were doing:
>
> Yes, I want this THANK YOU and this GOODBYE to be a "GOD BLESS" for you, too, because in God's face I see yours.
>
> May we meet again as happy thieves in Paradise, if it please God, the Father of us both.[27]

This is not the stuff of moderation or harmony, but how can it not move and awe us? Think also of the great Jewish sage Rabbi Akiba, who was said to be grateful to now fully understand the meaning of the Shema, which he devoutly uttered, while being tortured by the Romans: "Hear O' Israel, the Lord is our God, the Lord is One. . . . You shall love the Lord your God with all your heart and with all your soul and with all your might. Take to heart these instructions with which I charge you this day. Impress them upon your children. Recite them when you stay at home and when you are away, when you lie down and when you get up. Bind them as a sign on your hand and let them serve as a symbol on your forehead, inscribe them on the doorposts of your house and on your gates" (Deut 6:4–9).[28]

Such a call to fidelity was later reimagined by the atheist, writer, scientist, and Holocaust survivor Primo Levi. He altered the biblical call to that of the witness of the Shoah, demanding we, who only read about such horrors, must remember their traumas and strive to seek justice, or, as he writes in the poem "Shema,"

27. Salenson, *Christian de Cherge*, 199–201. See also the 2010 film *Of Gods and Men*.

28. For analysis of this rabbinic story, see Braiterman, *(God) After Auschwitz*, 45.

. . . may your house crumble,
Disease render you powerless,
Your offspring avert their faces from you.[29]

This, too, may seem extreme, but can there be harmony after catastrophic crimes like the Shoah? Jewish post-Holocaust philosopher and theologian Emil Fackenheim, who had been imprisoned in Sachsenhausen, believed we should always seek to mend the world, practicing *tikkun olam*, even as the post-Shoah world remained, and would ever remain, broken. No real harmony was thus possible.

More prosaically, do we not admire those who push their bodies and minds to the limit, whether on a sports pitch, acting on a stage, or straining to craft and fashion a work of art or literature, no matter the emotional, physical, or even personal and social costs? Think of Milton or Joyce straining to write as their eyesight dimmed, or the professional athlete gritting through blood and agony to reach that first-down marker, clear the ball away from the goal, or land that triple double.

And don't we all want the bliss and joy of young love; to revel in the moment or even idea of some so-called extreme feelings and experiences; the rare highs in life when some success or accomplishment sends us soaring in pride and self-satisfaction? Do we really want to resemble a Stoic ideal, taking anything life hurls at us with the same, even-tuned, apparent indifference—all the same whether hail, sleet, sun, or thunder? And should there be a limit to compassion (discussed, for example, in chapter 7), or to love—whether of one's spouse, children, parents, self, or if a theist, God? How do we find the balance and harmony within such virtues without undermining their evident value and worth?

Is There a Middle Way between Theism and Atheism?

An article in the *Catholic Herald* contains the headline "'There Is No Middle Way between Atheism And Catholicism,' Says Harvard Professor Who Has Converted."[30] While those who convert especially later in life to any belief (or unbelief) can be given the space of the fiery novice, the headline is of particular importance both to this chapter and the work as a whole. An argument could contend that theistic faith has caused much harm in the world (especially exclusivist, monotheistic versions) that have spread, promoted, defended, and monopolized their faith positions, leading to cultural,

29. Levi, *Survival in Auschwitz*, 12.

30. Teahan, "'There Is No Middle Way.'"

if not economic and social, devastation—even wars and genocides. Yet, is not atheism also an unhealthy alternative, some may counter, as it implies or states there is no ultimate meaning or value in the world, perhaps even doubting the integrity and substance of everything—even morals? The "without God, all is permitted" line—as espoused in *The Brothers Karamazov*—was a genuine fear of its author, Fyodor Dostoevsky.

Both descriptions above are gross caricatures, and yet whether there can and should be harmony between atheism and theism, or whether both are extreme points needing a midway vantage point are questions worth pursuing. In the sections remaining, and bearing in mind both the Harvard professor's claim and the sections above, I will sketch what moderation, and the virtue of harmony, can mean in the context of atheist-theist dialogue and in terms of religious belief and practice, bearing in mind the reality of our Anthropocene Age and the destruction we are unleashing on the Earth, and one another.[31] Again, if the world is burning and in agony, should not our energy and focus be on achieving harmony with one another and with all of life, especially as advocated in so many Indigenous faiths?

The Middle Way between Faith and Doubt

I worry that I sometimes have both too little faith and too little doubt—so reaching no mean or median in either case separately. And together? First, is there such a thing as extremity in religious faith? Here I am not referring to religions advocating violence, holy wars, or intolerance; I take such expressions as clearly wrong and so extremist in only a negative way. But, what of the spiritual call to "pray without ceasing"—a lived spirituality that aims to focus and steer all our actions, thoughts, words, and deeds towards, and in, the presence of God? Such is to contend we are rife with disordered desires and it is only in our return and immersion in a life of God-belief and practice that our inner spiritual harmony and wholeness are restored. What seems extreme or even unhealthy is only from the vantage point of a society focused on ephemeral pleasures and false promises of meaning and purposes. What is labeled extreme is actually our true home, to live always in the presence of a God of love ("the kingdom of God is within you," Luke 17:21). Building on that Lukan passage, recall, for example, the words of Tolstoy in *A Confession*. Despite the renown he earned through novels like *War and Peace* or *Anna Karenina*, he claimed he was drifting in

31. Kolbert, *Sixth Extinction*.

deep depression, unmoored. But when he realized his yearning for God and accepted this need, he felt liberated.[32]

I also have in mind religious individuals who profess and exhibit peace and contentment in their faith, who are not hypocrites or do not wield the outward expression of such faith against others or for personal gain. They seem deeply spiritual and committed, exude peace and kindness, but there is no compartmentalizing of their religious life—it is their life, whether amidst family, friends, or work. Is that a different kind of (unhealthy) extreme, or a type of harmony? Almost two decades ago, I taught parts of Augustine's *Confessions* in a freshman composition class in York College in Jamaica, Queens. As we sampled some initial chapters and I asked their opinions and interpretations, there was an unusually heavy silence. Finally, one of the students, a bit sheepishly, stammered, "It just seems the guy's [Augustine] obsessed with God or something."

There were nods in agreement. There is much about Augustine I can query and challenge, from his unhealthy views of sex and his treatment of his unnamed concubine, to his damaging views of human nature. I also believe his views of original sin and his flirting with doctrines like double predestination have been harmful. Nevertheless, I remain in awe about his steely and pervasive focus on God. His prayers are moving and genuine—and his focus on God, pervasive.

Writing these chapters as a theist, I feel I'm a fraud when I think not so much about a major figure like Augustine, proclaimed saint and father of the church, but upon writings from many theologians. Their works are steeped in biblical quotations and piety, references to the catechism, and the encyclicals of popes. They reflect a language and vocabulary that speak repeatedly of God's grace, or delve—without any modicum of doubt or discomfort—on the Trinity. They speak of the Catholic Church as "she" and seem to uphold church decrees and proclamations with reverence, if not exactitude. Such is simply part of their vocabulary and vision. There are also the genuinely pious, simple believers, whose language is not adorned or obfuscated by theological study, but who pray fervently in front of the tabernacle or shrine of a saint; who say rosaries and novenas with acceptance and humility; and who, on the whole, experience few pangs of doubt. They are, mostly, at peace in their religious faith. If one thinks of harmony in musical terms from the word's Western origins in the fourteenth century, there is a feeling of concord and agreement—where, it seems, doubt would only propel discord and disharmony.

32. Tolstoy, *Confession*.

As I will note in my discussion of humility in chapter 4, my theological work and immersion in what I call "the testimonies of mass atrocity"—memoirs and accounts of catastrophic and horrific mass suffering and death, from the gulags and Shoah, to inner-city violence and poverty and the ravages of earthquakes, disease, and societal neglect—can only seem to fuel doubt, if not dismissal, of any faith in God. When reading such accounts, especially if written from those who can no longer, or never, believe in any loving God on account of the atrocities they have witnessed or experienced, I can feel guilty that I don't, or can't, fully echo their outrage, let alone level of doubt.

Here, especially, I take solace in the wounded faith of an Elie Wiesel, a faith rooted in questioning and doubt as much as in hope and trust in God, despite evils like the reality of Auschwitz. Is there too much faith in such contexts, or insufficient doubt? What is, or should be, the mean or point of harmony?

I am skeptical of any rigid certitude, whether of a theist or an atheist, that exhibits or praises the need and role of doubt in their position. Such is not to say everyone should always be agnostic, which is the usual midpoint or mean between faith and unbelief. It seems more reasonable that positions and identities would be fluid, showing sympathy and solidarity with elements of all three broad positions even as, ultimately, we come down on one of those three sides (note: I see little credence in a position like misotheism—hatred of God). Despite my theistic doubt and faith struggles—which tend to be more passionate regarding certain triumphalist decrees of the Catholic Church (or any soteriologically exclusivist claims)—I do not see a universe and worldview completely mechanistic, atomistic, or materialist.

How, then, can the virtue of harmony aid my role as a Catholic theologian in a theist-atheist dialogue, and in applying that dialogue to our urgent need to face and address the devastation we are causing to our planet? A start is to listen and enact much of the ecological wisdom of Indigenous traditions.

Indigenous Peoples and Ecological Harmony

The ongoing destruction of Indigenous ways of life is linked with our world's ecological crisis, a process that exploded with so-called "New-World" discoveries by Europeans in the fifteenth century and which shows little sign of abating today. To put this in perspective, it was only in 2007 that the United Nations published and ratified the "United Nations Declaration on the Rights of Indigenous Peoples." Article 8 of the "Declaration" decrees that states, in consultation with Indigenous groups, should prevent or seek redress for:

a. Any action which has the aim or effect of depriving them of their integrity as distinct peoples, or of their cultural values or ethnic identities;
b. Any action which has the aim or effect of dispossessing them of their lands, territories or resources;
c. undermining any of their rights;
d. Any form of forced assimilation or integration;
e. Any form of propaganda designed to promote or incite racial or ethnic discrimination directed against them.[33]

Economic interests of governments and corporations, and the poverty (often choiceless choices) faced by many local, non-Indigenous (and some Indigenous) people, often mean business as usual for those who most benefit from the land and resource spoils—furthering the destruction of Indigenous land and ways of life. As Dina Gilio-Whitaker writes in her book tracing the Indigenous fight for environmental justice, "As 'the people,' our common enemy is the entrenched corporate power of Big Oil and other toxic industries that buy political influence to protect their own corrupt interests, in collusion with government, all in the name of democracy."[34] Regarding destruction of the Amazon in Brazil, Indigenous leader and nonagenarian Raoni Metuktire testifies, "I have seen many presidents come and go, but none spoke so badly of indigenous people or threatened us and the forest like this. . . . Since he [Bolsonaro] became president, he has been the worst for us."[35]

Can the world get worse for Indigenous people, after all the broken treaties, forced removals, disease, coerced Western schooling, language and religious practices, and dismissals of their dignity, equality, and basic human rights as individuals and peoples? What remains inspiring, certainly, is the Indigenous resolve for resistance and what Jonathan Lear calls a "radical hope" even "in the face of cultural devastation."[36] Such a hope, like theistic faith in the midst of despair, is also radical. Or as Nick Estes, citizen of the Lower Brule Sioux Tribe, writes, "Our history and long traditions of Indigenous resistance provide possibilities for futures premised on justice." In the

33. United Nations, "United Nations Declaration," 10.
34. Gilio-Whitaker, *As Long as Grass Grows*, ix.
35. Watts, "Amazonian Chief Raoni Metuktire."
36. See Lear, *Radical Hope*.

hope of such justice, he even cites "kinship relations between Indigenous and non-Indigenous and the lands we both inhabit."[37]

From Native American spirituality to the Dreaming of Aboriginal peoples, the principle of human interconnection with all of nature is reflected in all aspects of Indigenous life, from hunting and foresting, to art, prayer, language, and literature. For Native American thinkers and theologians, both Native and nonnative peoples must remember and sustain the rich and deep legacy of Indigenous wisdom, resilience, and morality despite what can seem never-ending persecution, racism, and exploitation. Tink Tinker, for example, highlights an Indian liberation theology that is deeply cognizant of how "American Indians represent cultures and communities that predate by thousands of generations the euro-western invasions of the Americas. We were people who knew the spiritual side of all life, who had firm experiential connections with the Creator, who had well-developed ceremonies to help us maintain harmony and balance in the life of communities and the world around us."[38] Lies and slander have hidden or denied such truths. As Tommy Orange writes in his acclaimed novel *There There*, "We've been defined by everyone else, and continue to be slandered despite easy-to-look-up-on-the-internet-facts about the realities of our history and current state of our people."[39]

Through the work of Pope Francis, and especially his landmark encyclical *Laudato Si'*, the call for ecological harmony and a deeper respect towards Indigenous ways of life are finally reaching up and trickling down from the institutional church. In December 2019, for example, the Catholic Bishops' Conference of the Philippines issued a document: "Dialogue towards Harmony." As they note, "Throughout history, there has been found among indigenous people, a certain awareness of a hidden power which lies behind the course of nature and the events of human life."[40] The bishops note this power is often linked to a Supreme Being. There is a holiness imbued in all of creation, and human beings are just one part of a vast and sacred whole.

Again, *Laudato Si'* was a revolutionary doctrinal document towards the greening of the Catholic Church and the process of moving ecological morality and awareness to the forefront of the Catholic conscience and focus. For our purposes, note that "harmony" appears twelve times in the

37. Estes, *Our History Is the Future*, 256.

38. Tinker, *American Indian Liberation*, 128.

39. Orange, *There There*, 7. See also Dunbar-Ortiz and Gilio-Whitaker, *"All the Real Indians Died Off."* For a fascinating account of basketball "on the rez" among the Navajo people, see Powell, *Canyon Dreams*.

40. Catholic Bishops' Conference of the Philippines, "Dialogue towards Harmony." See also: Liljeblad and Verschuuren, *Indigenous Perspectives on Sacred Natural Sites*; and Deloria, *God Is Red*, 296.

encyclical. Not surprisingly, Francis turns to the legacy of his namesake, Saint Francis of Assisi, a symbol of Catholic ecological integrity from the twelfth century. About the Italian saint, Pope Francis writes, "He was a mystic and a pilgrim who lived in simplicity and in wonderful harmony with God, with others, with nature and with himself. He shows us just how inseparable the bond is between concern for nature, justice for the poor, commitment to society, and interior peace."[41]

Francis also uses the word "harmony" to describe how the book of Genesis depicts humankind's origins and role with creation, which we have broken through excessive pride. He writes, "The harmony between the Creator, humanity and creation as a whole was disrupted by our presuming to take the place of God and refusing to acknowledge our creaturely limitations."[42] This call for proper humility will be a focus I'll return to in chapter 4.

Section 2.4 of the encyclical is titled, "The Message of Each Creature in the Harmony of Creation," highlighting the interconnectedness of all life. Francis stresses that "an integral ecology includes taking time to recover a serene harmony with creation, reflecting on our lifestyle and our ideals, and contemplating the Creator who lives among us and surrounds us."[43]

Challenging my initial assessment of Jesus above, Francis pens, "Jesus lived in full harmony with creation, and others were amazed: 'What sort of man is this, that even the winds and the sea obey him?' (Matt 8:27)."[44] Francis stresses how Jesus was no extreme ascetic or dualist who denigrated the body as the majority of Jesus' life was spent as a carpenter. Echoing God's "And it was good" decree over creation in Genesis, the incarnation further testifies to the sanctity of creation and the integral relationship of God and God's creation. Francis thus closes the encyclical with "A Christian Prayer in union

41. Francis, *Laudato Si'*, §10. For additional commentary on the encyclical, see McKim, *Laudato Si' and the Environment*; O'Hara et al., *Integral Ecology*; and Miller, *Theological and Ecological Vision.*

42. Francis, *Laudato Si'*, §66.

43. Francis, *Laudato Si'*, §225.

44. Francis, *Laudato Si'*, §98. I think better citations would be Jesus' reference to "the birds of the air; they neither sow nor reap" (Matt 6:26); his comparison to a mother hen (Matt 23:37)—which is often cited in feminist Christologies—and his role as a shepherd protecting and seeking the lost sheep (Matt 18:12–13). Such harmony is more indicative in these passages than one of nature obeying, which points more towards mastering nature—part of our environmental failures. The passage of Jesus cursing a fig tree (Matt 21:18–22), or sending the demons of Legion into the swine (Mark 5:1–20), would be even less auspicious from a nature-loving standpoint (note: both stories are usually read symbolically, with the latter, especially in postcolonial biblical writing, as an anti-Roman and anti-imperial trope).

with Creation," which includes the lines that Jesus, in his birth, "became a part of the earth" and "gazed upon this world with human eyes."[45]

The encyclical also highlights how "it is essential to show special care for indigenous communities and their cultural traditions." Francis contends such communities "should be the principal dialogue partners, especially when large projects affecting their land are proposed. For them, land is not a commodity but rather a gift from God and from their ancestors who rest there, a sacred space with which they need to interact if they are to maintain their identity and values."[46] The Indigenous people are also praised in the encyclical for embodying key values, which include their example to "instill a greater sense of responsibility, a strong sense of community, a readiness to protect others, a spirit of creativity and a deep love for the land."[47]

Echoing the call for church repentance and the need for Christians to seek forgiveness for past and present crimes, Pope Francis apologized to Indigenous groups in Bolivia in 2015 for the "'grave sins' of Colonialism."[48] Ecological harmony and solidarity with Indigenous peoples have been ongoing features of his ministry. Indigenous leader Gregorio Diaz Mirabal, general coordinator of the Coordination of Indian Organizations of the Amazon Basin (COICA), for example, praises "Brother Francis" for "risking his life" for the Amazon.[49]

Sadly, some conservative Catholics have criticized Pope Francis for such acts, even rebuking him in 2019 for being "sacrilegious and idolatrous for embracing indigenous symbols."[50] They remain, however, a (vocal) minority. At the 2019 Synod of Bishops for the Amazon, the bishops echoed and called upon Francis to see protecting the rainforest as a global core of climate change advocacy.[51] As Felicio Pontes Jr. writes,

> The bishops . . . voted overwhelmingly to recognize Amazonian society as multi-ethnic and multicultural. They recognized the rights of Nature and embraced three fundamental rights for indigenous peoples and local communities—the right to self-determination, the right to the recognition of their traditional territories and the right to prior and informed consent whenever any development project threatens to impact their way of life.[52]

45. Francis, *Laudato Si'*, §246.
46. Francis, *Laudato Si'*, §146.
47. Francis, *Laudato Si'*, §179.
48. ICT Staff, "Pope Francis Apologizes to Indigenous Peoples."
49. Martín, "Indigenous Leader."
50. Squires, "Conservative Catholics Accuse Pope Francis."
51. Wooden, "Indigenous Vow."
52. Pontes, "Lessons for COP 26."

In 2019, encouraged by proposals from the Amazon synod, Francis signaled his support of adding and defining "ecological sins" to the catechism of the Catholic Church.[53] For Francis, ecological sin is a social justice issue, as the most vulnerable are the most negatively affected. While the language of sin can sometimes alienate more liberal Catholics, what is important here is a clear condemnation of why and how harming the environment or excessive materialism is wrong and immoral—or sinful. While skeptics and supporters of Francis question whether Catholics will heed and follow Francis's ecological blueprint,[54] there is no denying that at an institutional level, combating climate change and making ecological justice part of the larger Catholic social justice focus has become a bedrock of the Francis papacy.

Conclusion: Harmony without God?

While writing this chapter, I have been challenging myself to decide whether harmony means more, or demands more, from a theist. Harmony with creation but no Creator seems to be missing a key rung or feature. I can feel a deep sense of spiritual inertia, doubt, or dark nights, but such language is linked to the hope and aim of relationship with what is beyond the physical and material. Is not something missing from harmony without this chord of "creative tension" between our human, finite striving and the infinite boundlessness that is God?

More narrowly, must such spiritual harmony require belief in Jesus and the language of the church to be whole, or as whole as possible in our flawed world? I will come back to questions of religious pluralism and being Catholic later in this book, but I again want to stress how the Indigenous traditions have so much to teach the Abrahamic faiths in particular. Does such teaching also include atheists, who would (by most definitions) seem forced to deny any (science-tested) spiritual link with animals, plants, and the ecosystem? Such is not to say atheists do not employ the language of the spiritual in many of their descriptions and observations of the natural world. Such is commonplace. We go to the forest and forest-bathe, feel awe in the raging of the sea, the intelligence of ravens, or the intricacies of a butterfly. I'm also thinking, for example, of the poetic musings of atheist naturalist Loren Eiseley or of atheist philosopher Ronald Dworkin writing about "religion without God."[55] What do such words like

53. Esteves, "Catechism Will Be Updated." As of August 2020, debate remains ongoing.

54. See, for example, Sweetser, *Can Francis Change the Church?*; and Teirstein, "Pope Might Make Destroying the Earth a Sin."

55. See Eiseley, *Star Thrower*; and Dworkin, *Religion without God.*

"spirit" or "spiritual" really mean, though, if there is no God, or nothing that can be objectively provable in claims like the "sacredness of life," as depicted by many Indigenous peoples?

What does harmony mean in a world solely of chance and contingency? What is one seeking harmony with or towards?[56] A concept like harmony seems to imply some system of meaning and stability. Even in Eastern worldviews that are nontheist, implied is some cosmological order and higher purpose—the Tao or Way, which while mysterious, unknown, indescribable, and untestable, still seems to operate from a holistic vantage point which connects and includes all of creation. Any total dependence on science and rationality could not coherently hold to such claims (it would seem). If such is dismissed as scientism or extreme, are we not again back to some nebulous middle ground (or way) between theism and atheism or faith and doubt?

To be clear, I'm asking such questions out of genuine curiosity and not judgment. Why? Because the world is burning, in agony, and drowning. Making an all-or-nothing argument for why harmony is best or most layered in a theistic framework when human beings, mostly through greed and willed ignorance, destroy our seas and mountains, our air and grasslands; eradicate habitats and species; and live blissfully in some parts of the world without any consequence or empathy for others seems misplaced—unless I genuinely believed that only those who believe in God can really work for ecological change and social justice. Who could sustain that idea with most climate change deniers or advocates for change being numerically and proportionately religious?

We fashion and sustain a world of such insidious inequality that language of harmony (whether secular, spiritual, or religious) seems laughable. There can be little talk of real harmony when our world is burning, in agony, and drowning.

And yet, "radical hope," a hope despite the hopelessness, a hope fueled by creative tensions, is finally uniting many religious and philosophical worlds, as people of all faiths and empathic ethical systems demand ecological change.

If ever there is common ground where we—theist and atheist—dwell, this is it.

56. The problem of evil is sometimes placed in an aesthetic category, claiming a balance of evil and the good (so all is needed) for a cosmic harmony. In the face of atrocities and genocides, I find such language morally harmful.

Response

ANDREW FIALA

I ALSO HOPE FOR harmony—with the world and with my fellow human and nonhuman beings. This hope must be present in any dialogical encounter. Without hope for finding common ground, there is little point in dialogue. The hope of harmony is that there might be some consensus, some understanding, some revelation of the other that gives rise to a kind of sympathetic vibration. This is an ancient idea. In Greek, the word that is often translated as harmony is *symphonia* (συμφωνίᾳ)—a word that has obvious musical overtones.[1] Plato—and his Pythagorean predecessors—were interested in the question of how diverse notes, strings, and ratios worked together to give rise to something larger and more meaningful (Plato discusses this in *Phaedo*, for example). Beautiful music—and inspiring dialogue—happens as something arises and emerges out of a symphony made up of diverse parts. Of course, this is not an easy task. In *Republic*, Plato shows how harmony breaks down, as the parts of the soul and the parts of the city get out of balance, culminating ultimately in tyranny. In *Symposium*, where harmony is also discussed, the dialogue is ultimately disrupted by the appearance of Alcibiades. The Platonic ideal of harmonious concord inevitably gives way to its opposite: to discord, strife, and violence.

Peter acknowledges that harmony remains an elusive ideal. It is especially difficult to find harmonious common ground in theistic and atheistic worldviews. Peter puts it this way: "What does harmony mean in a world solely of chance and contingency? What is one seeking harmony with or towards? A concept like harmony seems to imply some system of meaning and stability." A theist has faith that there is a God-ordered whole, which provides a larger structure of harmony. An atheist rejects this. Peter directs our attention to the problem of evil in a footnote here;

1. See Nikulin, *On Dialogue*.

he also directs our attention to Dostoevsky. Dostoevsky puts this problem in the mouth of Ivan Karamazov. Ivan rejects the idea that suffering—especially the suffering of children—can be justified from the standpoint of a "higher harmony." He says:

> If all must suffer to pay for the eternal harmony, what have children to do with it, tell me, please? It's beyond all comprehension why they should suffer, and why they should pay for the harmony. Why should they, too, furnish material to enrich the soil for the harmony of the future? . . . Too high a price is asked for harmony.[2]

Ivan Karamazov's complaint has been reiterated in various ways by atheists, who reject the "ultimate harmony" theodicy along with every other attempt at theodicy.[3] There is a vast literature on theodicy and the problem of evil. We cannot get into these questions in any detail here. But let us only note that any attempt to discover harmony in a dialogue between an atheist and a theist will have a difficult time negotiating this issue. This is a place that the atheist and the theist must agree to disagree.

Another point of disagreement will likely occur with regard to the question of whether there is, as Peter puts it, "a system of meaning and stability" in this world. A glance at the natural world—and the looming catastrophe of climate change—calls that idea into question. The world that is described by natural science is not one of stability or of any transcendent meaning. The system of natural laws does provide structure. But that system is indifferent to human beings and to evil. The earth and its galaxy congealed and evolved through billions of years. The crust is fractured by earthquakes and volcanoes. The climate is unstable: there have been hotter epochs and ice ages. There have been mass extinctions. And the human race will also go extinct. Civilization—including philosophy and religion—is a vanishingly small moment in the context of geological time. At some point all of this will come to an end. The world of "chance and contingency" that Peter points to as the world of atheism is indeed a world of radical finitude. All men are mortal, as are all human constructions—including art, religion, philosophy, and love. There is a kind of ecological harmony in which human bodies become food for worms and the ecosystem goes on without us. But that idea of harmony lacks the consolations provided by theistic religion. The challenge of atheistic humanism is to find the courage to embrace radical finitude—to live without appeal, as Camus puts it. It is difficult to imagine finding a way to harmonize an atheistic humanism that accepts radical finitude with the

2. Dostoevsky, *Brothers Karamazov*, 272.

3. See for example, Michael Martin, who describes one attempt at a theodicy as the "ultimate harmony theodicy" in Martin, *Atheism*.

hopefulness of a theology that sees harmony in nature and which finds a larger sense of purpose for human life in the cosmos.

Of course the hopeful harmony envisioned by the two Francises is inspiring (by both Francis of Assisi and by Pope Francis). Pope Francis writes,

> Our insistence that each human being is an image of God should not make us overlook the fact that each creature has its own purpose. None is superfluous. The entire material universe speaks of God's love, his boundless affection for us. Soil, water, mountains: everything is, as it were, a caress of God.[4]

I understand these words. They are reassuring. And I do feel an affinity with the material universe on certain days, when I hike on a bluebird day in the Sierra Nevada, as I pluck a juicy orange from a tree, or when I watch the sun set across the Pacific Ocean. There are moments of harmony and joy. I understand what it means to experience soil, water, mountains, and everything as if it were a caress of God. But that experience of harmony is momentary and metaphorical. I don't believe that humans were created in God's image. I believe that we evolved to fit our ecosystem. Where a theist sees God's love at work in all of this, I do not. And the value of the natural word is ambiguous. Mountain storms are brutal and dangerous. Rats and pests afflict my garden. And the Pacific coast is afflicted by forest fires and earthquakes. I relish and cherish moments of harmony and joy. But I also know that all good things end, that disease and winter will come, and that the natural world is simply not here for my enjoyment.

Peter offers us "radical hope" in connection with an inclusive vision of resistance to ecological disaster. He suggests that maybe we can find a way to unite the world's philosophical and religious traditions around the need for ecological harmony. I share that hope: we ought to pursue this vision of a common and global human embrace of the wisdom of ecology. But I worry that it remains quite difficult (if not impossible), given the historical evils that Peter recounts—reminding us of genocides and ecocides.

But—and here perhaps is a strange and sad point of common ground—the history of evil is broadly damning. No one has the moral high ground here. Theists and atheists have each engaged in evil—toward persons and toward the planet. In accepting this, we might find a kind of harmony of mourning, grief, responsibility, and regret. Perhaps the songs we should sing together are not merely joyful songs of triumph and praise—but dirges, requiems, and lamentations. Perhaps the common ground is found in our acknowledgement of evil and in our sense of failure and responsibility.

4. Francis, *Laudato Si'*, §84.

Chapter 3

Courage and the Existential Leap

Andrew Fiala, Primary Author

I am often the only atheist in the room. I have been involved in interfaith meetings. I have moderated panels of religious leaders. I have taught classes on religion. I have given sermons in churches. This may seem odd, but I wrote a book about Jesus and ethics and talk a lot about the Christian tradition in my work on pacifism and nonviolence: it is this material that I have been invited to present to Bible study groups and to congregations. I have also been an active supporter of interfaith efforts and efforts to reduce hate crimes against Jews, Muslims, and Sikhs in our community. I was recognized for my work by our local mosque, where I received a "Spirit of Abraham" award. I was also recognized at a local Sikh gurdwara for my efforts. I've worked with Jews and Christian Scientists, Hindus and Mormons. I've spoken at Catholic, Presbyterian, Mennonite, Lutheran, Unitarian, and nondenominational events. In most of those circumstances, I am the only atheist in the room. At first this was intimidating. But I have learned that with a bit of courage and a lot of faith in the goodwill and humanity of other people, it is possible to have productive conversations across the religious/nonreligious divide.

Atheism, nonbelief, and secularism are growing. But it is still unusual for many people to meet an atheist. For many years now, the media and the academy have been reporting and commentating on the rise of the "nones"—those with no religious affiliation. A recent report from the Pew Center concludes, "Telephone surveys conducted in 2018 and 2019 show that 4% of American adults say they are atheists when asked about their religious identity, up from 2% in 2009. An additional 5% of Americans call themselves agnostics, up from 3% a decade ago."[1] Atheists typically do not participate in religious events, interfaith panels, or give lectures in

1. Lipka, "10 Facts about Atheists."

churches. But I am convinced that there is a need for atheists to be present and to participate in this sort of thing. And while some atheists are quite outspoken and inflammatory in their denunciation of religion, there is also an important place for a more modest atheism that, rather than disparaging religion, engages in heartfelt, thoughtful, and human dialogue. The outspoken atheists do not help to remedy the deep-seated antipathy toward atheism that is prevalent in society. There are still some people who think that atheists have horns and tails and are evil. Psychological and social science research shows that people tend to distrust atheists and suspect them of immorality.[2] And until very recently in the Western world, atheists were ostracized, persecuted, and burned at the stake. This kind of violence continues to plague atheists in the non-Western world. It takes courage to speak up and speak out with this in the background. And it takes tact and civility to represent atheism in a public world that until very recently had no sympathy for nonreligion.

At one point I was fairly reserved about my atheism. But I have learned that most people in my part of the world are tolerant and hospitable. And I have discovered what religious people might call the power of testimony: when I admit that I am an atheist, I have found that this helps me feel more at home in my own beliefs. I have also been thanked by other closeted atheists who are empowered to learn that there are others like them. While I do not believe that my own experience compares with the kinds of oppression that are experienced by other marginalized folks—people of color, LGBTQI persons, as well as Jews, Sikhs, Muslims, and other minority religions—I have learned much about dialogue, testimony, and structural injustice in my position as an outsider to the mainstream. Cultural, institutional, and structural elements make it very difficult for there to be open dialogue across the religious divide. For the dialogue to become more equitable, the mainstream must take steps to be inclusive—and those of us who are able must be willing to speak up from the margins.

Here's one example of why this works and why it is important. A couple of years ago, I taught a class for adults on religion—a learning-in-retirement class for about 125 senior citizens. I discussed a variety of religious topics including differences among world religions—and the differences among monotheism, polytheism, pantheism, atheism, and agnosticism. At one point after class a woman in her sixties or seventies came up to me and thanked me for helping her understand her own atheism. She grew up in a religious family, had religious friends, and lived in a

2. See Moon et al., "Religious People Are Trusted." This article summarizes similar results from a number of other studies.

generally religious community. She did not really believe any of this, she said—and had not for a very long time. But she didn't feel that she could speak out or ask questions about religion. My class, she said, gave her the vocabulary—and the courage—to better understand and express herself. We talked for a while after class about the experience of being an atheist in a religious community. One take-away from this encounter is that it is possible for people to remain in the closet for a very long time. It is also possible that we fail to understand ourselves and our own beliefs when we have no one to talk them over with. Furthermore, we can easily assume that our communities are inclusive, when we fail to take stock of who is missing, who remains silent, and who is left out.

That small story gives a sense of the importance of courageous dialogue. Courage helps us become who we are by giving us the strength to wonder who we are and what we believe. There are complex social and political and religious forces that stifle this sense of wonder. In the United States, while atheists remain a small minority, outright persecution is illegal. So it does not take too much courage to admit one's atheism. We have a secular system that encourages freedom of religion. There are still challenges here for atheists in a culture that for the most part takes religion for granted. Your colleagues and family members may view you differently if they discover that you do not share their theological assumptions. But in other parts of the world, atheists need even more courage. Nearly half of the countries on earth—47 percent, according to one report—have laws that punish blasphemy and apostasy.[3] A 2019 report from Humanists International indicates that there are seventy countries that have laws against blasphemy and apostasy.[4] The report points out that in some places conditions have become harsher for free thinkers, humanists, and atheists: in 2019 Brunei instituted the death penalty for apostasy and blasphemy (along with homosexuality and adultery); in 2018 Mauritania did something similar. In a number of places, atheists and unbelievers face death threats, persecution, and murder. The *Atlantic* recently profiled an Iraqi student, Lubna Yaseen, who was outspoken in her criticism of religion and who was subject to death threats.[5] She fled Iraq with the help of Secular Rescue, an organization that helps to save nonreligious people who are being persecuted. There are grisly details about the murders of journalists, bloggers, and authors in places like Bangladesh who question

3. Fiss, "Anti-Blasphemy Offensives in the Digital Age."

4. Summary here: Humanists UK, "Non-Religious Continue to Face." Original report here: https://fot.humanists.international/.

5. Robson, "Underground Railroad to Save Atheists."

religious dogma—hacked to death by machete-wielding fundamentalists who are seemingly encouraged in their violence by the indifference of the police and political authorities.[6] In places that do not have robust secular protections of freedom of speech and freedom of religion, it takes great courage to speak your mind in public about nonbelief.

But speaking your mind is essential in genuine dialogue. The participants in a dialogue put themselves at risk by exposing their beliefs and identities. Courage is needed in order to take that risk. When I say that courage is an essential feature of dialogue, I draw upon the resources of the Western philosophical tradition. Let me confess one of my fundamental beliefs here—since dialogue of the sort we have in mind is about exposing our commitments—which is that I believe that it is possible to gain enlightenment through dialogue. Not everyone believes that this is true. There are those who embrace ignorance and who would prefer conformity and obedience. Martin Luther King Jr. described this as "sincere ignorance and conscientious stupidity."[7] He said that there was nothing more dangerous in the world than this kind of "intellectual and moral blindness."

The cure is open-minded inquiry and genuine dialogue. Immanuel Kant explained this in his essay "What Is Enlightenment?" Kant said that many people prefer to remain immature by remaining under the authority of someone else. But enlightenment requires courage: the willingness to dare to be wise, to grow up, and to use our own understanding. Kant wrote,

> Enlightenment is man's emergence from his self-incurred immaturity. Immaturity is the inability to use one's understanding without the guidance of another. This immaturity is self-incurred if its cause is not lack of understanding, but lack of resolution and courage to use it without the guidance of another. The motto of enlightenment is therefore: *Sapere Aude!* Have courage to use your own understanding![8]

This chapter is about courage as an essential component in dialogue. We must dare to know, dare to think, and dare to discover wisdom. Kant tells us we should have the courage to use our understanding. As we shall see, we also need the courage to face the existential risk of dialogue, which exposes us to the other and asks us to think critically about our beliefs and identities.

6. See Fiss, "Anti-Blasphemy Offensives in the Digital Age."

7. King, *Strength to Love*, 79.

8. Kant, "What Is Enlightenment?," 54.

Existential Courage

While I began here with a description of why courage is needed and how it functions in the life of a nonbeliever, courage is needed on all sides. Faith traditions often begin with a courageous affirmation: seen in the life of the prophets and martyrs who start a tradition—often in opposition to the status quo. Jesus exhibited courage in his life and through his crucifixion; something similar occurs in the life of the prophets, the apostles, and the martyrs of the early church. Denials of faith exhibit a similar sort of courage. This is the courage of one's convictions, the fortitude to assert oneself in opposition to the faith of the status quo. Socrates demonstrated this kind of courage when he challenged the beliefs of the Athenians and endured with equanimity his execution; this kind of fortitude was celebrated by the ancient philosophical schools such as Stoicism. But Jesus and Socrates are more than human—the one is supposed to be the incarnation of God, the other is supposedly possessed by a spiritual guide, the *daimonion* who whispered in his ear.

Human courage is harder. It is found in the middle of things, where outcomes are uncertain and doubt is pervasive. Human courage is existential: we need it in order to make a "leap of faith," to borrow a phrase from Kierkegaard—whether this leap of faith leads us to affirm a religious tradition or whether it leads us to atheism. In his book *Fear and Trembling*, Kierkegaard speaks of faith as a kind of "humble courage." He explains, "A paradoxical and humble courage is required to grasp the whole of the temporal by virtue of the absurd, and this is the courage of faith."[9] This is the humble courage of Abraham and Mary—both of whom are asked to believe that their sons will not die; it is an openhearted courage that is receptive to something wonderful.[10] And while this may make most sense in the theistic tradition, a similar sort of humble courage is required of the atheist, who must find a way to "live without appeal," as Camus put it. Camus explains that the absurd man "prefers his courage and his reasoning. The first teaches him to live without appeal and to get along with what he has; the second informs him of his limits."[11]

The parallel between Kierkegaard and Camus is informative: one is a theist who understands that faith requires the humble courage of believing that which defies belief; the other is an atheist who understands that a similar sort of courage is needed in order to find meaning in mortal finitude

9. Kierkegaard, *Fear and Trembling*, 49.

10. See Carlisle, "Humble Courage."

11. Camus, *Myth of Sisyphus*, 66.

and a universe emptied of God. And most important for our purposes here, both Kierkegaard and Camus understand the role of courage in dialogue, love, and solidarity. For Kierkegaard, this means putting himself in dialogue with the characters and ideas of the tradition—and with his reader—in a way that is acutely self-conscious and aware of the paradoxical impossibility of the task of communication. Kierkegaard's contribution to our understanding of dialogue has to do with his emphasis on the subjectivity of what he calls "indirect communication."[12] It is one thing to convey in words some objective content—say, for example, that "Jesus is the messiah" or that "God is dead." These propositions can be repeated in ways that reflect objective truth. It is objectively true to say, for example, that Christians believe that Jesus is the messiah. It is objectively true to say that Nietzsche said "God is dead." But what does it mean to actually believe that Jesus is the messiah or that God is dead? And how do we communicate the subjective depth and inwardness of the lived experience of one who affirms such a truth? Kierkegaard, of course, focuses this on the problem of communicating faith. But a similar problem holds for the atheist. To merely state that God is dead does not convey the subjective inwardness of the atheist's lived experience in a world that is godless and devoid of messiahs. The problem is that subjective inwardness is left out of direct, objective communication in every case. But in genuine dialogue, the subjective aspect must be present, that is, if dialogue is not merely an exchange of objective statements but also a meeting of minds, hearts, and souls.

And here is where existential courage comes in. A dialogue is not merely a debate about objective truths. One can debate without being personally invested in the propositions being debated. This is what students do on a debate team, what academics do at conferences, and what lawyers do in a trial: they make an argument and defend a position. But defending a position is not the same as exposing one's identity and belief in genuine dialogue. Debate requires the virtues of cleverness and quick-wittedness. But dialogue requires virtues such as magnanimity, receptivity, and, yes, courage. The courage I have in mind here is the willingness to expose who you are and what you believe to another person (along with your own doubts, questions, and misgivings).

The value of Kierkegaard for our understanding of this process is that in his discussion of indirect communication he reminds us that what we are aiming at is an expression of inwardness. One limitation, however, is that Kierkegaard tends to view the problem of communication from the vantage

12. This is an important theme in Kierkegaard's *Concluding Unscientific Post-Script*. See Herrmann, "Kierkegaard and Dialogue," 71–92.

point of an author/speaker. But the problem of dialogue also includes the vantage point of the listener. Courage is not only a virtue for a speaker who exposes him or herself, it is also needed for those who listen and receive. This is courageous receptivity or brave being-with. A hint is found in Camus, who points us toward the virtue of solidarity and love in his late work *The Rebel*. The lonely courage of the absurd man that Camus emphasizes in *The Myth of Sisyphus* gives way to the need for revolt, compassion, and solidarity with suffering others in *The Rebel*.

Camus's thinking is informed by his understanding of the master-slave dialectic and his reading of Hegel and Nietzsche. The drive to mastery is connected with the desire to deliver a monologue that reduces one's audience to silence. Camus sees this sort of silencing monologue in totalitarian political systems, in domineering religious systems, and in totalizing philosophical systems. What is needed as the antidote is "the mutual recognition of a common destiny and the communication of men between themselves."[13] Camus explains: "The mutual understanding and communication discovered by rebellion can survive only in the free exchange of conversation."[14] The courage of rebellion evolves into the courage to express oneself and to bravely seek to understand the other. Camus says, "I rebel, therefore we exist," to which he adds the following: "We have to live and let live in order to create what we are."[15] In courageous dialogue we expose ourselves in a creative act. We discover who we are and what we believe by listening to the other in a way that lets her be who she is, by courageously exposing our own inwardness to the other, by bravely bearing witness to the identity of the other, and by allowing something new to develop through this process of interaction.

While I have focused here on Kierkegaard and Camus, the model of dialogue that I have in mind has been fleshed out in a variety of ways by other thinkers—as we discuss throughout this book. But let's pause here to bring in another important voice, who is associated with the European existentialism of Kierkegaard and Camus—and who provides a bridge between Kierkegaard's theism and Camus's atheism.

Let's turn to Martin Buber, a Jewish philosopher whose post-Kantian religiosity offers a further source and explanation for the kind of dialogue we have in mind. Buber is famous for focusing our attention on the I-Thou relationship, which has both ethical and theological significance. It is no surprise then that Buber was also a great scholar and advocate of dialogue. He distinguished, for example, between technical dialogue (which merely

13. Camus, *Rebel*, 283.

14. Camus, *Rebel*, 283.

15. Camus, *Rebel*, 252.

conveys information) and monologue disguised as dialogue (in which each person takes a turn speaking but without listening). But what Buber calls "genuine dialogue" is what we have in mind here. Buber explains that genuine dialogue is "where each of the participants really has in mind the other or others in their present and particular being and turns to them with the intention of establishing a living mutual relation between himself and them."[16] In genuine dialogue, the "thou" of the other is fully present.

Buber points out that in our civilization (the civilization of the European twentieth century), genuine dialogue has become increasingly difficult because of a pervasive mistrust of our neighbor. Buber maintains that great civilizations, when they are healthy, are communities of genuine dialogue. But European civilization is plagued by existential mistrust, which undermines dialogue and prevents community from developing. To overcome this requires that we allow ourselves to genuinely encounter one another in our fragility and finitude. Buber explains: "We wish to trust him, not blindly indeed but clear-sightedly. We wish to perceive his manifoldness and his wholeness, his proper character, without any preconceptions about this or that background, and with the intention of accepting, accrediting and confirming him to the extent that this perception will allow."[17] For this sort of genuine dialogue to occur, we need "far-sightedness," "independence," "trust," "unreserved honesty," "good-will," and "courageous personal engagement."[18] Courageous personal engagement of the sort Buber is describing occurs when we expose ourselves to one another in our fragility, finitude, and with hope of finding some mutuality of regard.

Buber articulates this from the point of view of a secular Jewish philosophy. Buber's conception of the dialogical situation—of the I-Thou relation—develops out of his reading of Kant, Feuerbach, Nietzsche, and Marx.[19] While Buber speaks of God and the human-God relation, this is a humanistic reinterpretation of the religious tradition that emphasizes the importance of dialogue, the experience of transcendence, and the primacy of community. For Buber, this is a god of "religiosity" that is distinguished from the God of "religion." And, as we see in Buber's thinking, the secularized and humanized god exists in dialogue with the God of religion—and in our own dialogical encounters with self, world, text, and other. In a dialogue about religion between an atheist and a theist, all of this is on the table: what we mean by God, what we mean by self, and what we mean by transcendence

16. Buber, *Between Man and Man*, 22.

17. Buber, *Pointing the Way*, 226.

18. Buber, *Pointing the Way*, 227.

19. See Margolin, "Implicit Secularism of Martin Buber's Thought."

and community. To confront those big questions in their depth requires the kind of courage I am describing here.

Dialogical Courage

It is often very difficult to think about, talk about, and defend your deepest beliefs. Dialogue requires courage. Indeed, thinking and speaking depend upon courage. The same is true for relationships. Friendship and love require courage. When we expose ourselves to another, there are risks and dangers. To have trust, hope, and love requires courage. If dialogue is about thinking, speaking, and developing relationships, then dialogue rests upon courage.

Courage is required when we exhibit toleration and extend hospitality to strangers. We don't know, after all, whether the stranger poses a risk. Toleration in its most basic sense can be understood as a kind of fortitude: we tolerate something when we have the strength to endure and forbear. Dialogical encounters require us to have this kind of strength and forbearance, which is also related to patience. And hospitable dialogue demands that we have the courage to open our hearts and minds to another person. We must also have the courage to admit our own limitations, fallibility, and failures. Finally, *in extremis*, courage is related to the existential comportment of both believers and nonbelievers. Common ground for atheists and theists is found in the fact that belief requires a kind of courage. This is the theistic courage to make the leap of faith, as Kierkegaard might put it, or to submit to God's will. This is the atheistic courage to live without appeal, as Camus might say, or to resolutely embrace death, as Heidegger might put it. The object and context of courage will be different for theists and for atheists—with the choice between God or a God-shaped hole (as it is sometimes put)—as a dividing point.[20] But the spiritual/psychological virtue of courage provides a place of commonality that also allows dialogue to happen.

In thinking about the virtue of courage, it is useful to consider courage, as Aristotle did, as in the middle between the two vices of cowardice and rashness/recklessness. We can understand these two vices in relation to dialogue and to thinking as follows. Cowardice is a kind of apathy and disinterested laziness. The slothful indulgence of ignorance and unthinking indifference represent one way that we may lack courage. The ignorant and apathetic lack the existential courage to stake a claim and defend it; they lack the "courage to be" (as Tillich might put it—we will return to Tillich

20. See Fiala, "Militant Atheism, Pragmatism, and the God-Shaped Hole."

below). Martin Luther King Jr. explains this more clearly, I think, than Tillich (whom he studied). King explains courage as:

> "the power of life to affirm itself in spite of life's ambiguities";
>
> "the exercise of a creative will";
>
> "an inner resolution to go forward in spite of obstacles and frightening situations";
>
> "creative self-affirmation"; and
>
> "the zest for living."[21]

To say that courage is connected to creative affirmation and zest helps us understand one feature of dialogue, which is that it must be a creative and vigorous interaction. Desultory, superficial, and cursory conversation is not what we have in mind: not small-talk but deep talking and thinking. It takes courage to bring all of one's energies to bear on a problem and to dive into the depths.

At the other extreme lies reckless and rash self-assertion. This is the excess that in dialogue can occur when speech becomes dogmatic and self-righteous. It may seem that the dogmatic absolutist possesses the courage of her convictions. But dogmatic self-assertion is a kind of reckless carelessness that takes fearless fortitude too far. Dogmatic self-assertion quickly becomes a diatribe and a tirade. Instead of listening to the other, a monologue ensues. It may seem that this stems from courage. But it takes things too far. Reckless self-assertion is connected to hubris, that tragic flaw that haunts Greek tragedy. Oedipus, Creon, and the other characters in Greek tragedy provide a caution. They pontificate and harangue their interlocutors. But they fail to listen—and tragedy ensues.

The kind of courage that is found in dialogue and in critical thinking is moderate and humble. Dialogue involves an openness to the other that requires trust, hope, and faith. But this can only develop in a context of moderate self-restraint. Genuine dialogue with the other should also prompt inner dialogue. One must question oneself while attempting to respond to and relate to the other. This self-questioning requires courage: to admit one's own ignorance and limitations. But courage demands that we avoid self-abnegation and apathetic indifference. It is important to courageously admit what we do not know. It is also important to courageously defend an idea or an identity. There is a dance here, a movement, and a process. The subtle dance of the dialogical process is destroyed by reckless self-assertion and by apathetic

21. King, *Strength to Love*, 207.

indifference. Dialogue proceeds when each partner is attentive to the other while also seeking insight, common ground, and wisdom.

From my vantage point as a philosopher, this kind of courageous play is central to the process of philosophy. We certainly see this in Plato and in Plato's Socrates—who courageously pursues questions in dialogue, while also admitting his own ignorance. Let me cite two contemporary sources here to make my point: Michel Foucault, an atheist, and Cornel West, a Christian. Both agree that courage is a central ingredient of dialogue and of philosophy itself. But both remind us that there is often more to the picture. While Foucault reminds us that we must be cautious about making any such declaration as a dogmatic and universal claim, West warns that the rationalistic presuppositions of the philosophical tradition may need to be supplemented with something other than reason.

Foucault reminds us that the norms and practices (the disciplines) of dialogue are not stable or universal.[22] Dialogue itself is a practice that has a genealogy and which is located in concrete situations. Dialogue partners are embodied human beings, who come to dialogue with background knowledge, social status, and a whole set of historically conditioned preconceptions. Foucault's general approach is to expose all of this through genealogical critique. He shows that there are struggles for power at play in all human interactions. There is, from this perspective, no such thing as a perfectly reasonable, emotionally satisfying, egalitarian, and mutual dialogue. In fact, the ideal of such a frictionless dialogical space is itself socially constructed: an ideal that has a history and that carries with it explicit and implicit sets of values. Nonetheless, Foucault suggests that in our part of the world—in the modern, Western world—there is a specificity to this history. For us—well, for me, as a twenty-first-century, American philosopher—there is a presupposition that dialogue is used to disclose truth and that there is value in courageous conversations and in speaking truth to power. But that presupposition has a history and a location: it is a legacy of the European Enlightenment, which is itself dependent upon a Christian and Greek pre-history.

In lectures from the early 1980s, Foucault provides an outline of the history of this ideal, tracing it back through Kant to the Greeks. He describes the Greek ideal of free, frank, bold, and courageous speech (which he locates under the term *parrhesia*). He argues that "dialogue is a major technique for playing the *parrhesiastic* game."[23] The practice of dialogue depends upon the ability to speak freely, frankly, boldly, and courageously. But, as Foucault

22. See Falzon, *Foucault and Social Dialogue.*

23. Foucault, "Meaning and Evolution of the Word Parrhesia."

points out, the game of dialogue and courageous speech presupposes a whole bunch of other practices and disciplinary assumptions: about the nature of political power, about human subjectivity, and about the power and value of truth. Foucault also points out that philosophical dialogue always occurs at a given time and place in history (what he calls, using the Greek, the *kairos*—the opportune moment).[24] Philosophy has a "reality" and work to do in the real world, from Foucault's perspective: dialogue is not merely abstract wordplay—it has embodied reality. And, as Foucault argues, what is crucial for this reality is that there are those who listen to or are receptive of philosophy. In the jargon of Foucault, there is a kind of subjectivity that is created by and developed within the disciplinary structures of philosophy. In other words, dialogue only occurs when those who engage in it affirm the values of listening carefully and speaking courageously that are assumed by the practice of dialogue. Foucault describes a "circle of listening" as part of the structure of philosophy. This circle of listening is disrupted by violence, by political posturing, and by mere rhetoric. Foucault explains:

> This is the circle of listening: philosophy can only address itself to those who want to listen. A discourse which only protested, challenged, shouted, and raged against power and tyranny would not be philosophy. No more would a violent discourse, which forces its way into the city and spreads threats and death around it, find its philosophical reality.[25]

And here we return to the importance of courage. Dialogue can easily devolve—under threats of violence, tyranny, and oppression. We know these dangers from the history of philosophy (which Foucault himself discusses here): Socrates was executed by Athens, and Plato was imprisoned by Dion, the tyrant of Sicily. When bold, courageous, frank, and free speech encounter resistance and violence, there are dangers. Courage is required. But as Foucault reminds us, all of this is dependent upon contexts and opportunities that are historically constructed and dependent on a whole world of lived reality.

One important point to make here is that philosophical dialogue is quite specialized. Socrates, Plato, Kant, and Foucault are privileged in relation to the rest of the world. So, too, am I. Those of us who do philosophy for a living—who engage in dialogue with students, colleagues, and the community—have a privileged vantage point from which to discuss this issue. We must remember that none of this comes naturally or easily. We must be trained in the art of dialogue. And the practice is selective: tyrants are not invited, nor are those

24. Foucault, *Government of Self and Others*, 227–28.

25. Foucault, *Government of Self and Others*, 235.

who fail to play the game of providing reasons and listening to the other. The courage that is part of this, along with the other virtues of dialogue, is developed over time, with disciplined practice.

Another point must also be emphasized, which is that there is in all of this a presupposition about the importance of rational discourse. The authors and exemplars we have discussed so far have been men of status and power whose power rests in their ability to master the game of rational dialogue. But life is more complicated than that—and involves more than just rational dialogue. Let's turn to the work of Cornel West to see one part of the problem. Cornel West is an African American philosopher and a Christian—a Black man who works in a profession that is predominantly white and which has often looked askance at religious belief. As a philosopher West shares much of the Kantian and Socratic spirit. But he adds an interesting wrinkle. He puts it this way in describing the kind of courage that he sees as essential to the life of philosophy.

> A philosopher is a lover of wisdom. It takes tremendous discipline, it takes tremendous courage to think for yourself, to examine yourself. The Socratic imperative of examining yourself requires courage. William Butler Yeats used to say that it takes more courage to examine the dark corners of your own soul than it does for a soldier to fight on the battlefield. Courage to think critically. Courage is the enabling virtue for any philosopher, for any human being I think in the end. Courage to think, courage to love, courage to hope.[26]

West links thinking with loving and hoping here in an especially provocative way. Of course, West is a Christian, so this makes sense. And he also offers a critique of the philosophical tradition that he locates in what he sees as a key difference between Socrates and Jesus. Jesus cries, suffers, and loves; but Socrates never weeps. West described this difference in an interview where he said:

> Socrates didn't have as much compassion as he should have. He was arrogant. He never cries. He never sheds one tear. Jesus wept. That's a big difference. People who never cry never love deeply. Socrates lived too much in the mind. Questioning is very important, but you have to wed the spirituality of questioning with the spirituality of loving, and if they don't go hand in hand, you're missing something.[27]

26. West, "Cornel West: Truth," 6 (an interview in Taylor's *Examined Life*, which is a companion to the film of the same name, *Examined Life*.)

27. Cornel West in Morrison, *Cornel West*, 69.

Here is something worth considering in terms of dialogue across the atheist-theist divide. Is our dialogue to be merely rational—or is it also emotional? If it is to be inclusive of both perspectives, it must likely involve all of this. We need both intellectual courage and emotional courage—the courage to think and the courage to weep. This may not come easy to the atheist and philosopher, who is trained in the art of thinking and is less adept at the art of feeling.

But of course, all of this is complicated: no one is entirely one thing or another. The process of speaking and listening that is part of dialogue is, after all, part of life—and life includes joy and sorrow, thought and emotion, bodies and minds. To enter into a dialogue is to bring all of life with you. This includes the disembodied rational and dispassionate parts as well as the deeply personal and affective parts of the soul. Philosophical dialogue is often merely rational and dispassionate. Religious life appears to include something else. And it is this, I submit, that often seems to leave philosophers and religious people inhabiting different worlds. To a certain extent atheism is connected to philosophical dispassionateness, while theism is connected to a more passionate, heartfelt experience. This is an exaggeration, of course; there are passionate atheists and indifferent theists. But my point is that a genuine dialogue must also bring together both the heart and the mind. And again, this requires courage: both intellectual courage—the courage to think, criticize, argue, and defend ideas—and spiritual/emotional courage—the courage to feel, relate, and suffer with the other.

I submit here that we might find the unity of passion and thought, love and reason, in what we might call wonder. When Plato suggests that philosophy begins in wonder, he reminds us of the importance of wonder in critical thinking and in philosophical dialogue (see *Theaetetus*). Philosophy is "love of wisdom" after all: it is a process of courageously wondering and talking over the things we wonder about with those who share our love of wisdom and passion for understanding. And Plato points toward the mystery of love that moves us from the body toward the mind (in *Symposium*). Aristotle connects wonder to the human tendency to dig deeper and deeper in the meaning of things, their origin, and purpose. He implies that religion and myth also begin in wonder—since, as he says, "myths are composed of wonders."[28] But philosophy continues to probe, question, and wonder. The courage of wonder—the courage that it takes to keep wondering and the courage that is developed when we wonder—is an essential part of philosophy and of dialogue. But wonder involves unrest, uneasiness, and the uncanny. It takes effort and courage to hover in wonder. In a sense, courage is a presupposition of

28. Aristotle, *Metaphysics*, 982b.

wonder: we must overcome fear—of uncertainty and uneasiness—in order to experience wonder. But the courage I have in mind here also develops from wonder and belongs, in a sense, to the act of wondering. When we wonder, we discover a kind of freedom from fear that is found in the freedom of hovering outside of the realities we wonder about.

Kant famously said that two things fill him with wonder: the starry heavens above and the moral law within.[29] These two things point in the direction of the sublime, which threatens to annihilate us. Contemplating the starry heavens reminds us of our finitude; contemplating the moral law reminds us of our infinite responsibility. Both can be overwhelming. If we dare to be wise, as Kant suggests is the key to enlightenment, we must courageously face the paradoxical confluence of our finite existence and our infinite responsibility. The need for such courage is only apparent when we begin to wonder about our own existence—and about the meaning of life, the existence of God, and the nature of morality. And paradoxically, we discover courage in coming to understand this in a self-critical way, that is in discovering the will to think for ourselves. In this way, we can connect Kant's account of wonder with his call for courage in "What Is Enlightenment?": we must dare to be wise; and in digging into the depths, we discover a sense of wonder that gives us hope and the courage to persevere. In the same way, it takes courage to enter into dialogue. The other presents a challenge and a risk. But what we discover in confronting this challenge—when the dialogue is genuine, mutual, and courageous—are sources of wonder that give us further encouragement.

Courageous Dialogue vs. Disciplined Debate

Let's dig even further and consider the extent to which this kind of courage—the courage of wonder—is present in most dialogical situations. For some people (perhaps for most people), courage is less wonder-filled than this. They enter into dialogue in order to courageously defend their beliefs against the other. But this sort of "dialogue" ought properly to be described as a "debate." The sort of dialogue we have in mind here is not about courageously defending one's beliefs. Rather, it is a process of wondering about belief and identity. And in this process of wondering with others, a different sort of courage emerges. This is the courage of hovering, wondering, and thinking self-critically. It is in this sense that the courage

29. Kant, *Critique of Practical Reason*. See also Frierson, "Kant and the End of Wonder."

of wonder actually belongs to wonder: it is discovered and developed in the very process of wondering.

To say this in another way, consider a remark made by Giorgio Agamben when asked whether he was a pessimist. He said: "Thought, for me, is just that: the courage of hopelessness. And is that not the height of optimism?"[30] His playful and paradoxical point seems to be something like this: the more we think about things, the more complicated and convoluted they become—and the more pessimistic things seem to be; but the more we think, the more hope we have that thinking can help us find meaning and purpose and a solution to the difficulties of life. In the context of dialogue, a similar point holds. The more we talk and explore our differences (and what we have in common), the more we discover that those things that keep us apart are less important than they appeared, while those things that hold us in common are less substantial than we might have suspected. There is no guarantee that dialogue will help us discover common ground. But so long as we engage in dialogue, we continue to explore the possibility that we might discover common ground. Indeed, what we discover is that it is in the dialogue itself that common ground, wonder, and courage are discovered and sustained. A dialogical situation such as this is clearly not a debate. It does not seek victory or certainty. Quite the contrary, a dialogue based on courageous wondering provides no guarantee of a conclusion or hope that we will remain who we were before we entered into the dialogue.

This sounds obscure, so let's ground this in a real-world example. In the interfaith dialogues that I (Andrew Fiala) have participated in, something is found in the dialogue itself: a common humanity that is seeking meaning. The meaning that each of us will ultimately derive about the world will be different. But this difference need not keep us from recognizing the other's aspiration to discover and affirm meaning. These dialogues are not debates. The parties do not come together in order to establish supremacy or defend their ideas. Rather, such a dialogue begins, typically, with breaking bread and sharing a song. And it depends upon vulnerability, intimacy, friendship, playfulness, what King calls (as quoted above) zest, and what others have called *joie de vivre*.[31] This is different from debate. On the one hand, dialogue involves this playful vulnerability; on the other hand, debate involves serious defensiveness. Each supposes a kind of courage. But the openhearted courage of wonder—the courage of dialogue—is different from the competitive courage of debate.

30. Skinner, "Thought Is the Courage of Hopelessness."

31. For an interesting discussion of joie de vivre, the importance of song and breaking bread, as well as other dialogue values, see hooks and West, *Breaking Bread*.

Another way of considering this idea can be found in Paul Tillich's idea of the courage to be. Tillich explained: "The courage to be is the ethical act in which man affirms his own being in spite of those elements of his existence which conflict with his essential self-affirmation."[32] This links courage to doubt—and what we might call humility (see the discussion of humble courage above). The courage of self-affirmation occurs despite all that undermines the self and its certainty about its identity and belief. Tillich is a Christian theologian. So it should come as no surprise that he links courage to religion. He says: "Every courage to be has an open or hidden religious root."[33] He means that the courage to be is grounded in some affirmation of being—what religious people call God. And for Tillich, even if one denies that this is God (as the atheist does), there is still some affirmation of transcendent reality that occurs when we affirm being. It is this movement of courage and faith that prompts Tillich to speak about "theism transcended" and "transcending the theistic idea of God" and moving toward "the God above God."[34] But—and here is the crucial point—all of this talk of theism transcended and the God beyond God puts the firm ground of courage into question. With Tillich in mind, dialogue cannot be a matter of defending basic principles of theology. Rather, the humble, existential courage that we find here is simply the courage to persevere in the attempt to find meaning.

Now, atheists like myself will wonder whether it is really necessary to move into the theological register, as Tillich does. Camus and other existentialists share much with Tillich in terms of the need to have the courage to persevere in pursuit of meaning; but for the atheist, this occurs without invoking God or the God above God. Paul Kurtz, one of the prominent defenders of atheism and humanism in the twentieth century, offered a response to Tillich in his book *The Courage to Become*. While Tillich emphasizes the need for a transcendental ground for the courage to be, Kurtz argues that human existence consists only in becoming. Kurtz writes: "The affirmation of courage is not simply the 'courage to be,' as Paul Tillich called it, but the courage to become, because it is the latter, not the former, that is the essence of the species."[35] He continues:

> We have no clearly defined essence to fulfill, only an existence to create. Humans are able to conceive or invent their own destinies. All other species have natures, which they seek to realize. Human nature is in the realm of consciousness, freedom,

32. Tillich, *Courage to Be*, 3.

33. Tillich, *Courage to Be*, 156.

34. Tillich, *Courage to Be*, 182.

35. Kurtz, *Courage to Become*, 23.

> autonomy, and creativity. We are free to decide who we shall be, where and how we shall live.[36]

Kurtz explains that this kind of freedom requires a kind of courage—the courage of creativity that embraces freedom. And he declares in opposition to theism:

> Anti-humanistic, transcendental theism is the polar opposite of human freedom. For there is a collapse of courage, a failure of nerve, an escape from freedom, and a retreat from reason into the myths of consolation. Transcendentalism is unable to face the reality of human finitude.[37]

This dispute (or is it a dialogue or a debate?) between Tillich and Kurtz is helpful in fleshing out the dialogue between theists and atheists. There are deep disagreements here and strong language. But could there also be common ground? This common ground can be found in the very question about the larger structure of being or becoming. This question is shared by both the theist and the atheist, and it works itself out in the psychological, spiritual, and existential structure of the lived experience of both theist and atheist. Tillich reminds us that atheism is often only the rejection of simplistic theism—that kind of theism that turns God into another object in the world, who is understood by way of simplistic analogies with ordinary objects. But Tillich, of course, is not a traditional theist. The God beyond God of Tillich's theology is not merely the tyrant who rules the universe. Nor is he merely an object among other objects. Tillich implies that this means that there is something deficient or immature in a theology that sees God merely as an object to be defended in an abstract debate about objective principles; there is also something deficient or immature in an atheism that merely rejects this simplistic theology by knocking down the straw man of simplistic theism. Kurtz may be attacking such a straw man. However, and here is my point, Kurtz and Tillich—to the extent that they are talking about the importance of courage in pursuit of meaning—may have more in common than is often admitted. A courageous theism (and a courageous atheism) must remain open to that which is larger, more mystical, and more wonderful. It is here that we find—and create—the possibility of common ground: in recognizing that there is much to talk about in terms of the difference between theistic and atheistic responses to being and to becoming.

Now this turn to theology and humanistic philosophy may seem obscure. So let's return to a concrete example. When I (Andrew Fiala) have

36. Kurtz, *Courage to Become*, 23.

37. Kurtz, *Courage to Become*, 24.

been involved in genuine dialogue with theists—whether with students, scholars, or religious practitioners—these dialogues unfold in a space of wonder and openness that takes courage to confront and sustain. But these dialogues are different from the kinds of debates that sometimes occur in similar contexts. A debate ensues, for example, based upon readings of key texts or when directed to arguments for the existence of God (say, the cosmological argument) or against the existence of God (say, the problem of evil). I have had students and colleagues who enjoy that sort of debate. I also enjoy it myself. But the spirit of debate, the existential feeling or phenomenology of debate, is different from what we find in dialogue. In dialogue, it is not a matter of seeking to defeat an opponent or attempting to defend a proposition. Rather, it is a practice of wondering, questioning, and playing with ideas, while also seeking common ground and being willing to expose oneself while also remaining receptive to the other.

Concluding Note on Social Justice and Equity

Of course, dialogue is a special moment that occurs at a given time and place. Foucault reminds us that all of this is embodied and situated. Ordinary daily practice for me, as an atheist academic living in California, does not require any special effort. Life unfolds in its ordinariness. No one is trying to kill me for my beliefs—as happens to atheists in other parts of the world. I have tenure and academic freedom. I can say and think what I want. I can also remain silent, if I choose. Sometimes I am challenged in my beliefs—by students, by colleagues, and by those I encounter in community activism and interfaith events. When I am challenged to think about the meaning of life, suddenly the ordinary is set aside. Sometimes the challenge aims to provoke a debate—and then I work through the arguments and seek to defend propositions. But at other times there is a spirit of wonder in the air and ideas unfold in a more humane and existentially uplifting way. And even though, in the end, my fundamental beliefs about reality tend toward the naturalistic, humanistic, and materialistic, I find that in dialogue about these beliefs they lose their firmness. The world and the self become less certain in dialogue. The same is not true in debate, since the goal of debate is to courageously defend a position. The courage that it takes to engage in dialogue is different: it is the courage to open oneself to wonder and potentially to lose the kind of certainty that debate rests upon.

Before I conclude this section, let me address a concern regarding social justice issues that rest in the background here. I mentioned that I have quite a privileged position in all of this—as a white, straight, male academic living in North America. It is easy enough for me to talk about courage in dialogue—since no one is trying to kill me for my beliefs. This is not true of atheists in other parts of the world. While there is residual distrust of atheism in the United States, our fundamental law of religious liberty—in the First Amendment to the Constitution—protects me in my atheism. Furthermore, in the twenty-first century, there is increasing tolerance. And my own intersectional identities allow me to deflect intolerance, distrust, and violence. I can go quite easily through my daily life without any worry about my identity. It is easy enough to keep quiet about my atheism and simply rely upon my class, education, gender, and racial identity to protect me in my privilege. The same is not true for atheists (and for theists) of different backgrounds. While it is easy for me to speak of courage and wonder—it may not be so easy for a non-white, gender nonconforming person who is also an atheist.

This means that we must take proactive steps to help change remaining inequities and that we must continue to defend basic principles of secularism and religious liberty. Let me return, in closing, to the voice of Martin Luther King Jr. King suggests that courage is an activity that demands that we speak truth to power and that we challenge injustices and inequities. And indeed, this demand to courageously speak up in the name of social justice is essential for genuine dialogue. A dialogue implies that there is a meeting of mutuality. But when there are inequities and injustice there can be no mutuality. Those of us who are privileged to engage in wondering dialogue owe it to those who are less fortunate to find ways to share this privilege.

Response: What Am I?

Peter Admirand

In *Game of Thrones*, Samwell Tarly is initially portrayed as a blubbering, docile, and frail man-child, banished to the Wall by his "masculine" father. In the midst of the rebellious and violent wildlings, and expected to live as a soldier with no further ties to his former life and forbidden any future family, the banishment was really a death sentence. Sam does not become a warrior like Jon Snow, but amidst all his whimpering and stumbling, when any courage is desperately needed, Sam somehow shows enough resolve and fortitude (even if he never recognizes it as such). More importantly, he is guided by a strong moral compass, where his true courage lies—not in any ability to wield a sword or bow.

In the book of Genesis, the patriarch Abraham shows remarkable courage when he heeds the word of an unproven God and leaves his homeland of Ur for some promised land. More awe-inspiring, Abraham challenges God when that biblical being speaks aloud about plans to destroy Sodom. Mere mortals addressed, let alone challenged, divine beings at their peril. Yet, Abraham spoke for the innocent. "My Lord, what if there are only fifty righteous ones?" The Lord responds: "For the sake of those fifty, I will not destroy it." Abraham probes further. Does the same promise apply if there are only forty-five? Forty? Thirty? Twenty? What if only ten? This seems reckless, yet Abraham persists—a heroic courage. God agrees to spare destruction even for ten individuals.

Alas, Sodom and Gomorrah are still destroyed, though God sends an angel to warn Lot and his family (Genesis 18 and 19). They were apparently the only good people in the cities (rabbis later argued that even the babies in the womb could be considered wicked in Sodom because they would be raised in the ways of their parents). While the biblical God plays a modern-day villain, Abraham is again the hero. And yet, when traveling with his wife Sarah through foreign lands, he twice pretends she is his sister so no harm will apparently befall him because of her beauty. She is subsequently taken into the harems or households of Pharaoh and Abimelech (Genesis 12 and 20). Courage, this is not.

Abraham is also silent when God supposedly called him to sacrifice his son, Isaac. This is the focus of Kierkegaard's *Fear and Trembling*, the famous "leap of faith" line, and the very problematic "teleological suspension of the ethical"—as if ethics—love of neighbor—were separate from love of God. Such instead is a leap into what Phyllis Trible calls a "text of terror." We know there was human sacrifice in the Near and Middle East—but if the moral was to say Yahweh forbids such sacrifice, why have a bound Isaac stare up at the glinting knife held by his father, poised to come down? This is faith as failure, not leap.

Courage, though, is a virtue many of us are scared to acknowledge or seek. Worries, fears, and previous failings have such a strong pull.

"I am often the only atheist in the room," Andy begins his chapter. Not sometimes—but often—Andy acknowledges, explains, defines, or defends his position—the "only atheist in the room." While Andy praises "modest atheism" and one may be lulled in the genuine modesty (and learnedness) he shows in these chapters, note his courage and belief that atheists should be present, active, and included in interfaith dialogue—an idea some of his fellow atheists and some of my fellow theists challenge or undermine through sneers or silence.

He calls for a dialogue of both reason and emotion (the mind and heart), sourced in wonder, that is "courageous, genuine, and mutual." Such a call, echoing Kant, must have the courage "to use your own understanding," and as importantly, "to admit what we do not know." It challenges us to practice being active listeners—and here, active readers. A "genuine dialogue," Andy writes, should have the "courage of hovering, wondering, and thinking self-critically." I can only sing "Amen" to so much of this chapter, but let me highlight areas mentioned that (taking the theme of courage) scare me.

Andy wonders if it is "really necessary to move into the theological register." This is a question that demands courage from theists—and so must be asked and reflected upon. Above I opened with a story from popular mass fiction and a story from the Bible. Abraham is hailed as a father of faith. His moral failings and dearth of courage towards his wife and son rest side by side with his bravery in advocating for strangers. The courage of Jesus in the garden of Gethsemane to face his likely crucifixion is also part of the theological register. Are such theological stories necessary—in a different way—from the courage of "purely" literary figures like Samwell

Tarly, the Tin Man, Henry Fleming, or Antigone? Are they potentially more harmful or liberating? Both?

On the challenging and time-worn question of "being or becoming," I have to confess my ignorance, curiosity, and fear in dipping into such waters. I hold to the belief that all of creation, but especially human beings, are created by a holy God. This God of Love has fashioned beings made in God's image and likeness. We are thus intrinsically holy and dignified, entailing rights and responsibilities for all. It means our hours and days should be lived through seeking, and living toward, a God that is love. Because of our finitude and frailty, we are always becoming and striving, which is best expressed for the good of others (and which for theists is linked to love of God). While we are not born equally in terms of capabilities or favorable contexts, all human life is valued, and to weigh (without fear and trembling) any life against another is at the cost of moral trauma and decline.

What, moreover, of the same privileges (minus the atheism) that I also have, which Andy acknowledges? We are thus two white, male, educated, straight, non-disabled, and blessed (and/or lucky) tenured academics. Is it really surprising we agree on so many issues—even if disagreeing on the following True or False question: whether God exists? Aren't such privileged voices (especially mine as a theist in the West) suspect?

Further scarier questions: Should our voices still be heard in light of all these privileges? Does the God question become paramount in the midst of so many similarities—or (rightfully) subsumed and minimized? Such is to say, I don't know of my own courage, but I have a lot of fears, so if neither a Samwell Tarly nor an Abraham, what am I (the courage question par excellence)?

Chapter 4

Humility through Dogs and Dickens

Peter Admirand, Primary Author

The story about the Leningrad dog was what did it. I was reading Svetlana Alexievitch's *The Last Witnesses*, a hope-shattering but illuminating oral history of childhood memories about life in the Soviet Union during WWII. These are tales about mamas and papas murdered before their children's eyes by the *Einsatzgruppen*; witnessing torture and mutilation—unending cries of agony and murdered gods—starvation and bloated bodies—stories of a world not just upside down but so brutal that everything seems subsumed in a vacuum of despair and meaninglessness. But then there is always a worse story. And for me, it was the one about the dogs—"My dear dog, forgive me"—as recounted by Galina Firsova.

As I type these words, I glance at my German short-haired pointer, Sally, who adores me and my wife and kids with all the clichés of canine love. She is slumbering on the couch but if I call her name (I won't) she'll bounce over to me, ready to go wherever I want. Seeing Sally while reflecting on the story adds to my discomfort, especially those haunting words: "My dear dog, forgive me."

Galina was ten years old. It was during the Siege of Leningrad—nine hundred days—bodies were piling up—accounts of cannibalism common. Anything was desperately eaten—tree bark, grass, dirt. . . . Soon there were no cats in Leningrad—and the dogs were also rarely seen. Galina would have died twice over if a neighbor had not first given her their family cat—and then dog. Many couldn't kill and eat their own pets, but Galina was suffering from blindness (and previously, hearing loss). Reluctantly, after three days, her mom tied the dog to the family radiator. She told Galina and her sister to leave the room.

Galina still remembered "those meatballs."[1] Her vision returned.

1. Alexievich, *Last Witnesses*, 267.

But there are worse stories.

Sometime later, again, on the verge of death, Galina had just received her daily ration at the bakery when a dog approached her. "This dog . . . our salvation!"[2] She gave him bits of bread, leading the dog to the family's apartment. The dog was rightfully leery—but was also starving. Up four flights. More scraps. One more flight of stairs, but Galina was out of food. "There he stopped and wouldn't go any further. He looked at me . . . as if he sensed something. Understood, I hugged him, 'My dear dog, forgive me . . . my dear dog, forgive me.'"[3]

It meant her family survived a few more days of the nine hundred they had to endure.

Can a dog be more loving than God? Any theist should be careful in responding quickly—but the answer seems evident. It leads a theist like me to another question—how can religious faith not be humbled, if not extinguished, by such stories?

This chapter focuses on humility, which also leads to many questions: Is humility not a so-called virtue that sometimes masquerades as a vice? Does it not tend to be in short supply in those who most need it, while grinding and smothering the frail and breathless? Is not humility mostly a weapon of the arrogant to sustain their power against those deemed beneath them, another way of speaking about Marx's "opium of the people" regarding religion? Is it not a mere platitude, an empty word one hears or says, or even claims? The answer, I'm afraid, is mostly yes, but humility is also so much more.

And what would it mean to really live humbly? To believe humbly, to learn, listen, and question humbly?

Religions all value humility, sometimes bordering on depravity—seeing the human as a vessel of sin, puffed up in pride or emptiness. Theists are often reminded we are nothing before God, nothing without God—think of the tradition of paintings of saints contemplating dead bones, a skull. Such is a shock treatment form of humility—and may be necessary for some individuals to see through their so-called autonomy, permanence, and accomplishments.

In my previous writing on humility, while not hiding its flaws, I stressed how I advocated a spunky humility that does not denigrate self or others, but, balanced by other virtues, is an honest assessment of the self. Intellectual humility is particularly relevant in our context—where theists and atheists acknowledge gaps and breaks in their knowledge, the mountain

2. Alexievich, *Last Witnesses*, 269.

3. Alexievich, *Last Witnesses*, 269. See also Peri, *War Within*.

of ignorance still to overcome, and the need to be open for corrections, unanswered questions, and growth. It is a virtue that can help unite all sides to learn and to listen to one another.

In this chapter I first analyze humility in three classic Christian thinkers: Benedict of Nursia, Anselm, and Benedict of Clairvaux.[4] Using literature as a common ground between atheists and theists, I will then examine a few scenes involving key female characters in some works of Charles Dickens; namely, Florence Dombey in *Dombey and Son*; Amy Dorrit in *Little Dorrit*; and Lizzie Hexam in *Our Mutual Friend*. From that final work I will also examine the Jewish character of Riah, which will further complicate and sharpen humility's portrayal, also providing an interfaith context.

I chose Dickens both for the richness of his characters and also for their flaws (and his own too[5]). Possibilities of literature as a common ground between atheists and theists are obviously endless; and I could have just as easily chosen a Cormac McCarthy or Maya Angelou. Also note that Florence Dombey and Amy Dorrit, much like Little Nell in *The Old Curiosity Shop* or Esther Summerson in *Bleak House*, embody the ideal feminine in much of Dickens's works. In calling them "ideal," other critics, as George Bernard Shaw points out, would call them "ridiculous idealizations of their sex."[6] They are all, thus, deeply loyal, nurturing, self-sacrificing, humble, and courageous. The humility of these characters can be defective, with traces of self-negation and self-deprecation. But there is still much to revere in their steadfastness and moments of rebellion.

First, though, I'll begin with one of the core founders of Western Christian monasticism who also happened to survive two assassination attempts on his life (by a monk and a priest, respectively).

The Humble Steps of Benedict of Nursia

Augustine's "Letter 221"[7] to a community he founded of women religious in Hippo made a deep impact on Benedict of Nursia (d. 543), often deemed the founder of Western monasticism. While we begin here in a cloistered setting, for Benedict such was rarely an escape from the chaotic political

4. For an examination on humility within other seminal Christian thinkers (like Augustine, Aquinas, Ignatius of Loyola, and Teresa of Ávila), see the first chapter of Admirand, *Humbling Faith*.

5. While rightly praised as a social reformer, Dickens has been criticized for some hypocrisy, especially in the treatment of his first wife, Catherine Hogarth. See Nayder, *Other Dickens*; and Wilson, *Mystery of Charles Dickens*, 97–141.

6. Shaw, "Introduction to *Great Expectations*," 638.

7. Augustine, "Letter 221." See also Fortin, "Saint Augustine's Letter 211."

situation in Rome.[8] From monks who tried to poison him with wine; to a priest, Florentius, who tried to poison him with a loaf of bread; to battling lusty visions of a woman that sent him running in a field of thorns as punishment; to encountering a mad woman who stumbled into his cave (and was subsequently cured), Benedict's life was eventful. An example of the radical conversion, he grew tired of his studies in Rome and headed for the solitude of caves in Subiaco, Italy. Attracting followers, he established cenobitic monastic groups and then a Grand Monastery at Monte Cassino, where he wrote his *Rule* around 530.[9]

In the *Rule of St. Benedict*, Benedict refers to degrees or steps of humility, borrowing biblically from the image of Jacob's ladder (Gen 28:12), and from Jesus' words: "For all who exalt themselves will be humbled, and those who humble themselves will be exalted" (Luke 14:11).[10] The first step is that a man keeps the fear of God before his eyes without fail. Here we may be reminded of *The Way of a Pilgrim* and the quest to pray continually.

"The second step of humility," Benedict tells us, "is that a man loves not his own will nor takes pleasure in the satisfaction of his desires," but submits to God's will.[11] The third step is to obey one's superiors. The fourth step is to submit to any suffering, even unjust suffering that may accrue from obeying one's superiors. The fifth step is to confess everything to one's abbot, even a stray, unhealthy thought. The sixth step calls the monk to be "content with the lowest and most menial treatment, and regard himself as a poor and worthless workman."[12] Here one may think of Buddhist instruction to look upon oneself as a rotting corpse, though as Catherine Cornille notes: "Within Buddhism, the term 'humility' is scarcely in use" because there is neither "a permanent abiding self" nor "personal creator God."[13] Pride, however, is a deep cause of ignorance and craving which must be overcome.

Returning to Benedict, the seventh step further accentuates a break with any pride and vanity, calling the monk not only to admit his low position but to believe it in his heart. The eighth step demands a monk act

8. Cunningham, "Cassian's Hero and Discernment," 234.

9. For the classic if hagiographic account of Benedict, see Book 2 of Gregory the Great's *Dialogue* with commentary in Kardong, *Life of St. Benedict*, 1–2. For an article comparing the leadership of Benedict, Confucius, and Francis (with helpful biographical details), see Garcia, "Brothers from Different Mothers."

10. For the influence of Cassian and especially the *Rule of the Master*, see Foulcher, *Reclaiming Humility*, 95–163. See also Pardue, *Mind of Christ*.

11. Benedict, *Rule of St. Benedict*, 18.

12. Benedict, *Rule of St. Benedict*, 19.

13. Cornille, *Im-Possibility of Interreligious Dialogue*, 48.

according to the monastery's common rule and the actions of one's superior. The ninth step demands silence, except when asked a question. The tenth step is to restrain from senseless laughter, while the penultimate step is to speak modestly, briefly, reasonably, and gently (and without laughter). The final step is to do everything with a sense of humility. Perhaps ironically to many contemporary listeners, such a seemingly punitive process is a means to "cast out" fear and "arrive at the perfect love of God."[14] For many practitioners, peace and joy result.

In this way, one performs these steps, ideally and ultimately, purely from a love of God and not out of any fear of hell, though such fears are prominent in the early steps.[15] For Trappist monk Thomas Merton (d. 1968), such steps are means of uplifting human beings. While Merton (and I) would accentuate humanity's inherent dignity as creatures made in the image and likeness of God, Thomas More adds: "It makes psychological sense to affirm our inferiority, thus grounding our confidence in an accurate view of ourselves."[16] Such so-called monkish virtues, famously rebuked by David Hume, still need to be carefully calibrated and assessed. Can such humility be supported by contemporary theists, let alone (somehow) secularized for nontheists in a healthy way? For now, though, let us advance six centuries and move to France and England and see how the virtue further developed.

Anselm and the Mountain of Humility

Geographic and epochal jumps have advantages and disadvantages. It may speed things along but at a great cost to depth and nuance. In this case, as Darby Kathleen Roy writes, the time of Anselm (d. 1109) is "a period of stunning change. . . . In nearly every area of life—politics, economics, and social relations, and religion—Europe was dramatically transformed."[17] While the Christendom of Augustine and Benedict was in its early stages, in the time of Anselm we have a pervasive "imperial spirit"[18] and what Joerg Rieger calls "medieval empire formation—the Norman conquest of England, the First Crusade, the expansion of the lands of 'Latin Europe,' and the extension of the power of the pope."[19] It is also a feudalistic world

14. Benedict, *Rule of St. Benedict*, 20.

15. Benedict, *Rule of St. Benedict*, 16–20.

16. More, "Preface," xv–xxv.

17. Ray, "Anselm of Canterbury," 123.

18. Ray, "Anselm of Canterbury," 124.

19. Rieger, *Christ and Empire*, 14.

which shapes nearly every aspect of people's lives, and certainly contributes to Anselm's understanding of God and the atonement with its language of honor, satisfaction, and debt. Shawnee M. Daniels-Sykes argues that because of Anselm's immersion in feudalistic thinking and a high Christology approach, he "neglects a Christology from below, which challenges Eurocentric superiority and envisions Jesus as a liberator of the oppressed."[20] Such an approach may also have had an upside, however, as Anselm was, at best, a reluctant supporter of the First Crusade in 1096, forbidding fellow monks to go, and in one well-known earlier case, encouraging a noble layman to become a monk for the heavenly Jerusalem rather than joining his brother to fight in Byzantium in 1086.[21]

Theologically, Anselm's ontological argument for the existence of God and his interpretation of the atonement are still widely studied, along with their many famous critiques by the likes of Hume and Kant.[22] From our contemporary post-Auschwitz, post civil-rights, human rights vantage point, we can easily spot the historically and contextually moral flaws of medieval thinkers like Anselm. Such flaws need to be addressed to prevent undiscerning support or accept hidden assumptions. Anselm's atonement theory, as I have argued elsewhere, has caused much damage to women and the marginalized in its argument for necessary suffering. Its depiction of God demanding satisfaction in the death of Jesus has also been a major barrier to Christian interfaith agreement with Jews and Muslims.[23]

Despite these serious flaws, in Anselm we see further development of the Benedictine tradition of examining humility.

Anselm was born in Aosta, a town bordering the kingdom of Burgandy, in 1033. Turned away from his local monastery, he became one of the wandering scholars seeking study as there were no formal universities yet established (the University of Bologna and the University of Paris were founded in 1088 and 1150, respectively). Unlike Benedict, Anselm thrived in his formal period of study. At the Benedictine monastery of Bec, he became the prior and schoolmaster and wrote classic works like *Monologion* and *Proslogion*.[24] Anselm's willingness to include his own ideas and original thoughts were met with criticism from his mentor (Lanfranc), misunderstanding, and

20. Daniels-Sykes, "Anselm of Canterbury," 40. For a contrary view (arguing the feudalist approach is outdated and one needs to read Anselm through his monastic background), see Hidden, "Alleged Feudalism."

21. Cowdrey, "Pope Urban II's Preaching."

22. See Davies, *Philosophy of Religion*, 304–55; and Oppy, "Ontological Arguments."

23. Admirand, "Healing the Distorted Face."

24. Anselm, *Monologion and Proslogion*.

even calls of heresy.[25] Reluctantly transferred to Canterbury to serve as archbishop, Anselm had to endure numerous rows with kings William Rufus and Henry I, leading to periods of exile in Rome.

For Anselm, as for all these Christian thinkers, Jesus' life and thought are the cornerstones and guides of reflection. As he asks in the *Meditation on Human Redemption*: "Good Lord, living Redeemer, mighty Savior, why did you conceal such power under such humility?"[26] Anselm contends it was not to deceive but to redeem human beings.

Anselm treats the theme of humility through using the metaphorical images of a mountain with seven levels, which one ascends from a plane (representing pride) below. As we read in *Dicta Anselmi* (*Anselm's Sayings*; composed and redacted by the monk Alexander): "But humility is a great mountain, at whose summit there is full light, and a crowd of very good persons, that is the holy virtues. It is climbed by seven levels."[27] Interestingly, Anselm shortens Benedict's twelve steps into seven stages, but never cites Benedict explicitly. The first level is "to acknowledge oneself contemptible"; followed by grieving about this reality (step 2); confessing it (step 3); convincing others of this contempt and wishing for their agreement (step 4); "bear[ing] patiently that this be said of us" (step 5); "suffer[ing] oneself to be treated with contempt" (step 6); and finally, "loving being thus treated."[28] Persevering in one's suffering with patience and humility is grounded in Paul and other foundational Christian thinkers like John Cassian (d. 435).[29] What is particularly helpful about Anselm is the linking of humility and mercy. As Gregory Sadler comments, for Anselm, a humble regard for oneself does not equate to critical vehemence of others. Recognizing and praising others' virtues can have an alleviating or didactic influence on the sinner, penitent, and the one tempted. As Sadler comments: "So, each person should pay attention to the other's virtue, not their vice, and to their own vice, not to their virtue."[30]

Returning to Anselm's metaphor, the valley (as noted) represents pride. Ironically, what seems to promote great altitude (pride) diminishes and lowers. We instead climb a mountain through the virtue of humility which helps us confront, heal, and surmount egoistic, self-centered, and

25. For concise overviews, see Evans, "Anselm of Canterbury"; and Sadler, "Anselm of Canterbury 1033–1109."

26. Anselm, *Prayers and Meditations*, 233.

27. Translation from Sadler, "Anselm and the Seven Levels of Humility."

28. Quoted in Aquinas, *Summa Theologiae*, 2.2.161.6.

29. See, for example, Cassian, *Institutes*, 4.7 and 12.33.

30. Sadler, "More on Anselm and Humility."

self-seeking tendencies. Such a metaphoric image is used to visualize Jesus' saying highlighted above from Luke and here in Matthew: "All who exalt themselves will be humbled, and all who humble themselves will be exalted" (23:12).[31] Interestingly, Anselm also includes two guardians of the mountain: "Modesty that is before God, and modesty that is among human beings."[32] Unfortunately, it is the latter that can lead one astray, even after ascending the mountain. One must always be on guard. As he writes: "Behold how the poor man is deceived, how quickly he is conquered, how cunningly he is overcome!" For Anselm, a person may rationalize that no one will see a certain sin I may do and I can then "correct myself so that by suffering enough, I will make myself better than I am right now."[33] In the climb of humility—and as Aragorn told Théoden in *The Lord of the Rings*—"there is no rest yet for the weary."[34]

Bernard of Clairvaux: Seeking Humility by Truthfully Studying the Steps of Pride

I could certainly apply Aragorn's warning to theologian and mystic Bernard of Clairvaux (d. 1153). He was a member of the Cistercian Order, which sought a deeper return to the *Rule of St. Benedict*.[35] As a founder of the monastery of Clairvaux, Bernard was profoundly committed to the Cistercian reform and to the affairs of the universal church. Such ambitions brought him into a number of political and theological quarrels. Emero Stiegman calls Bernard a "watchdog of orthodoxy. . . . [yet] he is himself a theologian whose originality and intellectual daring sometimes surpasses" those he accused of heresy or unorthodox thought (notably Peter Abelard).[36] In Bernard we have a preacher who led the call for the Second Crusade (including the battle at Lisbon in October 1147[37]), but also a figure who helped heal the church schism of 1130 and rose from his sickbed to defend Jews attacked in

31. This biblical passage is followed by anti-Pharisee and Scribe denunciations, embarrassing to Christians attuned to the Jewishness of Jesus and the importance of interfaith dialogue; Jews would be justly offended.

32. Sadler, "Two Guardians of the Mountain of Humility."

33. Anselm, *Dicta Anselmi*, para. 4.

34. Tolkien, *Lord of the Rings*, 676.

35. See Matarasso, *Cistercian World*.

36. Stiegman, "Bernard of Clairvaux."

37. See Phillips, "St Bernard of Clairvaux." See also Scales, "Central and Late Medieval Europe," 297.

the Rhineland.[38] Even here there is much grey area, as he argued Jews should not be killed as they are still being punished by God but will eventually be led to conversion as God is merciful.[39] For many Jewish people, there would be little distinction between conversion and killing, and Bernard's depiction of Jews aligns with the *adversus judaeos* tradition. Nevertheless, he has a more positive record than his contemporary Peter the Venerable (1156).[40] Bernard's view of Muslims was even more severe, though he focused on defending Jerusalem; otherwise Muslims could be left alone.[41] As with many of these proponents of humility, Bernard's moral failures and biases must be highlighted and rebuked. As Jane Foulcher astutely (and rhetorically) asks: "Did Bernard ever admit to being wrong?"[42]

Bernard examined humility throughout his life and writings. Foulcher, for example, highlights not only the importance of truthfulness and authenticity in his reflections, but a gradual nuancing of humility as cold and warm, linked with reason and the will, respectively. She writes that for Bernard, "Cold humility, arising from 'truthful reasoning,' . . . [is] a step towards warm humility, the humility infused with love."[43] Such humble love is steadfast and sure,[44] a key feature of the Dickensian female characters further below.

In Bernard's first published work, *On the Steps of Humility and Pride* (*Liber de gradibus humilitatis et superbiae*), he assesses twelve steps (or degrees) of humility by way of the twelve steps of pride. He traverses this course, as he tells the abbot of Fontenay, Godfrey of Langres (who had requested the work), because he has more experience falling down the steps of pride than rising on the path of humility.[45] This is a shrewd and humble approach.

Bernard organizes these steps further into three subgroups: the first six entail contempt for one's brothers, the next four towards one's superiors, and the remaining two, for God.[46] In this way, the path of humility begins

38. For helpful historical context, see Chazan, "From the First Crusade to the Second"; and Boys, *Has God Only One Blessing?* 57–64.

39. Bernard of Clairvaux, *Letters of St. Bernard of Clairvaux*, 1953.

40. Chazan, "From the First Crusade to the Second," 49–50.

41. See Kroemer, "Vanquish the Haughty"; and Phillips, "St Bernard of Clairvaux."

42. Foulcher, *Reclaiming Humility*, 239.

43. Foulcher, *Reclaiming Humility*, 203.

44. Foulcher, *Reclaiming Humility*, 203.

45. Bernard of Clairvaux, "Steps of Humility and Pride," 142.

46. Bernard of Clairvaux, "Steps of Humility and Pride," 137.

with one's attitude towards God, and so is the foundation for one's attitudes towards, and treatment of, one's fellow human beings.

Bernard highlights our dependence and weakness before God. This awareness counteracts any attempt to justify a false freedom and independence.[47] Otherwise, sinners would show no shame and slide into habitual sin. As Aristotle had earlier noted in the *Nicomachean Ethics*, character, habit, and virtue (or vice) are intertwined. Aquinas, of course, would emphasize this a century after Bernard, upon Aristotle's rediscovery in the Christian West.[48] Bernard, as Martin Luther pointed out, did not read Aristotle, but if he had (contra Luther), he would have found much of it fitting here.[49]

As a quick overview, Bernard's steps of pride are the following: the proud are overly curious (step 1).[50] They are not content where their attentions should lie—"concentrat[ing] hard on the state [they] are in."[51] Such unhealthy curiosity is followed by being frivolous and shallow, falling into useless (or derisive) laughter (steps 2 and 3). The proud are boastful and overly chatty (step 4); seek uniqueness (step 5); claim superior holiness (step 6); are nosey in others' affairs (step 7); justify their sinfulness (step 8); confess without sincerity (step 9); rebel against superiors (step 10); claim full independence to act as they want (step 11); and sin as habit (step 12). The steps of humility, then, promote the opposite tendencies, but their numbers correspond in the reverse order.

The first step of humility is watchfulness and an awareness and fear of God's presence. This sense of mindfulness, similar to the Buddhist context of Thich Nhat Hanh,[52] defends against habitual sin (the twelfth degree of pride). With such attentiveness, participants focus on their own state and condition. Bernard's counter examples are Dinah, Eve, and Satan, though we may want to rehabilitate the first two cases from their patriarchally-biased stumbling. Keys are to recognize our frailty, weakness, and inadequacies as we encounter individuals who do not share our own religious or ethical lenses.

47. Bernard of Clairvaux. "Steps of Humility and Pride," 138.

48. MacIntyre, *After Virtue*, 71.

49. As Brian Daley clarifies, *The Nichomachean Ethics* became widely available again in the 1240s from the translation into Latin by Robert Grosseteste (Daley, "'To Be More Like Christ,'" 15). In reflecting on the Nicene Creed's opening "I believe in God the Father Almighty, Maker of heaven and earth," Luther writes that "this article ought to humble and terrify us all if we believed it" (Luther, *Large and Small Catechism*, 76; see also 34, 49, 87, and 102).

50. Being curious is one of the virtues praised in our book.

51. Bernard of Clairvaux, "Steps of Humility and Pride," 123.

52. Hanh, *Living Buddha, Living Christ*, 20.

The second step of humility is deeply challenging, for we are not to take joy in fulfilling our desire or loving our own will. We hear this beautifully interpreted in the blogposts of the Benedictine Nuns from Holy Trinity Monastery: "After mindfulness of God comes mindfulness of self in relation to others. What I want to do isn't necessarily the best thing I could do, and what's good for me isn't always good for others."[53]

The humble person, then, experiencing freedom in obedience and habitual serving of God (third step of humility), is all too aware of his sins and so acknowledges and repents of such failings candidly. Contra, for example, "insincere confession," the ninth step of pride, the corresponding fourth step of humility calls for forbearance even in the face of false accusations.[54] In the context of confession (the fifth step of humility), moreover, Bernard points to the pitfalls of a "prideful humility," where one can confess one's sins proudly or falsely.[55] In expressing sins honestly, one takes responsibility for them and avoids self-justification and excuses.[56] Thus, the humble person shows no presumption and takes no excessive initiative (sixth step of humility), of placing himself above others, showing arrogance (against the sixth step of pride). He not only asserts his frailty but accepts it (the seventh step of humility). With such acceptance, he knows that any praise he receives is owed to God.[57] Not claiming such specific praise is also linked to being content with oneself and one's ties with others and so does not seek to be different (eighth step of humility).[58]

Contra the fourth prideful step of boasting, the humble person in the ninth step of humility cherishes and practices silence. Such is a core feature of his repentance, watchfulness, and learning.[59] Silence enables listening to others, especially one's superiors. When one speaks, recalling Benedict, one speaks moderately.[60]

The next step of humility (the tenth), also reminiscent of Benedict, opposes foolish merriment. We should not be glum and gloomy but avoid the reality of sin, suffering, and loss. The humble are immersed in reality,

53. Benedictine Nuns from Holy Trinity Monastery, "Self-Will by Bro Duncan PBGV." In this particular post, the nuns pretend it is their beloved hound dog writing, which is a nice link to the ninth step of humility, rebuking laughter (think scorn or derision).

54. Bernard of Clairvaux, "Steps of Humility and Pride," 136.

55. Bernard of Clairvaux, "Steps of Humility and Pride," 136.

56. Bernard of Clairvaux, "Steps of Humility and Pride," 135.

57. Bernard of Clairvaux, "Steps of Humility and Pride," 134–35.

58. Bernard of Clairvaux, "Steps of Humility and Pride," 133.

59. Bernard of Clairvaux, "Steps of Humility and Pride," 132–33.

60. Bernard of Clairvaux, "Steps of Humility and Pride," 131.

as Jon Sobrino notes. Sobrino's liberation theology speaks in solidarity with the poor and oppressed. It does not shield their cries and pains from its impact on theology and praxis.[61] Yet the poor, liberation theologians, and monks also laugh. Aware of evil and misery, they find great joy and comfort in their faith, in one another, and those they serve. And sometimes, all you can do is laugh. The Benedictine nuns from Holy Trinity Monastery clarify: "Humor misused easily becomes cruel, and what began as one of God's pleasantest gifts is warped into something horrible. It is not being a killjoy to suggest that we need to watch our laughter and ensure that it builds up rather than destroys."[62]

The eleventh step of humility further focuses on one's own need for penance and repentance instead of judging others (and so avoiding lightmindedness), a sure means to combat envy and depression. The twelfth step calls for living and being humble in all one does, not out of fear of God, but love of God. It is also linked to the love and care of others. According to Mark Button, such openness can be a great asset in our contemporary pluralist society.[63] Bernard's interpretation of humility prepares the way for a "fraternity or neighborliness with others and seeks to understand and listen to our fellow human beings."[64]

Also crucial is Bernard's focus on authenticity and truthfulness as part of this humbling.[65] Such authenticity and truthfulness are also key features of the female characters I will now highlight in the fictional worlds of Charles Dickens. How do such characters both embody and challenge the humility presented above, and what kind of humility results from such mixing?

Let Us Now Praise Humble Women: Humility among Dickens's Female Characters

Little Dorrit

Little Dorrit, rarely called Amy, endures her proud father's often inconsiderate treatment, but heroically tries to help maintain his sense of pride, despite living in the Marshalsea debtor prison. This was also Dickens's prison as a child

61. See, for example, Sobrino, *No Salvation Outside the Poor.*

62. Benedictine Nuns from Holy Trinity Monastery, "Of Clowns."

63. Button, "'Monkish Kind of Virtue,'" 841.

64. Button, "'Monkish Kind of Virtue,'" 850.

65. Foulcher, *Reclaiming Humility*, 179 and 187.

when his father fell into debt in 1824. It was an experience that shadowed him. Unsurprisingly, Amy is painted in an almost ethereal light.

In the first scene examined below, Arthur Clennam, having had pangs of conscience that his family fortune was earned through dubious means, has befriended Little Dorrit and is instrumental in quietly working towards freeing and economically rejuvenating the Dorrits (indeed, they eventually became wealthy). Once released from the debtor's prison, Mr. Dorrit wastes no time: only the best dresses and other fashionable joys of life are good enough for his three children. Anyone, including Clennam, who knows of their life in the Marshalsea must be removed and silenced from their rising family orbit. As the father remarks to his children in his stuttering fashion: "It would appear that Mr. Clennam is put altogether out of the question, and that we have nothing to do with him or he with us."[66]

Clennam had performed untold acts of kindness to Mr. Dorrit when he was languishing in prison, but now the father feels he must uphold the pretence that Clennam was the one always seeking his "society": "He knew my society to be-hum-sought."[67] Soon, the family is off to the Continent as fashionable people must (and to escape knowing connections remaining in London). In one key section of the book, Little Dorrit closes a letter to Mr. Clennam: "That you will think of me (when you think of me at all), and of my true affection and devoted gratitude, always without change, as of / Your poor child, Little Dorrit."[68]

The letter drips with self-effacement and modesty, but recalling her father's clear warning to sever any contact with Clennam, it becomes an act of rebellion, integrity, and courage. She will not forget Clennam's steadfast kindness. As an aside, note that Clennam could also be a model of humility, but of the kind that comes from a catharsis and moment of crisis. Amy is humble and humbled from birth; Arthur's humility solidifies as he meets Amy and in his quest to right past wrongs. They are an admirably romantic, if not humility-infused, pair.

To return to Amy: yes, she is unknowingly humble and in love, and even here she cannot fathom that Clennam would have any such mutual feelings for her. While at this point in the narrative, Little Dorrit needs to be inflated, moving away from identifying herself as a child and embracing a richer picture of her self-worth, of key importance is her humility that seems immune to all forms of potential corruption, especially that most unyielding one of sudden riches, recognition, and status. Her

66. Dickens, *Little Dorrit*, 435.

67. Dickens, *Little Dorrit*, 434.

68. Dickens, *Little Dorrit*, 448.

unabashed, enduring loyalty to helpless individuals like Fanny (even after Amy's joyous marriage to Clennam) testifies to key components of humility: integrity and steadfastness.

Heart's Delight: Florence Dombey

In *Dombey and Son*, Florence Dombey is the neglected and forgotten child who had the temerity to be born female. Yet, she loves her irascible, cold-hearted father with a daughterly love that borders on, if not exceeds, the heroic. Mr. Dombey is consumed with having a son and heir. When Florence is born, she is a disappointment and an opportunity wasted. Like Henry VIII, only a son matters; only a son is demanded. When Paul is born, Florence is all the more shunned and insignificant. Their beloved mother dies shortly after childbirth, but Mr. Dombey still has plans and ambitions to fulfill. The business will be Dombey and Son and nothing can dim that reality. He remarries a beautiful woman (Edith Granger) whom he neither loves nor who loves him: but what matters is that she is beautiful and (he assumes) obedient.

Paul, meanwhile, is groomed to take over his father's firm ("girls have nothing to do with Dombey and Son," as Mr. Dombey intones), but unlike his father, Paul deeply loves and admires Florence, or Floy as he calls her. He is also doomed to a short life. On his deathbed, Paul's last words are spoken to Florence about their mother,[69] whom he never knew but sees reflected in Florence's face. He was six years old. The father isolates himself even further in his grief. The mere sight of Florence repels him. Yet, she can only love her father and worry about him. Her childish naïveté and low self-esteem yearn for her father's love: "And now Florence began to think, if she were to fall ill, if she were to fade like her dear brother, would he then know that she had loved him; would she then grow dear to him, would he come to her bedside, when she was weak and dim of sight, and take her into his embrace, and cancel all the past?"[70]

Florence is worth ten of her so-called father. Fortunately, she also has the motherly affection of Edith, the care and concern of Captain Cutler, and the (eventual) love of Walter. Though Mr. Dombey had exiled Walter at sea to spite Florence, she remained loyal. Only the spunky Susan Nipper, who had been Florence's caretaker for twelve years, berates Mr. Dombey. She tells him: "You don't know your own daughter, sir, and you don't know what you're doing, sir, I say to some and all . . . that it's a

69. Dickens, *Dombey and Son*, 211.

70. Dickens, *Dombey and Son*, 325.

sinful shame."[71] Foaming, Mr. Dombey cannot believe such a person had the audacity to speak to him, asking the head of the household: "Do you know this woman?" His ignorance of Susan only further testifies to his unrecognized, unrepentant, "sinful shame." Matters grow darker. Edith, initially threatened by Dombey to cease all contact with Florence, finally ends their loveless marriage. She demands divorce. When the exasperated Mr. Dombey scoffs, she flees into the arms of Mr. Dombey's smooth, calculating, and corrupt right-hand man, Mr. Carker.

Florence knew none of the details, acting only from her all-embracing love. Mr. Dombey, out of pride, seeks to fetch back Edith. When he instead returns alone, Florence

> hastened towards him unchecked, with her arms stretched out, and crying "Oh dear, dear Papa!" as if she would clasp him around the neck.
>
> And so she would have done, but in his frenzy, he lifted up his cruel arm, and struck her, crosswise, with that heaviness, that she tottered on the marble floor.[72]

He then insulted her and Edith. Florence shed no tears. "She saw him murdering that fond idea to which she had held in spite of him."[73] Florence fled and eventually is taken in and protected by Captain Cuttle.

The captain's second mentioning is a perfect time to "make a note of" that irrepressible sea dog, who is "one of those timber-looking men, suits of oak as well as hearts,"[74] and "with a hook instead of a hand attached to his wrist." In short, he was deeply deserving of a daughter like Florence, the father figure she had so desperately sought. "It's Heart's Delight" said the captain, looking instantly in her face, "it's the sweet creetur growed a woman!"[75] Florence had initially sought Walter's uncle, who was in search of finding Walter, feared dead from a shipwreck. Florence begs the captain to safeguard her and ensure no one knows her whereabouts. Captain Cuttle pledges that she can tell her story whenever in the future she is ready and asks no questions: "And as to giving you up. Or reporting where you are, verily, and by God's help, so I won't, Church catechism, make a note on!"[76] He would do anything for his Heart's Delight and hopes beyond hope that

71. Dickens, *Dombey and Son*, 570.
72. Dickens, *Dombey and Son*, 615.
73. Dickens, *Dombey and Son*, 615.
74. Dickens, *Dombey and Son*, 113.
75. Dickens, *Dombey and Son*, 618.
76. Dickens, *Dombey and Son*, 619.

poor Wall'r will resurface. When Walter is found alive, it is Florence who asks Walter to marry her; her plea again has all the marks of humility but is all the more bold for her taking action: "If you will take me for your wife, Walter, I will love you dearly."[77] They get married and name their son Paul in honor of her deceased brother (and father).

While Florence's father is now alone and ruined financially, she still returns to see him. Mr. Dombey, as ever, remains proud in her long absence and amidst his social fall. But her unrelenting and consummate forgiving love (like the Taoist image of water wearing down the roughest of stone) finally breaks through. The proud man is humbled by her kindness; the "better angel"[78] forces the proud devil to submit. Florence had felt remorse for having left him alone. She begs his forgiveness, when he should have implored hers. As an aside, I must admit I found it refreshing that Edith would not forgive Mr. Dombey so easily: "Tell him I am sorry that we ever met,"[79] she tells Florence. She then relents somewhat for Florence's sake (who can resist her humble persistence?), saying that his love for Florence can be a means of their mutual need for repentance.

Florence's humility is inseparable from her boundless love of others. But while a deeper, healthier self-love could be sought, there is a fierceness and resolve in her ways that are ultimately commendable. She may be an angel and a heart's delight, but she enlivens all those she encounters and is instrumental in a lost, broken man being restored. If there is a moral failure, it is her separation from Edith. This issue touches on the hypocrisy of Victorian society: Edith is a "fallen" woman for having left her husband for another man (even as she ultimately rejects Carker, who dies a wretched and violent death). Edith lives out her remaining years alone, insisting that she was "innocent."[80] Her situation touches on Victorian discrimination against women and Dickens's own double standard in this regard. Edith, though as proud as Mr. Dombey, had never committed such reprehensible acts. Mr. Dombey, though, spends his remaining days with his grandchildren. Perhaps this is the father in me, but I read Florence's forgiveness of him with much astonishment and rancor. Is her humility excessive, or must it be so to be truly humble?

77. Dickens, *Dombey and Son*, 657.

78. Dickens, *Dombey and Son*, 798.

79. Dickens, *Dombey and Son*, 801.

80. Dickens, *Dombey and Son*, 798.

Gaffer's Daughter—and the Old Jew

In Dickens's *Our Mutual Friend*, Lizzie Hexam is another exemplar of the heroic female whose beauty is only matched by her humility and sacrifice. She serves her father as his companion and helper while he prowls the river Thames in search of lost and valuable refuse, especially cadavers. Cadavers paid well as loved ones sought the missing. Here is an early exchange between Lizzie and her father after another body had been found (initially believed to be the promised heir of a fortune, John Harmon):

Lizzie's father, nicknamed Gaffer, grunts: "Here. And give me hold of the skulls. I'll take the rest of the spell."

"No, no father! No! I can't indeed. Father—I cannot sit so near it!"[81]

Not your typical father and daughter collaboration, but Lizzie—like Nell, Esther, Little Dorrit, and Florence—is dedicated to her family and endures much grief despite her sacrifice for them. She repeatedly defends her raspy, growling father and often ingrateful brother.

Her father, though, is later murdered, and despite the suspicion that he played a role in the young heir's death, Lizzie remains loyal. At the same time, she supports the education of her younger brother Charley, not only against Gaffer's wishes but through her own labor. Soon after Gaffer's drowned body is found entangled in nets, Charley tries to control and parent Lizzie, pressuring her to marry his apoplectic and prone-to-fits tutor, Bradley Headstone. Instead, Lizzie confesses to an angry and perplexed Charley, "I mean that I do not like him, Charley, and that I will never marry him."[82]

While Lizzie's hard edge of humility here resembles the other humble female characters above, the character Riah is more complicated. He is an old Jewish moneylender, and a pointed contrast from the Jewish criminal Fagin in *Oliver Twist*, twenty-six years earlier.[83] Fagin is such a repellent and immoral character that his constant description as "the Jew" caused much consternation among the Jewish community in England after the book's serial publication. Such complaints were periodically brought to Dickens's

81. Dickens, *Our Mutual Friend*, 3.

82. Dickens, *Our Mutual Friend*, 401.

83. "'Aha!' said the Jew, shrugging up his shoulders, and distorting every feature with a hideous grin." See Dickens, *Oliver Twist*, 54. Fagin is brandishing a knife as he exclaims that "aha," admiring his valuables and other trinkets stolen from associates, conveniently put to death by the State. Fagin's physical grotesqueness and odd mannerisms are accentuated, much like they will later be (to more comic and horrific effect) in the character of the "dwarf" Daniel Quilp in *The Old Curiosity Shop*. Leering at Little Nell, and forcing a kiss on her cheek, we read: "'Ah!' said the dwarf, smacking his lips, 'what a nice kiss that was—just upon the rosy part. What a capital kiss!'" See Dickens, *Old Curiosity Shop*, 97.

attention. It is also possible, as Heather Abrahamson, a Jewish colleague of mine on the Irish Council of Christians and Jews, reminded me, that Dickens created all sorts of unsavory and despicable characters, most of whom were presumably Christian. Such scoundrels lurked and skulked in the shadows and bowers of Dickens's worlds, so it wouldn't be surprising that one of those villains would also be Jewish. Nevertheless, Riah initially seems too morally perfect, even if serving as Dickens's apology for Fagin. In fact, in later editions of *Oliver Twist*, Dickens removed those ubiquitous "the Jew" references. James D. Mardock contends that Dickens goes further than criticizing his own bias, and so intends Riah is an anti-Shylock figure to "critique his own society's depiction of the stage Jew."[84]

Leaving aside this debate, our next scene involves Lizzie Hexam, distraught after having rejected Headstone's marriage proposal while remaining adamant against her brother Charley's threats: "'And this girl,' cried the boy contemptuously, throwing her off again, 'calls herself a sister!'" And more stinging: "I'll not unsay them. I'll say them again. You are an inveterately bad girl, and a false sister, and I have done with you. Forever, I have done with you!"[85]

As Lizzie is lost in melancholy, Riah approaches her (Dickens's London is conveniently provincial, when needed).[86] "'My daughter,' said the old man, 'I stand amazed! I spoke as to a stranger. Take my arm, take my arm. What grieves you? Who has done this to you?"[87] Notice that Riah is so kind-hearted that he had reached out to comfort an apparent stranger. Lizzie tells Riah of her brother's words. Riah remarks strongly that Charley "is a thankless dog." He entreats that she let herself be escorted by Riah and protected in his home. "For it is past your usual time, and will soon be late, and the way is long, and there is much company out of doors to-night."[88]

As if on cue, Eugene Wrayburn appears (just as Lizzie and Riah "passed out of the churchyard"). Wrayburn is initially portrayed as a dandy whose interest and attraction in Lizzie has been rising (confer the heat in his name, of a ray and a burn). He inquires what is wrong. At various points he wants the old man dismissed so he can be the gallant savior. After inquiring who the man is and being told by Lizzie that he was a "trusted friend," Eugene

84. Mardock, "Of Daughters and Ducats."

85. Dickens, *Our Mutual Friend*, 403.

86. For a contemporary look at the marginalized in London, see Judah, *This Is London.*

87. Dickens, *Our Mutual Friend*, 404.

88. Dickens, *Our Mutual Friend*, 404.

comments: "I will relieve him of his trust."[89] The narrator had previously noted that "the Jew having taken in the whole of Eugene at one sharp glance, cast his eyes upon the ground and stood mute."[90] This deferential, humble posture will be maintained by Riah throughout the encounter but he will not relinquish Lizzie to Eugene's care unless Lizzie advises him to do so. They share a few words, but Riah's calm manner seems to affect the normally careless and carefree Wrayburn: "Even Eugene was checked in his light career, and subsided into a thoughtful 'Humph.'"

"With an air of perfect patience the old man, remaining mute, and keeping his eyes cast down, stood retaining Lizzie's arm." Eugene, annoyed and "fatigued" at his stubbornness, calls him "Mr Aaron and remarks that he must have an engagement at the synagogue and so to ' . . . have the kindness.' But the old man stood stock still."[91] Again, Eugene tries to have him dismissed, even asking if Riah is mute as he does not reply to some of his queries. There is a hint of Jesus before Pilate, perhaps. Riah also anticipates Dostoevsky's portrayal of Jesus in the "Grand Inquisitor" section of *The Brothers Karamazov* (published in 1880), though Jesus does not speak at all in Ivan's tale.[92]

Eugene, realizing he will not convince Riah to leave, proposes they both escort Lizzie to her home. Lizzie cannot refuse and so the destination is changed. As the narrator remarks, Eugene cannot but know of his superior "sallies and self-possession to the gloomy constraint of her suitor."[93]

After Lizzie is inside her home, Eugene and Riah exchange brief but telling words:

"'Mr Aaron,' said Eugene, when they were left together in the street, 'with many thanks for your company, it remains for me unwillingly to say Farewell.'" So suave, so measured, so ironic, and dismissive: Eugene willingly wanted to say farewell to Riah when they first met. Feeling and acting the superior to a much older man, Eugene presumes to have the last word. But Riah again reveals a moral fire underneath the calm, patient humility: "'Sir,' returned the other, 'I give you good night and I wish you were not so thoughtless.'" Of course, Eugene must reply: "Mr Aaron . . . I give you good night, and I wish (you are a little dull) that you were not so thoughtful."[94] Again, it seems the humbled are vanquished by the

89. Dickens, *Our Mutual Friend*, 405.
90. Dickens, *Our Mutual Friend*, 404.
91. Dickens, *Our Mutual Friend*, 405.
92. Dostoevsky, *Brothers Karamazov*, 273–93.
93. Dickens, *Our Mutual Friend*, 406.
94. Dickens, *Our Mutual Friend*, 406–7.

proud, but the stirrings of further questions and thoughts in this apparently thoughtless man linger and burn, especially as Eugene feels drawn to Lizzie. In the spirit of *Jane Eyre*'s Mr Rochester, Eugene will also be humbled before his love accepts him.

Returning to Riah, I am reminded of Joseph Telushkin's comments regarding the first-century context of the great Jewish sage Hillel: "The Talmudic tradition hails bashfulness as a lauded trait, and one that characterizes the ideal Jew: This people [Israel] are distinguished by three characteristics: they are merciful, bashful, and perform acts of kindness (*Yevamot* 79a)."[95] Riah seems to exemplify these traits, and yet, he is mired in a culpable relationship with the Christian usurer, Fledgeby. Toward Fledgeby, Riah is excessively patient and accommodating despite all his insults and dastardly plans. In fact, Riah inexplicably allows himself to be an accomplice and front for Fledgeby's illicit schemes, serving as the mean, stern Jewish moneylender.

Riah's redemption is made possible by Jenny Wren, a disabled doll maker and friend of Lizzie whom Riah had protected, even becoming Jenny's "Godmother." (Note the feminine name, which may justify my including Riah in this section on female Dickensian characters, but it also raises questions, in Dickens's Christian patriarchal world, of Riah's outsider status as Jewish.)[96] Tragically, Jenny witnesses Riah's usury role. Even though she later suspects he was taken advantage of, she rightly rebukes Riah for following Fledgeby's orders to act the part of a cutthroat moneylender.[97] Responding to her lost trust, Riah resigns from his post. Fledgeby, meanwhile, is conveniently beaten to a pulp by one of his debtors, the schemer and fraud Mr. Lamme. Riah apologizes to Jenny and so resumes his cherished role as her "fairy godmother." He even admits that "I was hateful in mine own eyes. I was hateful to myself in being so hateful to the debtor and to you."[98] He then adds that "in bending my neck to the yoke I was willing to wear, I bent the unwilling necks of the whole Jewish people."[99] Here, perhaps Dickens is quintessentially too dramatic and saccharine (and unfortunately echoing the problematic passage in Matt 27:25). But Riah is right to acknowledge that his allowing Fledgeby to use him as an image of the evil Jewish usurer would damage Jewish lives and dignity. He is lucky to be forgiven so easily. The reader is then reminded of Riah's own saintliness when he plans to go to Fledgeby, "that beaten cur," to nurse him in his wounds. Jenny, though,

95. Telushkin, *Hillel*, 156.

96. See, for example, Baumgarten, "Seeing Double."

97. See, for example, Grossman, "Absent Jew in Dickens," 37–57.

98. Dickens, *Our Mutual Friend*, 726.

99. Dickens, *Our Mutual Friend*, 727.

"irritably" retorts: "Godmother, godmother, godmother! . . . I really lose all patience with you. One would think you believed in the good Samaritan. How can you be so inconsistent?"[100] Riah refers to a Jewish call to help the needy, but she again interrupts, saying Fledgeby is undeserving and wants to be left alone. She is also right to call Riah "inconsistent." He will help the "cur" but had allowed him to lord his wealth and interest over debtors. Yet, despite Riah's flaws, his love of one's enemies exposes the un-Christlike acts of Christians (Lammel, Fledgeby, etc.). In accepting his imperfections and taking responsibility for them, Riah can still serve as an exemplar of humility. The humble, like the Christian saints above, are not perfect and are often in need of forgiveness.

A Humble Conclusion: Going to the Dogs

The portraits of fictional characters embodying humility help to deepen and nuance the humility elevated, but what precisely is being raised? Challenging subservience, such humility must stand up to injustice, and where someone fails, to make reparations and signs of repentance, as with Riah. Thus, the humility I see worthy of being elevated is necessarily scrappy, rugged, and obdurate, willing to be fierce in the midst of oppression and injustice. All the fictional characters above exemplified this, with Riah (a male godmother) a more complicated but ultimately relevant example because of his working for Fledgeby. All had to struggle and endure difficulties, vexation, and uncertainty. Theologically, here one may speak of a faith wounded or broken as Elie Wiesel and Irving Greenberg have noted, or refer to a fractured theodicy,[101] or theological "limping."[102] Yet, it is still resilient and alive.

In this chapter, I first examined how humility was depicted in three foundational, male, Christian theologians, whose theology, rooted in the life and action of Jesus as the highest image and reality of humility, remained fairly consistent throughout Christendom. Today, we are rightfully hesitant and a bit skeptical about humility. We can point to the self-righteous and call for them to be humbled, or those who need a dose of humility, but we know too many who have been told for too long to be quiet, to silence themselves, to just endure. From Black Lives Matter to #MeToo, we now proudly praise those who assert their once disempowered voices and demand respect, equality, and justice for all. Yet, humility can still play an important role in that process. For all its flaws, humility remains a timeless virtue, as

100. Dickens, *Our Mutual Friend*, 727.

101. See Admirand, *Amidst Mass Atrocity*.

102. Vanhoozer, "Scripture and Tradition," 168.

alive in fiction as in theology, for the believer as much as the nonbeliever, the practitioner as much as the recipient.

As a theist, though, in light of what we have read of humility from a few novels of Dickens and three Christian foundational thinkers, what should my response be to real stories of abject tragedy and suffering—to witness and oral testimonies to mass atrocity like Galina's in the introduction? When a dog seems to show more empathy, kindness, and sacrificial love than any God, how should a believer try to respond? Do we:

1. Try to justify the evil experienced?
2. Focus on free will or evil as mere privation and perversion of what is essentially, intrinsically good?
3. Place the blame (primarily) on human beings for choosing harm or apathy?
4. Highlight a God who suffers in the face of such corrosive evils, in solidarity with all of creation, but especially the victims, whether human or nonhuman?
5. Trust in postmortem justice, and a God who will right wrongs and heal the despair and abandonment that contaminate many lives in this world?

Theists will often employ one or all of these ideas—but we are fooling ourselves if we think such attempts fully solve the mystery, remove all legitimate doubt, or justify any triumphalist religious faith. Stories like Galina's deeply humble, if not silent, theistic belief. Theists may stress a God of love and perhaps see a divine reflection in the act of Galina's neighbors who gave away their beloved pets so another family could live; or in the unnamed, unknown "dear dog," even if we can never fully know his reason for entering Galina's apartment.

But this too leaves scars without healed wounds, gaps without bridges, oceans of doubt. The spunky humility advocated here may cobble together, bravely or foolishly, reasons to keep believing in God despite stories of horror and useless suffering. Yet, the virtue also commends silence, acknowledgement of failures, and so deep understanding for those who cannot believe because of the evidence before them.

This robust but flawed virtue can still guide how believers approach the believer-nonbeliever dialogue, aware their own "answers" are unsatisfactory, their positions faulty, their faith fractured. My hope is that such a humble awareness will nurture kindness and understanding, whether exemplified in Little Dorrit, St. Benedict, or that dog in Leningrad following an emaciated girl to her apartment.

---- * ----

Response

ANDREW FIALA

I ADMIRE PETER'S CONSIDERATION of the virtue of humility. I am humbled by his scholarship and erudition. I also believe, as I think Peter does, that a kind of humility is essential for living well—and for engaging in a dialogue across the religious/nonreligious divide. My approach is fallibilistic and pragmatic. My understanding of humility here is connected to what is often called intellectual humility. I admit that there are mysteries and questions that leave us without answers. But intellectual humility is not the same as skepticism. Humility is a virtue that lies between arrogance and self-abnegating diffidence. There are some things we do know. About those things, humility is not proper. But we ought to be humble about the things we do not know. The challenge, of course, is knowing what we know and knowing what we do not know. This was in fact the challenge laid out for us by Socrates.

My own version of atheism is connected to different levels of agnosticism. This is in turn related to intellectual humility. Anthony Kenny put it this way in describing his own agnosticism toward religion: "If we look at the matter from the viewpoint of humility it seems that the agnostic is in the safer position."[1] Church and Samuelson have pointed out that the relationship between agnosticism and intellectual humility is more complicated than we might think.[2] Intellectual humility requires us to admit what we do not know; but it does not prevent us from affirming what we do know. From my vantage point, it seems fairly clear that the sky-God of ancient theism does not exist. With regard to that God, I am firmly atheistic. But I admit that when we wander into the thickets of modern theology, things get more complicated. With regard to the God of theology, I remain more agnostic.

1. Kenny, *Unknown God*, 108.
2. Church and Samuelson, *Intellectual Humility*.

Let's begin with the God of traditional ancient theism: the judgmental and capricious sky-God who controls the weather, who requires sacrifices, and who punishes us and plays with us. This is the God I see, for example, in the book of Job, where God allows Satan to harm Job as a test of faith. Such a God is not acceptable from a moral point of view, since God in this story explicitly allows Satan to inflict suffering on Job and his family. And the idea that God and Satan can intervene in the affairs of the world in this way also is not acceptable from a metaphysical vantage point that takes the laws of nature as fixed and views miracles as violations of these laws. Of course, the more fully developed theism of modern Christian theology offers a more complicated story. In some versions of theology, miracles get reinterpreted in ways that are more mysterious and texts like Job are reinterpreted as allegories and metaphors. There is no room to provide detailed arguments here or recount the arguments of a number of philosophers and theologians who have worked on these texts and problems, for example, Plato, David Hume, Paul Tillich, or John Shelby Spong.[3] My conclusion is this: about the existence of the philosopher's God, a "God above God" (as in Tillich) or a "God beyond theism" (as in Spong), I remain humbly agnostic; but about the sky-God of the revealed religions, I am more definitively a nonbeliever or atheist.

But let me make a point about this agnosticism, which is that it leads me to turn aside from theology and focus my attention on the human world. As Peter suggests, theologians have dealt with the problem of evil in a variety of ways, for example by providing a theodicy or even by offering a notion of a God who suffers. There are technicalities here that fascinate philosophers and theologians. Alvin Plantinga has tried to show, for example, that there is no logical contradiction between the idea of the philosophers' God (who is omniscient, omnipotent, and omnibenevolent) and the existence of evil.[4] Jürgen Moltmann has attempted to provide a theology after Auschwitz that turns away from the philosophers' God in order to focus on a suffering God who is also a loving God.[5] But these theological revisions are unsatisfying from my point of view. These ideas could be true. But how would I know? And what difference would they make to my daily life? In asking these questions, I move in a pragmatic direction. The point, for me, is not to try to figure out whether God is compatible with Auschwitz or to

3. See Fiala, *Against Religions, Wars, and States*. Plato's *Euthyphro* is an obvious source, as are Hume's *Natural History of Religion* and *Dialogues Concerning Natural Religion*. Also see Tillich, *Courage to Be*; Spong, *Why Christianity Must Change or Die*; and Spong, *New Christianity for a New World*.

4. Plantinga, *God, Freedom, and Evil*.

5. Moltmann, *Crucified God*.

look at Auschwitz as an opportunity to learn about God's suffering, love, sacrifice, and redemption. Rather, what seems to matter most is how human beings can prevent another Auschwitz. One of my areas of research is peace and conflict studies. I have had the opportunity to visit a number of places of great suffering, including Auschwitz and Hiroshima. The questions that arise for me in these places are not theological. They are moral, political, and entirely human. The humanist question is how we prevent violence, evil, and atrocity, not how we justify God in the face of evil.

Let me make one further methodological point here, which is that the multiplicity of religious claims—the plurality of religions—makes it difficult to believe that any one of them is true. Christians say that we are created in the image of God and that God loves us so much he sacrificed his Son; but Buddhists say that there is no self and that life is suffering; and the ancient Greeks and other polytheistic animists hold that we are the playthings of the gods and spirits who haunt the mountains, forests, and oceans. Given the multiplicity of theories about God, self, and world, it is wiser to admit that we just don't know—and then to get to work in the human world on the project of preventing evils and atrocities.

This conclusion, I think, is a place to find common ground. We can set aside unresolvable disputes about dogma, metaphysics, and the meaning of life if we humbly agree to disagree about theology. To agree to disagree requires a kind humility associated with being reserved, patient, tolerant, kind, and taciturn. Silence is often wiser than insistence. It is kinder to hold back than to argue against. And it is usually better to listen than to pontificate. A Christian, Buddhist, or animist might, in the end, be right about what they claim. I happen to think that the natural sciences make more sense—the big bang theory of the cosmos, the Darwinian account of life, and a brain-based theory of the mind. But most of the time there is no need to insist on this, when we are focused on the project of alleviating evil. A bit of humility should lead us to admit that, ultimately, we do not know with absolute certainty which theory is true. And since there is often no use in insisting dogmatically about these things, let's find other things we can productively talk about. Instead of pontificating, let's seek out what we have in common in terms of lived experience, aesthetic experience, psychological well-being, and moral and political values—including especially the need to prevent evil.

With all of that being said, let's consider three questions prompted by Peter's contribution.

1. Does humility mean the same thing for a theist as it does for an atheist?

2. What exactly is the solution to the problem of evil, which Peter discusses here?
3. And how does the history of power, oppression, and exclusion factor into the question of who ought to humble themselves?

These questions create difficulties in finding common ground. But they must remain on the table if we are to find common ground.

First, a Christian conception of humility may not be the same as philosophical intellectual humility. One problem is the theological issue of the humiliation of Christ, as the incarnate God who was crucified. This theological scheme (and the theodicy associated with it) is subject to atheistic and agnostic critique. A related concern is the problem of sin, which I see woven throughout Peter's account. In order for sin to be forgiven, a kind of humble confession of sin is required along with acceptance of the grace of God. This is clear in Peter's account of Bernard. We also see it in Jonathan Edwards, the early American Protestant theologian and revivalist, to cite an example from a different part of the Christian tradition. Edwards linked repentance and humility saying: "Repentance tends to humility; for no one can be truly sorry for sin, and self-condemned in view of it, without being humbled in heart for it."[6] There is a link between pride and sin, on the one hand, and humility and repentance (and grace and forgiveness) on the other.

Atheists reject the metaphysical and spiritual scheme of repentance, grace, and forgiveness. They also reject the idea that human beings are inherently sinful. Richard Rorty explains: "To have a sense of sin, it is not enough to feel guilty. It is not enough to be appalled by the way human beings treat each other, and by your own capacity for vicious actions. You have to believe that there is a Being before whom we should humble ourselves."[7] Rorty and the American pragmatists he cites reject this idea. To put this in a more positive way, atheistic humanists tend to believe that human beings are capable of good things as well as evil things. But we are not in need of divine forgiveness, repentance, or grace. What we need is better science, art, law, politics, and philosophy. This celebration of the human spirit in atheistic humanism is at odds, I think, with the Christian notion of sin. Thus, humility will mean something different for an atheist than it will for a theist. Indeed, humanists and atheists often avoid the language of humility for exactly the reason that it seems too steeped in incense and holy water. A critic of Christianity such as Nietzsche will see humility as part of what he calls "slave morality." Nietzsche says that the slave views the power of the

6. Edwards, "All the Graces of Christianity Connected," 393.
7. Rorty, "Pragmatism as Anti-Authoritarianism," 8.

master with envy and resentment, while extolling the mandatory weakness and humility of the slave.[8]

We need not accept Nietzsche's polemic against Christianity to understand that humility is sometimes psychologically damaging, especially when it is linked to a kind of self-abasement and self-abnegation. Some kinds of Christianity call for this, although it is also possible for Christian humanists to have a more affirmative approach to human pride. In the history of Christianity, this dispute can be traced back to the conflict between Augustine and Pelagius with regard to the notion of original sin. Pelagian Christianity held that human beings were good enough to solve their own problems without the need for divine grace; Augustine denied this, holding instead that we are born sinners in need of grace. Augustine says in an oft-quoted passage that the Christian path requires humility as its first step, its second step, its third step, and so on—in a letter to Dioscorus from AD 410.[9] Throughout that letter, Augustine vehemently rejects the pagan philosophical tradition—including the Epicureans and Platonists—for pridefully asserting humanity over against "the example of divine humility" seen in Jesus Christ, which Augustine describes as "an example before which, even in the mind of the most headstrong and arrogant, all pride bends, breaks, and dies."[10]

Christian humility goes so far in some cases as to include ascetic and mystical practices that demand active "humiliation": self-flagellation, mortification of the flesh, and so on. I take it that this is not Peter's point. Peter is not advocating a kind of Christianity that requires us like Job to repent in dust and ashes. Nor is he advocating the kinds of humbling practices found in the monastic tradition that he cites. But still, one wonders where an atheist might find common ground with a theist around the topic of humility, if Christian humility is fundamentally linked to original sin and asceticism.

8. Nietzsche writes: "Those qualities which serve to alleviate the existence of sufferers are brought into prominence and flooded with light; it is here that sympathy, the kind helping hand, the war heart, patience, diligence, humility, and friendliness attain to honor" (Nietzsche, *Beyond Good and Evil*, para. 260, p. 230).

9. Augustine says: "I wish you to prepare for yourself no other way of seizing and holding the truth than that which has been prepared by Him who, as God, saw the weakness of our goings. In that way the first part is humility; the second, humility; the third, humility: and this I would continue to repeat as often as you might ask direction, not that there are no other instructions which may be given, but because, unless humility precede, accompany, and follow every good action which we perform, being at once the object which we keep before our eyes, the support to which we cling, and the monitor by which we are restrained, pride wrests wholly from our hand any good work on which we are congratulating ourselves" (Augustine, "Letter 118").

10. Augustine, "Letter 118."

Let me move on quickly to my other two worries. The first follows from this discussion of the Augustinian account of original sin, which is part of a larger theodicy. Peter's account is different, I think. He leaves us with a kind of fear and trembling in the face of atrocity and with a humble admission of silent woundedness. But atheists have long been dissatisfied with this response. Peter recognizes that it is not sufficient simply to shrug and humbly appeal to the mystery of God. I appreciate this. If evil exists, the point is not merely to fret about theology but to go out and fight against it. Atheists and theists have often both seemingly ignored this point, retreating into smug self-satisfaction of theological (and a-theological) argumentation when in fact the world demands our active intervention. Evil won't go away unless we do something about it. Perhaps this is something both theists and atheists can agree upon. I know that many Christians have been at the forefront of an active response to the evils of the world. Maybe what we ought to focus on here is the fact that no theodicy (or anti-theodicy) provides us as much certainty as we have about the fact that right here, right now there are things we can all do to struggle against evil.

This brings me to my final question, which is about the role of humility in social and political life. For many millennia, it was common to claim that women, slaves, and "the other" ought to humble themselves before the pious and the powerful. The history of humility includes a whole series of practices of humiliation, by which peasants bowed to kings, priests lorded their holiness over the laity, and so on. Auschwitz provides one horrible example of hubris run amok. So too does human arrogance toward non-human animals, which is central to Peter's opening narrative. Humility is lacking in anthropocentric, racist, nationalistic, and xenophobic hierarchy. Atheists have often argued against the role of religion in supporting hierarchy, patriarchy, and authoritarianism. But we must also admit that state-sponsored atheism (as in the Soviet Union, for example) led to authoritarian and hierarchical outcomes. Perhaps a further kind of common ground can be found in the call for nonhierarchical, antiauthoritarian, and democratic values.

My focus here has been on a humble humanism and intellectual humility. This may overlap with Christian humility. But I suspect that fundamental differences remain. Nonetheless, despite these differences, we might humbly hope that there is enough here to allow us to find common ground in a critique of hierarchy and in concrete struggles against evil.

Chapter 5

Curiosity: Dialogues within Dialogues

Peter Admirand and Andrew Fiala

As curiosity has been placed in the center of our seven virtues, it seems to demand something different, especially in a cowritten book meant to be egalitarian and dialogical—in other words, equally borne and composed. As we are two people reflecting on seven virtues, the decision was to each write on curiosity and then reply to what the other produced. As I (Peter) compose these words, Andy has already sent me his section—and while I'm eager (and curious) to read it, I decided I'll first construct my piece, not knowing if what I'll write will overlap, parallel, build upon, or clash with what he's written. We'll then each reply to the other. Do we help forge common ground between atheists and theists through curiosity? Let's read and see.

Making Sense of the World: Beyond Naïve Religion and Normal Science

Andrew Fiala

Curiosity took me to the Holy Land. I spent a sabbatical in Israel several years ago, while I finished writing a book on atheism.[1] Living in the land of the prophets was an eye-opening experience for a scholar interested in politics and religion. I came away with a new appreciation of the history of the Bible, the complexity of history, and the difficulty of interfaith work. I talked with Israelis and Palestinians. I learned that Palestinians and Israelis are both unhappy with the political situation there. But I also learned that despite substantial conflict, Jews, Christians, and Muslims can coexist. My experience in

1. The book was Fiala, *Against Religions, Wars, and States*. I also began work on *Secular Cosmopolitanism, Hospitality, and Religious Pluralism*.

the Holy Land left me more skeptical of the truth of the revealed religions but also more hopeful about humanity. If we could replace fear and indifference with curiosity and compassion, we'd all be better off.

Curiosity between Fear, Evangelism, and Indifference

Curiosity is a central value of dialogue. In listening to the other, there must be an interest in what the other has to say. But we cannot listen if we fear the other (or fear that what the other might tell us will be damaging to us). In genuine dialogue, there must be a fearless hope to learn something new. And this shared love of learning must be mutual. Shared and mutual curiosity helps to create the common ground of dialogue. By focusing on curiosity, we can see three ways that dialogue fails:

1. because of fear of who the other is or what he or she might say,
2. because of an overly zealous need to convert the other, or
3. because of a kind of indifference to learning.

Curiosity lies between fear, evangelism, and indifference.

Dialogue requires a kind of courageous willingness to take a risk. Dialogue should not merely be viewed as a chance to proselytize on behalf of your preferred idea or to refute the other. Nor should dialogue be understood as mechanical debate in which each party gets a turn to make its point without ever really listening to the other. Dialogue requires mutual curiosity. It is easy to imagine examples of each kind of failure of dialogue.

In the first, case, with regard to fear, we might think of the kinds of problems we see in conflicts such as the Israeli-Palestinian conflict. When each side fears the other, there is no room for curiosity to unfold. When the other is viewed as a terrorist or an oppressor who cannot be trusted, dialogue cannot happen. When fear and distrust pollute the atmosphere, "dialogue" degenerates into name-calling and condemnation. When I lived in Tel Aviv, we spent a lot of time in the neighborhood of Jaffa, which is a predominantly Arab part of town. We enjoyed eating falafel and hummus, while listening to the muezzin (the Muslim call to prayer). One of the first steps in dialogue is to be open and curious about food, music, prayers, and rituals. When you do not understand (or bother to explore, experiment, and listen and learn), the alien and foreign can appear to be menacing and dangerous. But fear dissipates through experience and familiarity. To my mind, the hummus tasted better with the sound of the muezzin in the background. Unfortunately, the political and religious conflict in Israel has degenerated since then and anti-Arab leaders have attempted to silence the loudspeakers that call Muslims to prayer.[2]

Jaffa, by the way, is the location for a biblical story that appears to teach a lesson about food, dialogue, and fear (Acts 10–11). When Peter the apostle was in Jaffa, staying at the house of Simon the Tanner, he had a vision that led him beyond his fear of the gentiles and their "unclean" and foreign foods. An angel appeared and told Peter not to fear to eat these unclean things, since they all came from God. Peter was summoned to Caesarea to meet a gentile soldier named Cornelius, visiting him in his home. It is not clear whether Peter actually ate gentile foods. But we might learn from this, at least, that Peter needed to overcome his fear and prejudice toward the gentile world in order to pay his visit to Caesarea. Peter went on to become the first pope—and Cornelius was the first gentile (i.e., non-Jew) to convert to Christianity.

Now let's turn to the second case and the problem of evangelism. Peter's encounter with Cornelius was not exactly an open dialogue. Peter was not curious about Cornelius. He did not ask Cornelius about the Roman religion or indeed ask any questions at all. Instead, the story says that the Holy Spirit appeared and Cornelius converted. So fear is not the only impediment to dialogue. The evangelical spirit is also a problem. Missionaries and proselytes knock on doors and preach on street corners. The proselytizer may feign an interest in drumming up a conversation. But their motive is to share the good word as they understand it. The talk here is one-sided, the questions (if there are any) are loaded, and there is no sense that the proselytizer is interested in learning anything from those he (or she) seeks to convert. The most famous example of this is the episode in which Paul disputes with the philosophers in Athens. The story goes that Paul was moved by the spirit to engage in a "disputation" (Acts 17:16–34).[3] Paul's zeal moved him to preach about Christ and the resurrection of the dead to the Epicurean and Stoic philosophers of Athens. One of his main points was to condemn the religion of Athens—including its apparent worship of statues—as mere superstition (Acts 17:22). This was not a dialogue of the philosophical sort. I picture it as as a kind of harangue. Paul does not ask the Athenian philosophers to explain what they think or how they worship. This was not a two-way conversation. Rather it was an evangelical sermon. And it is not surprising that

2. See Diab, "Israeli Bill to Mute the Muezzin."

3. The words used here are interesting. The word used to explain his stirring of spirit is παρωξύνετο (*paraxyneto*), which is the root of the English word paroxysm—which means a violent and emotional attack or outburst. The word used to explain his disputation is διελέγετο (*dielegeto*), which is related to the English word "dialogue," but which can also mean to dispute and to preach.

the Athenian philosophers mocked him as a result—returning scorn to Paul in return for his own contempt for them.

This is perhaps the first historical example of a clear failure of dialogue between theism and atheism. The Epicureans were not exactly atheists in the modern sense. But they were often the subject of Christian scorn, since they saw no need for a savior, did not find value in the concept of sin, and were content to pursue happiness in this life. In a different version of this story, we might imagine a curious Christian asking the Epicureans why they believe what they do; and we could imagine the Epicureans responding in kind with a curious and open mind. But Paul's evangelic sermon to the Athenian philosophers was a failure of dialogue such as has often occurred between Christianity and its critics. When a disputation begins with the urge to save the other from what we see as ignorance and "sin," there can be no genuine dialogue. Each side expresses its own zeal and certainty in contemptuous terms toward the other, while forgetting the importance of curiosity.

Now let's turn to the third problem: indifference. Here we might imagine those excruciating kinds of pseudo-dialogue that occur in political debates, in bureaucratic consultations, and even unfortunately in some kinds of academic arguments. Each side comes to these kinds of discussions with a fixed set of arguments and without any expectation of converting the other. In the first case—that of the zealous proselyte—sermons and harangues appear to be motivated by a desire to save the other. We can imagine that there is a kind of compassion in such efforts. But in the pseudo-dialogues of indifference there is no apparent concern for the other or compassion. And certainly there is no curiosity in the dull and dry speech acts of bureaucratic consultation. Instead, the pseudo-dialogue of indifference is a kind of theater in which the participants say things out loud but without any expectation of learning or even being listened to. The audience for this kind of theatrical performance is often absent: in the US Congress, for example, the orators often speak to a nearly empty chamber. The point is to say something for the record in order to have something to share with the party bosses or the constituents back home. This kind of indifference is exemplified in the act of voting and in the procedures of criminal justice. To vote is simply to express one's opinion. This is a purely one-sided affair and does not involve dialogue or curiosity. Democracy understood in procedural terms merely as voting is a far cry from the more dialogical model of democracy known as "deliberative democracy," where each party is supposed to provide reasons and respond to the reasons provided by others. A merely procedural approach is also characteristic of criminal justice systems—whether adversarial (as in the American system) or inquisitorial (as in European systems influenced by

Catholic tradition, most notoriously in the case of the Inquisition). In these systems, the point is to establish guilt or innocence and not to learn something. In either system there is supposed to be a kind of official indifference on the part of courts and juries: they are open to evidence. But in such cases, this indifference falls short of curiosity to the extent that it is guided by the need to judge—and is thus not inspired by the desire to learn.

There must be fearless openness and a passion for learning in genuine dialogue. Curiosity is linked to care and concern. Most generally this is care for knowledge and concern for understanding. The etymology of the term indicates this connection with care and concern. And in fact that proverbial claim that "curiosity killed the cat" was originally rendered as "care killed the cat" in Shakespeare's *Much Ado about Nothing*.[4] The point is this: when we are curious, we are concerned and care about things. And in the case of care killing the cat, there is a sense that too much worry and concern can wear us out. When this gets transformed into "curiosity killing the cat" there is more of a sense that there are dangerous things that we ought not to pry into, and that the lust for learning can lead us astray. The most obvious case is seen in stories such as Faust and Frankenstein, where the curious desire of the scientific mind leads us to sell our souls and create monsters. Faust's curiosity is linked to a kind of pride. The Faust story originated out of the Reformation (under the authorship of Johann Spies) as a kind of warning against the kind of curiosity and critical engagement with tradition associated with the Lutheran protest against the Catholic tradition, as well as a general condemnation of the rest of modern, scientific, and enlightenment culture.[5]

This helps explain the problem of curiosity. Curiosity has often been rejected as perverse and transgressive by conservatives, while progressives have seen curiosity as rightfully leading us to transcend the fixed ideas that conservatives defend.[6] We will explore this ambivalence here. The hope is that we can find a way to understand theism that allows for curiosity, while also finding a way for atheists to remain curious about the theism that they reject.

4. The phrase occurs in act IV, scene 1. See Kenny, *Uses of Curiosity*.

5. See Heller, "Faust's Damnation."

6. As Barbara Benedict points out in her history of curiosity: "For conservatives, curiosity retained its moral taint: as curious people showed a perverse desire—the desire to know the forbidden. . . . For progressives, curiosity promised improvement. Both kinds of thinker, however, recognized that as humanity's traditionally insatiable appetite, curiosity is always transgressive, always a sign of the rejection of the known as inadequate, incorrect, even uninteresting" (Benedict, *Curiosity*, 4).

Curiosity Killed the Cat of Revealed Religion

The usual meaning of the proverb about cats and curiosity is that curiosity can get you killed. If you venture into high places, you may fall to your death. If you stick your nose into dark corners, you may be stung. The proverb means something like "mind your own business." It might also be related to other proverbs that say "what you don't know can't hurt you" and "ignorance is bliss." Philosophers, of course, reject this last one. Wonder and the urge to solve problems lead us into philosophy. When things don't make sense, philosophers want to know why. The lovers of wisdom want to resolve paradoxes and find solutions to logical, ethical, political, and metaphysical puzzles.

But this drive to make sense of things has often led to a critique of prevailing ideology and the status quo. Indeed, there is a sense in which curiosity killed religion. When Friedrich Nietzsche proclaimed that God is dead, he added: "and we have killed him."[7] One of the things that killed God was our curiosity about him. Throughout the modern period, we developed techniques of critical inquiry, including the natural sciences. At first, these techniques were employed in an effort to glorify God. But, from my perspective, the result has been just the opposite: curious inquiries into the truth of religion make it more difficult to maintain naïve faith in revealed religion.

Galileo provides an example. Galileo observed the heavens in order to better understand God's word and his creation. One of the puzzles that he attempted to solve was how God could have made the sun stand still in the sky as he supposedly did in helping Joshua slaughter his enemies (Josh 10:13–14). Galileo suggested in 1615, in his "Letter to the Grand Duchess," that God would have had to stop all of the motions of the planets in order for this to happen. He intended to use this to help bolster support for the Copernican or heliocentric model of the universe. But he also understood that this would require, as well, a revised approach to reading the Bible. In the letter, Galileo explained that errors would result if we read the Bible literally. Instead of beginning from the Bible and taking it as literally true, Galileo suggested, we ought to begin from sense experience and natural law and read the Bible in light of this. Galileo did not think that there was an insurmountable contradiction between the Bible and scientific reason. He thought that his method would aid in defending the Christian faith: "For the holy Bible and the phenomena of nature proceed alike from the divine Word."[8] Galileo's

7. Nietzsche, *Gay Science*, para. 125.

8. Galileo, "Letter to the Grand Duchess."

strategy backfired. His curiosity about astronomy led to his arrest by the Inquisition. By 1633, under threat of torture, he recanted and officially abjured the Copernican model of the universe.

The Galileo affair provides an example of how curiosity, which was intended to glorify God, ended up in conflict with faith. Eventually the heliocentric model was shown to be correct. Today the challenge for faith is that modern science and astronomy demonstrate that the earth is a small planet in the middle of an unimaginably vast cosmos. Traditional faith in the specialness of earth and humankind is harder to accept. And many of the Bible's miraculous stories cannot be literally true. Similar deflationary effects occur throughout the modern period. Critical philology and biblical exegesis led to a desire to apply scientific methods to the texts of the Bible and to explore biblical archeology. But as scholars dug into the depths of the texts and looked around the world for traces of the Bible's stories, naïve faith became more difficult. The experts have uncovered noncanonical works and they have offered an interpretation of the Bible that points toward a complicated history involving multiple authors and rival faith communities. This serves to undermine faith in the literal truth of the Bible.

The Joshua story provides an interesting example. After Moses died on the edge of the promised land, Joshua led the Israelites into the land of Canaan and, with God's help, killed or drove out everyone who lived there. But critical Bible scholars and archaeologists have concluded that this story can't be true. Not only is the astronomical miracle impossible, as Galileo suggested, but there is no archeological evidence of such an invasion. Some go so far as to suggest that Moses and Joshua did not exist—or that these figures were legendary heroes, whose "existence" is understood along the lines of Achilles and Odysseus. The most likely explanation is that the stories of Moses and Joshua were written down in the seventh and sixth centuries BCE, long after the events recorded were supposed to have taken place. The narrative of these books reflects the desire of the ancient authors to establish national unity and a claim to the land in a time of tumult that included the destruction of Israel and exile in Babylon.[9]

A similar hermeneutical approach can be applied to the whole of the Bible: reading the Bible not as a literally true document but rather understanding it as a compilation of Israelite and later Christian attempts to make sense of history, religion, politics, and the meaning of life. This approach helps explain the evolution of ancient Israelite religion from polytheism toward monolatry or henotheism and eventually to monotheism.[10]

9. See Finkelstein and Silberman, *Bible Unearthed*.

10. See Wright, *Evolution of God*.

The Bible seems to record the development of monotheism from a polytheistic background.

Genesis tells us that in the beginning *the gods* (in plural!) created the heavens and the earth. In the very first verse of Genesis, God is referred to in a plural form—as *Elohim*. Later in this story, the gods decide to create human beings in the image of themselves. "Let *us* make man in *our* image" (Gen 1:26). This story describes the creative activity of one of these gods in special detail. This is the god Yahweh or Jehovah, often translated as "the Lord God" (or perhaps the Lord of the gods—*Yahweh Elohim*). As the story unfolds, the creator god tells the humans not to eat the fruit of the tree of knowledge. This seems to be a warning against curiosity! But another spiritual being—the Serpent—tells the woman that the reason they shouldn't eat the fruit is that it would make them like the gods (*Elohim*) (Gen 3:5). The humans eat of the forbidden fruit. But then they are punished for attempting to become one of the gods. "The man has become like one of us, knowing good and evil" (Gen 3:22).

And so history begins with Adam and Eve condemned to a life of labor and reproduction in a hostile world, punished for their curiosity. This fall into history occurs because man—who was made in the image of the gods to begin with—had made himself even more like the gods by gaining godlike knowledge. It is significant that this original story begins with a recognition of divine plurality. Yahweh appears to talk things over with other gods—the *elohim* or council of divine beings.[11] Other evidence of divine plurality can be found scattered throughout the Hebrew Bible, including a remarkable story in Genesis 6 in which divine beings (sons of god or members of the divine council) have sex with human women, who then bear children who were the heroic warriors of old. It is a long way from these legends to full-fledge monotheism. Although some Christians interpret these indications of divine plurality as a sign of the Trinitarian view of God as three persons, it's hard to deny that monotheism develops from a polytheistic background. And indeed, it may be that the Trinitarian idea reflects a sense that God is more complicated than just one thing. Indeed, when it comes to the question of monotheism it seems that Islam and Sikhism have a purer brand of theology, since they simply assert the unity of God without the Trinitarian complication.[12]

The journey to monotheism can be explained as a product of curiosity. Polytheistic animism attempts to make sense of the natural world.

11. I borrow the idea of a council of divine *elohim* from Penchansky, *Twilight of the Gods*. For further discussion of ancient Hebrew polytheism see Schneider, *Beyond Monotheism*.

12. I discuss this in chapter 2 of Fiala, *Secular Cosmopolitanism*.

The result is a world where streams, forest, lightning, and earthquakes are embodied by spiritual beings. Monotheism develops later, when religion sought to make sense of things as civilization became organized under a central authority and with a singular cult based in the capital city. Versions of monotheism developed in a variety of ancient civilizations: from Egypt's cult of Akhenaten to the Babylonian cult of Ahura Mazda (the good god in the Zoroastrian dualistic system) to the Greek philosophical focus on unity. We might quibble over various details here. One focus is the emergence of "henotheism" (the idea that there is one supreme god among others, such as Zeus, the "father" of the Greek gods). Another version of the story emphasizes the development of "monolatry" (the exclusive worship of one god, which does not deny the existence of other gods). At any rate, there is no denying that monotheism is a later development that arises out of the human attempt to understand the world.

One cultural and historical explanation of Judeo-Christian monotheism is that the Jews would have absorbed some of this broader influence as they sought to make sense of their own experience of exile in Babylon, centuries after the world was supposed to have begun (and where they would have learned about Zoroastrianism). The attempt to make sense of exile and the destruction of the temple in Jerusalem led to reflection on the nature of God. For the Jewish God to remain significant for a people in exile, he must become a God that is separated from a specific geographical location. In this way, the local deity (Yahweh of Jerusalem) becomes more universal and transcendent. At the same time, this tribal deity continually struggles for supremacy against other local deities. This struggle ultimately leads to the idea that all other gods are false or nonexistent and that there is only one God.

Christian theology can be explained using a similar materialistic and historical hermeneutic. Critical scholarship of the New Testament tells us that the Gospels were written down after Jesus was killed by the Roman and Jewish authorities. For those searching for a messiah who would save the world, this required a theological leap. The Christian stories were likely further reinterpreted after the destruction of the temple in Jerusalem, which symbolized a clear loss of political and religious power for ancient Jewish and early Christian communities. Jesus was imagined as a new Joshua. But the historical situation made it necessary to provide a new understanding of "the kingdom of God." Christianity is not as fixated on Jerusalem as Judaism is. For the Jews, Jerusalem was the spiritual center, with the temple representing the holy of holies. But Christianity developed beyond that geographic location into a universal religion that had no single geographical center. As Jesus says: "The kingdom of God is within you" (or "among you"—depending on the translation of Luke 17:21). This claim makes sense given the historical and political circumstances in which Christianity develops—and from this interpretive point of view, the theological point follows from the historical situation.

And yet, Jerusalem remains a curiously important place. During my sabbatical, I toured the historical sites. What I learned from this experience is that theology and religious ritual and practice are influenced by history, politics, and geography. One example is worth noting, having to do with the question of where exactly the crucifixion and resurrection of Christ took place. The Church of the Holy Sepulcher in Jerusalem supposedly houses these original places. On one interpretation of this site, this is also where Adam's skull was buried: the site of Calvary was literally thought to be the place where a new Adam was born. Jerusalem is also, according to tradition, the location of Mount Moriah (thought to be the Temple Mount): the place at which Abraham's abortive sacrifice of Isaac took place. The Temple Mount lies just around the corner from the Church of the Holy Sepulcher. The Temple Mount is where the ancient Jewish temple stood (and where Jews continue to pray at the ruins of its Western Wall—the "wailing wall"). On top of this is the al-Aqsa Mosque and the Muslim Dome of the Rock. This is supposedly the place where Creation began and a central place for the Islamic faith, since this is where the Prophet Mohammed underwent his mystical "night journey" during which he communed with the rest of the prophets.

Of course, the archeologists disagree and debate whether any of this is true—a debate that began in earnest in the past couple of centuries with the advent of scientific methods for dating and interpreting ancient sites. If you go to Jerusalem, you will learn about the complicated and contentious history of these sites and the rest of the archeological history of the Bible. My own conclusion is skeptical. The more we search for proof of religion in the archeological record, the harder it is to retreat to naïve faith in the stories of the Bible.

At the same time as biblical archeology was developing, we were also developing tools of anthropological and sociological analysis. There is a growing awareness of the diversity of religions and the complexity of human religiosity. The other branches of natural science also make faith more difficult, including Darwinian evolution, medical science (including brain science), considerations of plate tectonics, paleontology, psychology, and so on. The more we looked for evidence of God and sought to understand his creation, the harder it became to cleave to traditional religion. And eventually, in the nineteenth century, Nietzsche and others came to the conclusion that God was dead. What killed God was our insatiable curiosity and effort to prove, vindicate, and understand God.

Curiosity, Theology, and the Evolution of God

Curiosity appears to lie at the root of religion. I mentioned how this shows up in the story of Adam and Eve, who are punished for their curiosity. But I am focused here on what is often called "the natural history of religion." A guiding idea holds that religion develops out of the human imagination and evolves by way of our innate curiosity about self and world. This story tells a tale by which God is invented by us to satisfy our desire to make meaning. The prevailing narrative of the natural history of religion holds that religion begins from the primitive animism of hunter-gatherers and moves toward the polytheistic pantheon and eventual monotheism of agricultural and city-based cultures. This story has been told in various ways by scholars such as Karl Jaspers, Robert Bellah, and Robert Wright.[13] Often accounts such as these are sympathetic to the impulse that drives the evolution of religion. The sympathetic interpretation maintains that the ethical universalism of monotheistic religion is the progressive result of this process. There is also a related story, more critical of religion, that has been told by critics such as Marx, Nietzsche, and Freud. Following upon the insights of Hegel and Feuerbach, who offered a developmental account of religion that was either spiritualized (Hegel) or based in the material interests of humanity (Feuerbach), these great critics of religion sought to push beyond religion in order to satisfy the human needs that gave rise to it. The critical approach is decidedly atheistic and anti-Christian. Marx, Nietzsche, and Freud viewed religion as a mechanism of psychological and social control that produces negative effects described as the opium of the people (Marx), slave morality (Nietzsche), and the repressive super-ego (Freud).

The story told by both the sympathetic theory and by the critical theory of religion revolves around curiosity. In seeking to make meaning out of experience and in order to fulfill our needs and desires, curiosity leads us to postulate the existence of spirits and gods. This is not merely intellectual inquisitiveness. Rather, it is perhaps better understood as the desire to make meaning. This way of defining curiosity—as the desire to make meaning—can be distinguished from what we might call "speculative curiosity." Speculative curiosity is abstracted from lived experience. But what we might call "existential curiosity" is interested in how our inquiries connect to lived experience.

This distinction shows up in a number of important places in the work of those who write about the natural history of religion. David Hume says that religion develops from a practical concern: "Not from a contemplation

13. Jaspers, *Origin and Goal of History*; Bellah, *Religion in Human Evolution*; and Wright, *Evolution of God*.

of the works of nature, but from a concern with regard to the events of life, and from the incessant hopes and fears which actuate the human mind."[14] Hume suggests that love of truth itself, what he calls "speculative curiosity," is not possible for primitive people who are immersed in existential need focused on the concrete hopes and fears of lived experience. The speculative turn only comes later, at a higher level of evolution. From this point of view, religion begins from a narrowly self-interested need to control nature and appease the gods. The story usually continues to suggest that monotheism and philosophical theology develop beyond this primitive, self-oriented, and narrow point of view. We see this point made by Freud in *Totem and Taboo*.[15] Freud connects self-interested religiosity to magic, which is the attempt to manipulate the natural world. Magic eventually gives way to a more abstract conception of religion, theology, philosophy, and science.

Hume and Freud remind us that curiosity and religious speculation are linked to our drives, interests, and existential needs.[16] It was Freud who suggested that religion was a useful illusion: a set of ideas and practices that

14. Hume, *Natural History of Religion*, "Section 2." Hume continues: "It must necessarily, indeed, be allowed, that in order to carry men's attention beyond the present course of things, or lead them into any inference concerning invisible intelligent power, they must be actuated by some passion which prompts their thought and reflection; some motive which urges their first inquiry. But what passion shall we here have recourse to, for explaining an effect of such mighty consequence? *Not speculative curiosity surely, or the pure love of truth.* That motive is too refined for such gross apprehensions, and would lead men into inquiries concerning the frame of nature; a subject too large and comprehensive for their narrow capacities. No passions, therefore, can be supposed to work upon such barbarians, but the ordinary affections of human life; the anxious concern for happiness, the dread of future misery, the terror of death, the thirst of revenge, the appetite for food and other necessaries" (Hume, *Natural History of Religion*, "Section 2"; my italics).

15. Freud follows Hume in recognizing that there is a tendency in primitive religion (what he calls animism) toward anthropomorphic explanations of natural phenomena. But Freud adds that the psychoanalytic method goes further: "Our psycho-analytic approach to the subject, however, is from another side. It is not to be supposed that men were inspired to create their first system of the universe by *pure speculative curiosity*. The practical need for controlling the world around them must have played its part" (Freud, *Totem and Taboo*, 90; my italics).

16. The difference between Freud and Hume is, I would suggest, that while Hume holds out the possibility that curiosity and the search for knowledge has a source in a kind of disinterested objectivity, Freud digs deeper into an account of curiosity that is based in psychological drives. But Hume can be understood as a source for the eventual Freudian approach. Hume understands reason as "the slave of the passions," for example, which points toward a psychological analysis of how we think. But Hume remains an Enlightenment thinker. He connects curiosity to the love of truth—a kind of innate passion to want to understand things. See Hume, *Treatise of Human Nature*, bk. 11, ch. 3, sec. 10. See also Gelfert, "Hume on Curiosity."

functions as a wish fulfillment.[17] But illusions leave us with dis-ease, since they conflict with reality. Reality and truth matter. Yes, curiosity satisfies our desires and inclinations. But what we are curious about is the truth. It brings us pleasure to know things and discover the truth. And when we settle upon something that is not true and discover contradictions and inconsistencies, we are driven toward further inquiry. The intellectual pleasure of learning and the desire for knowledge that is associated with curiosity is not easily divorced from the expectation or desire that what we learn is true.

Nonetheless, after Freud (and Nietzsche and Marx and the other critics of the Enlightenment tradition), it is not so easy to distinguish between the desire for truth and the desire for some other more selfish, culturally conditioned, or ideological satisfaction. This brings us to Marx's critique of religion as the opiate of the people. Marx suggests that religion provides a remedy for the unhappiness that is caused by the oppressed social condition of the masses. Marxists suggest that religion helps to keep those dysfunctional social conditions in place both by anesthetizing the masses and by empowering a dominant class who rules over them. The evolutionary account of religion has often focused on the ways in which shamans, priests, and prophets have exploited religious experience in order to serve their own self-interest. From this perspective, religion grows from the profit motive: it is profitable for the prophets! A related critique helps to explain religious conflict, which can be understood as the pursuit of power instead of the quest for truth. From this point of view, the Roman Catholic Church had a vested interest in controlling Galileo, whose ideas developed while the Reformation was challenging the church's religious and political supremacy in Europe. Also from this point of view, even biblical archeology can be criticized for merely serving the interests of ideology and power. The example of Jerusalem shows us this problem. Control of the Church of the Holy Sepulcher is divided among different sects, as is Jerusalem itself. Divergent religions and denominations make divergent claims about what the archaeology and history of Jerusalem mean for the Jews, Christians, and Muslims living and worshiping there today. Even science can be seen as ideological, despite the fact that science is often understood as a method of pure curiosity.

Conclusion: The Mythic Power of Religion

There are several drives or interests woven through our intellectual and religious lives: we desire truth and meaning, but we also desire power and

17. Freud, *Future of an Illusion*, ch. 6.

the satisfaction of our interests. We also fear what we do not know, desire to convert others to our own point of view, and are sometimes simply indifferent and uninterested in truth. All of this is at play in curiosity and dialogue. Curiosity grows from our effort to make sense of the world, which involves both our existential needs and our desire to know. Understanding this can provide us with a source of common ground: in the shared sense of curiosity as both speculative and existential. We all desire to make theoretical sense of things; we also desire to find sources of meaning.

Those sources of meaning include songs, prayers, stories, and even food. We need narratives, models, and inspiration. We might call this the "mythic" register of things.[18] This does not mean, I would argue, that religion can therefore be accepted at face value. Once we have reached the point at which we understand that science and religion both must be evaluated in terms of their ability to provide us with meaning, we have moved beyond the naïve faith of ordinary religiosity as well as beyond what is sometimes called "normal science." Normal science, like normal or ordinary religiosity, simply takes the metaphysical, ontological, and epistemological scheme in which it operates for granted. But philosophers take a step back and ask whether any of this is true and how we might decide between and among competing schemes. My own approach to religion comes at it from this philosophical angle. From this point of view, there is plenty of room for dialogue between religion, science, and philosophy. Such dialogue is moved along by curiosity. This is not merely curiosity about the literal truth of religion. Rather, it is about the *mythic power of religion*, what religion tells us about the meaning of life, ethics, political reality, and so on. And in fact, I still believe there is a lot to learn about religion—and by studying religion we learn a lot about ourselves, including about the ways we find and make meaning.

18. I discuss myth in Fiala, *Just War Myth*, where I connect it to the result of cognitive, emotional, social, and culture mechanisms. A number of philosophers have pointed out the importance of myth. One useful source is Mary Midgley, who connects this to the "hunger for meaning" and the idea of religion. Midgley says: "A hunger for meaning is central to our lives. It is not just an accidental, irrelevant emotion, needing to be brushed aside as an interference with thought. It is the wider motive of which our theoretical curiosity is only a part. It is the impulse of our imaginations to order the world with a view to understanding and contemplating it" (Midgley, *Evolution as a Religion*, 157). Midgley further explains: "Myths are not lies. Nor are they detached stories. They suggest imaginative patterns, networks of powerful symbols that suggest particular ways of interpreting the world. They shape its meaning" (Midgley, *Myths We Live By*, 1). Midgley's general point is that we need myths and stories to guide experience. Science alone is not sufficient for human life. As she puts it: "Whatever the faults of religion, science cannot sensibly be put in its place" (Midgley, *Myths We Live By*, 25).

In practical terms, let me put it this way, as I conclude my initial offering in this chapter: I remain curious about religion because I am curious (in both speculative and existential senses) about human beings. There is a vast variety of religions in the world. I am curious about what other people believe, where they live, how they pray, and what they eat. My speculative curiosity impels me to ask whether their beliefs are true. But religion is also more than merely a set of truth claims. It is also a system of practice, rituals, and mythic meaning, lived out in the real lives of people in places like Jerusalem and Jaffa. I agree with the general result of the critical theories of religion we have discussed here. But I remain curious about the human condition and about the various ways that human beings make sense of themselves and the world. It is this curiosity that drew me to the Holy Land. I became more skeptical there. But I also became more curious.

*

Response: Did Fear of Curiosity Kill God?

Peter Admirand

The experience of reading Andy's section felt as if two artists were given separate canvasses and told simultaneously to paint the same theme. Now they are coming together to see how and what the other composed, highlighted, and omitted. For me, it's been another enlightening, humbling, and fascinating experience. If curiosity killed God, as Andy wrote, then no wonder I questioned its claim as a virtue (!)—and while I wouldn't agree to the literalness of God's demise or nonexistence, I concede that curiosity helpfully killed certain (mis)conceptions about God, or at least, complicated and purified them. Paramount among them is again the question of theodicy and how a loving, omnipotent God can create and sustain a world of such acute, often needless, suffering. Curiosity likewise "kills" or "purifies" biblical and theological doctrines and statements, especially regarding the scientific workings of the world, outdated or immoral positions or implications against women or LGBQTI individuals, and whether certain biblical stories are historically true.

Regarding conceptions of God, in *The Female Face of God in Auschwitz*, Melissa Raphael argues that the God of many Jewish men (like Rabbi Richard Rubenstein) was only dead because the patriarchal God of military intervention and defeat of enemies never existed. The God many Jewish women had experienced, however, continued to be present, even in the camps—a soft, fleeting, tender presence, manifest in moments of solidarity and compassion, like one woman wiping the tears of another. She argued that the crucial question was not where was God, but who was God in Auschwitz.[1] Liberation theologians like Gustavo Gutiérrez similarly contend that the face and power of God is reflected in the poor and the oppressed,

1. Raphael, *Female Face of God in Auschwitz*. Raphael highlights the feminine face of God, the Shekhinah.

and that to live and know God, we must live and strive for justice and life with those betrayed and battered by the injustices of the world, practicing a preferential option for the poor.[2]

Andy and I both mentioned the story of Adam and Eve and Paul's encounter with the Athenians (see my main section below), but while I highlighted Paul's encounter as a moment of curiosity, Andy called it "perhaps the first historical example of a clear failure of dialogue between theism and atheism." This is just one of many insights and challenges I gleaned from his text. I want to hear even more about how "Curiosity lies between fear, evangelism, and indifference," and I fully endorse "If we could replace fear and indifference with curiosity and compassion, we'd all be better off."

Andy identifies one of his hopes in the chapter to "find a way to understand theism that allows for curiosity, while also finding a way for atheists to remain curious about the theism that they reject." Linking curiosity with compassion and contending how it can and should combat fear, indifference, and what I would call a closed evangelism certainly helps do that.

Openness and compassion are keys, and both die when we think we know all there is about another. But what if this does happen—can there be certainty in one's own position but a sustained compassion towards those (wrong) others, or does a healthy, holy, and positive curiosity (see further below) counteract such rigidness—because the world is always new and unexpected?

Speaking of the unexpected, there was one moment in Andy's essay that annoyed me. It was not when he said God was killed by curiosity (!), but when he mentioned visiting and living in Jerusalem. I had been avidly planning and anticipating my first ever trip to Jerusalem that was supposed to have happened in September 2020. I had a conference and, more importantly in my case, the research funding for it to happen—but it was not only cancelled because of the coronavirus but would not be rescheduled. It was one of many cases of holy envy while reading Andy's piece—but perhaps also fitting that a nonbeliever's visiting of Jerusalem only makes me more curious and hopeful when I will one day, too.

2. See, especially, Gutiérrez, *Theology of Liberation*.

---- * ----

Seeking Holy Curiosity

PETER ADMIRAND

IN "A MURDER OF One," a Counting Crows song about overcoming a wasted life of shame and regret (perhaps from an abusive relationship), Adam Durwitz croons that a curious kitten need not be alone.[1] It is a reminder that seeking something new need not mean you are alone. Yet, what kind of curiosity? In this book promoting virtues as common ground between believers and nonbelievers, it is not enough simply to state the virtue. Further questions arise in terms of how that virtue is described, naming the limitations and blind spots around the virtue, and perhaps more problematically, how that virtue is assessed and by whom and which standards. Neil S. Masson, for example, argues for a certain "epistemic restraint" when it comes to curiosity, not to stifle scientific discovery but to provide ethical guidelines and probe deeper into why certain knowledge is sought and the context by which it is sought.[2] Such restraint will not only require humility but discipline. Curiosity in certain contexts involving certain people should not be supported. This, too, involves further scrutiny and also raises difficult questions.

As made clear in Andy's response to my chapter in humility, that virtue will be presented and modeled differently by believers and nonbelievers—especially in how faith in God is essential in most theistic accounts. The end

1. Like most Counting Crows songs, it is the live versions—where lyrics are often modified, added, or extended—that provide the most pleasure. The song was initially from their 1993 album, *August and Everything After*. For an acoustic version, see: https://www.youtube.com/watch?v=NIUAWqLFU90 (from a bootleg 1994 album called *Carving Out Our Names*). My favorite live version is from a fan-compilation: *August & Everything After - Live Compilation—2-Disc Collectors Edition*, available here: https://www.youtube.com/watch?v=ZHSqGTdw9h4.

2. Manson, "Epistemic Restraint and the Vice of Curiosity," 258.

result (in forming a humble person) may be similar, but the grounding of the virtue varies. What about curiosity?

When Andy and I were tweaking this book's structure, we reached these seven virtues after various attempts. I had included "curiosity" as a supporting description of courage—which I saw as an intrinsic virtue needed to engage outside one's religious or ethical comfort zone. Courage made the final cut (see chapter 8), but then, interestingly, so did curiosity, which Andy had later promoted. I agreed to the term even as I felt some ambivalence towards it. Building from humility and compassion, I would have stressed the need for openness to other views and to recognize and accept my own tradition's failures. I would not have identified (mere?) curiosity as a key factor in engaging other ways. Reflecting further, I seemed to associate curiosity with a certain frivolity, or (at its worst) ill-intent. Why is that the case? As an omnivore reader, I'm obviously interested in learning but seem to prize wonder and not curiosity. Is it only semantics? I then fear I'm insufficiently curious. Is not empathy rooted in a certain curiosity, in seeking to learn about and know another?

I grappled further with my subjective definitions or perceptions of "curious." I also seem to associate the word with strange or odd, as in, "Isn't it curious that so-and-so never is seen with his wife anymore?"—a banal example that also elides the term with idle gossip. Gossip, so close to slander, which for Jews can be akin to murder (if you destroy someone's public identity and integrity) again seems to place the word far removed from a virtue.

In the realm of religion, is not curiosity suspect? Desire, which I attach to curiosity, is also mixed. Augustine spoke of "disordered desires"—when we elevate quotidian matters above our longing and seeking of God; desire as craving (thirst) in Buddhism is what must be overcome. In Judaism, desire can be more mixed, as sexual longing is seen as a somewhat necessary evil or is at least tainted, even as it is the drive in which humans respond to God's call in Genesis "to be fruitful and multiply." Society, of course, commodifies and packages desire in commercials, clickbait, and billboards—and often such desire is simply for objects (sometimes actual people) that promise to satiate pleasure.

Theologically, much is enveloped in mystery: grace, the afterlife, the Trinity, the incarnation, theodicy, God, our existence, the soul—and such claims can spill over into the universe, dark matter, quarks, our brains. Is it intellectual laziness in theists when we so often stop many inquiries with words like "God," "faith," or "trust"? Where most likely did my ambivalence towards curiosity arise, and why do I now feel both a holy envy and distance towards it?

I will first set out to trace such a path, beginning with the Bible and then turning to curiosity in Augustine, Aquinas, and Pope Francis. Could a better theistic understanding of curiosity help solidify common ground between atheists and theists?

The Bible and Curiosity

A survey of curiosity in the Bible yields mostly unfavorable results. In Genesis, humans are forbidden to eat of the tree of knowledge of good and evil. Eve's curiosity and disobedience (and Adam's unquestioning acquiescence) are both rebuked and punished (Gen 3:16–24). Also recall Lot's wife (Gen 19:26). While I am partial to Elie Wiesel's interpretation that Lot's wife witnessed horrible crimes and so was traumatized,[3] was it curiosity that rendered her into a pillar of salt? In the Tanach, there are clear limits to what should and can be known of the world. In the book of Job, part of God's response to Job's complaints is that he understands nothing of the majesty and mystery of the world which only God knows as the creator (Job 38:4–7). It seems such truths are beyond the scope of human beings, or mortals should humbly know their place and not reach beyond it. God is also said to conceal such mysteries.

While there is often a lack of curiosity in biblical figures—think of Abraham not questioning God when asked to sacrifice Isaac—this is praised in the tradition as faith and obedience. Fortunately, there are exceptions. Abraham asks God if the just will be smote with the unjust (Gen 18:16–33). Moses's curiosity is also rewarded. He sees a burning bush and wonders why it wasn't consumed: "I must look at this marvelous sight; why doesn't the bush burn up?" (Exod 3:3). As he reflects, God addresses him.[4] He then inquires of God's name, though is basically given a non-answer: "I will be what I will be" (Exod 3:14).

Elsewhere, there are clear fences around curiosity. In Psalm 131:2, we read: "I do not occupy myself with things too great and too marvelous for me." In Deuteronomy 29:29, there is a fairly common refrain: "The secret things belong to the Lord our God, but the things that are revealed belong to us and to our children forever, that we may do all the words of this law." Here note the division of the revealed and the secret: a boundary marker. In Numbers 4:20, the Kohalites (a division of the Levites) "must not go in to look on the holy things even for a moment; otherwise they

3. Wiesel, *Wise Men and Their Tales*, 38.

4. I thank my colleague Brad Anderson for pointing out this passage to me. Private email, May 20, 2020.

will die." Like the tree of the knowledge of good and evil, there is a cost if one delves too deeply into some matters.

In Ecclesiastes 3:11, we read: "Also, he has put eternity into man's heart, yet so that he cannot find out what God has done from the beginning to the end." This ignorance of human beings here seems ordained by God.

Returning to Abraham pleading for the innocent of Sodom and Gomorrah, there are moments of what Rabbi Anson Laytner calls the "Law Court Pattern of Prayer." Such includes theological protest, but because it is a prayer, trust and faith in God remain essential. Jesus' cry on the cross—"My God, my God, why have you forsaken me?"—is a clear example. In Psalm 22, the speaker states the grievance against or towards God, the areas of pain or need of help, but then asks and expects God to be the savior, and so promises fidelity and praise.[5]

Perhaps the most interesting anecdote is Proverbs 25:2–3: "It is the glory of God to conceal things, but the glory of kings is to search things out. As the heavens for height, and the earth for depth, so the heart of kings is unsearchable." While interpretation of this verse is widespread, the great Talmudic scholar Rashi contends this verse encourages searching out certain mysteries and answers.[6] Confer debates in the Talmud and rabbinic literature—where a voracious intellectual curiosity is evident—but there are still limits—and only what helps gain a better understanding of biblical commandments and meaning is what is pursued. Perhaps of note is that kings search, and even if this search is not just related to legal matters, the verse is not referring to the average person.

In the Christian scriptures, faith is a preeminent response to such mysteries. Recall, for example, the Reformation debate of whether faith or good works are needed for salvation. Curiosity only seemed a hindrance. I will highlight some other examples below, but consider Acts 1:7: "[Jesus] said to them, 'It is not for you to know times or seasons that the Father has fixed by his own authority.'" This is a fairly standard Gospel trope where certain knowledge—especially of the end times—is only known by God. The call again is trust, whether as praised in children (Matt 18:3) or the birds of the field (Matt 6:26). In Philippians 4:8–9, we read: "Finally, brothers, whatever is true, whatever is honorable, whatever is just, whatever is pure, whatever is lovely, whatever is commendable, if there is any excellence, if there is anything worthy of praise, think about these things."

5. See Laytner, *Arguing with God.*

6. Rashi's full commentary can be found with corresponding biblical verses on Chabad.com. See https://www.chabad.org/library/bible_cdo/aid/16396#showrashi=true.

Here again, we have a guide and standard for the kinds of matters to reflect upon—ultimately linked to love of God.

Jesus often asks questions in his parables—"With what can we compare the kingdom of God?" (Mark 4:30)—or in his many discussions, whether with Zacchaeus the tax collector (Luke 19:1–10), the Pharisee Nicodemus (John 3:1–21), or his disciples: "Who do people say that I am?" (Mark 8:27). While faith is demanded, is not a certain curiosity also present? As Garrick Allen reminded me: "Another good place is the questions that Paul answers in his letters, most of which are responses to letters he received asking questions. First Thessalonians, the earliest Christian writing still in existence, is key here: it's a direct response to questions on eschatology and what happens to people who die before Christ's return. Paul also quotes some of the questions he's asked in 1 Corinthians."[7] Also relevant is Paul's discussion with the men of Athens on the God he was preaching. While the Athenians were drawn to a certain novelty and fleeting curiosity, some still became disciples that day, "including Dionysius the Areopagite and a woman named Damaris, and others with them" (Acts 17:33).

Where curiosity and faith, then, reside can be difficult to unravel. Jesus praises Mary for choosing to sit at his feet when her sister chides her for not helping prepare the meal (Luke 10:41). While at the well in Samaria, a woman's curiosity and questioning about Jesus leads her to seeing him as the messiah (John 4)—though it is faith as the ultimate aim or means. Mary at Bethany wasn't curious about Jesus: she already believed and so wanted to hear his words. While the Samaritan woman at the well was amazed at what Jesus said, once she believed, it would seem such curiosity ends. Confer also the story of Thomas after Jesus' resurrection appearance. He doubts until he gets to probe the wounds on Jesus' body. I am not sure if curiosity and doubt can be clearly linked here, but it is faith that ultimately is lauded: "Blessed are those who have not seen and yet have come to believe" (John 20:29).

This emphasis on faith—and limiting or rebuking curiosity—becomes prominent in the early church fathers and medieval theologians, represented below in Augustine and Aquinas.

Lust of the Eyes: Augustine and the Curious Fish

While the Bible, as noted above, is cold if not critical of any extensive curiosity, Greek and Roman literature also reveals mixed feelings. While we may associate Socrates with wonder and seeking knowledge and recall Aristotle's opening line of *Metaphysics*—"All men naturally desire

7. Garrick Allen, private email, March 20, 2020.

knowledge"[8]—confer the tales of Cupid and Psyche, and Pandora, for example. Curiosity results in bad consequences. P. G. Walsh helpfully highlights a negative thread of curiosity from Plutarch and Apuleius, with mild rebukes from Cicero and Seneca,[9] to church fathers like Tertullian. In Augustine this negative thread becomes a dominant tapestry. While it is difficult to precisely date when Augustine wrote certain texts, his stance against curiosity was consistent after his conversion.

In his *Confessions*, Augustine highlights pride as the deadliest of sins, but it was lust that he most found bedeviling and dangerous.[10] Interestingly, he ties curiosity to both those perceived vices. He grounds his reflections on 1 John 2:16: "For everything in the world—the lust of the flesh, the lust of the eyes, and the pride of life—comes not from the Father but from the world." Such a world vision divides those in the light or darkness (1 John 1:4–7). On its own, the biblical quote is unnerving and jarring, subsuming everything in the world as vice—or at least everything linked to lust and pride. Much of John's letter resembles Gnostic or Manichaean tendencies with a hatred of the flesh and a separation of God and the world—even as there are also some moving and beautiful passages on love, especially the idea that God loves us, God is love, and we are called to love one another (1 John 1:16–21).

Yet, how this expansive love coheres amidst a vision and proclamation of a divided world is either paradoxical or self-defeating. Augustine parallels sexual lust of the body with an unhealthy lust for knowledge that stems from curiosity.[11] Just as physical lust renders us into slaves, Augustine implies, so, too, does this curiosity—which is "manifold in its dangers."[12] While sexual lust is straightforward, this lust of the eyes can be more easily rationalized or perhaps innocently undertaken. Yet it is a "diseased craving"[13] where individuals try to probe secrets of the universe without a higher purpose but

9. Aristotle, *Metaphysics*, 980a21.

9. See Walsh, "Rights and Wrongs of Curiosity." Walsh refers to "traditional conflict between Stoic and Aristotelian standpoints, with the Peripatetics sponsoring disinterested enquiry and the Stoics insisting that such investigation is justifiable only if it advances us on the path of virtue" (Walsh, "Rights and Wrongs of Curiosity," 80). Tracing a similar historical path, but contending how an ethics of curiosity (and dialogue) are often overlooked in science's unrestrained curiosity, see Sarukkai, "Science and the Ethics of Curiosity."

10. Augustine, *Confessions*, 210.

11. Augustine, *Confessions*, 210–11.

12. Augustine, *Confessions*, 210.

13. Augustine, *Confessions*, 211.

simply as "knowledge for its own sake."[14] Curiosity is also seen in those who try to gain knowledge by perverted or discredited means, as in the magical arts, or tempt God for a "thrill" and "not for any salvific end."[15]

Augustine was a slew of curiosities; he enfleshed his biographies with prayers as questions; he probed, pushed, and distended theological language; his life was one long search for God, who, once found, rendered any unrelated quest superfluous. Knowledge of the world, of how to read texts—all only served the purpose of understanding and maintaining that seeking of God. There was no knowledge for knowledge's sake, and there are limits to one's knowledge. Some truths are secret and so not meant for human minds, and some curiosity can be perverse, where God is not really sought in some demand for miracles, but is a mere presumptuous test, bereft of awe and longing.

The Psalms, so dear to Augustine, are another helpful source.[16] In his exposition on Psalm 8, highlighting the majesty of God and so the lowliness of human beings whom God crowned "with glory and honor," Augustine again links pride and curiosity. He rebukes those "who set their mouths against heaven," and the curious—whom he calls fish—who search in vain the bottomless depths of the sea and so "vanish and perish, as quickly as the water comes together again after it has given room, in their passage, to ships, or to whatsoever walks or swims." Curiosity is the seeking "after vain and fleeting things." It is a vice, he contends, again citing and analyzing 1 John 2:15–16 and conflating the world, lust, and flesh. Referring to Jesus' temptation by Satan in the desert, Augustine labels the third temptation—when the devil told Jesus to throw himself down from the mountain top (to be saved by angels; Matt 4:6)—as a temptation of curiosity, a hollow test of God.[17]

In *On Christian Doctrine*, Augustine speaks of "hurtful curiosity"[18] while in "Letter 118," he writes of his desire to Dioscorus (a Greek student at Carthage) to temper curiosity and avoid learning what is either unprofitable or a curiosity too inquisitive. He advises him to avoid mere intellectual games or ostentatious learning.[19] In the same letter he speaks of those "with idle curiosity" who "awaken anew controversies which have slept for

14. Augustine, *Confessions*, 212.
15. Augustine, *Confessions*, 212.
16. Brown, *Augustine of Hippo*, 168–69.
17. Augustine, "Exposition on Psalm 8."
18. Augustine, *On Christian Doctrine*.
19. Augustine, "Letter 118."

ages"—dredging up heretical arguments.[20] There is no need to retest or analyze what has already been decreed false.[21]

He extends his attack on curiosity in "Homily 2," focusing specifically on 1 John 2:12–17: "By the lust of the eyes, [John] means all curiosity. Now how wide is the scope of curiosity! This it is that works in spectacles, in theaters, in sacraments of the devil, in magical arts, in dealings with darkness: none other than curiosity." Curiosity seems the antithesis of the faith in God desired, an idle test or a proud ambition to gain power over this world, which is both vain and futile.[22]

Aquinas: Studiousness, Not Curiosity

In Thomas Aquinas's *Summa Theologica*, curiosity is first mentioned in his investigation of pride.[23] Highlighting how the devil promised Adam knowledge, Aquinas investigates whether it is curiosity and not pride that was man's first sin. He replies, though, that "the desire for knowledge resulted in our first parents from their inordinate desire for excellence. Hence the serpent began by saying: 'You shall be as Gods,' and added: 'Knowing good and evil.'"[24] He thus contends the initial sinful thrust was pride, trying to become a god. He raises pride as the vice par excellence, although this does not then exonerate curiosity.

While examining sloth (2.2.35), Aquinas cites Isidore, who believed curiosity was one of the negative effects of sloth as a way of contending that sloth was a distinctive vice. In his reply, Aquinas speaks of the "'wandering of the mind after unlawful things.' This tendency to wander, if it resides in the mind itself that is desirous of rushing after various things without rhyme or reason, is called 'uneasiness of the mind,' but if it pertains to the imaginative power, it is called 'curiosity.'"[25] The main point is whether sloth is more a sorrow than a "distinct vice," but for our context it is again curiosity that is rebuked. This is further clarified in his focus in questions 166 and 167 in the *Secunda Secundae*, where curiosity is deemed as the opposite vice to studiousness. As Gladden J. Pappen writes: "The term *studiositas* describes the regulation of man's desire for knowledge by something akin to temperance. Indirectly, it concerns things that presuppose knowledge (like

20. Augustine, "Letter 118."

21. Augustine, "Letter 118."

22. Augustine, "Homily 2."

23. Aquinas, *Summa Theologica*, 2.2.163.

24. Aquinas, *Summa Theologica* 2.2.163.1.

25. Aquinas, *Summa Theologica* 2.2.35.4.

the maintenance of the body or acquisition of gain)."[26] Thus, it is a moderate studiousness and not curiosity that must be fostered. At first glance, this might seem to be a semantic distinction.

In question 166, Aquinas first asks: "Whether the proper matter of studiousness is knowledge?" He contends that "curiosity is accounted to be about things pertaining to the body by reason of things pertaining to knowledge."[27] This in itself is not bad, according to Aquinas, as it is understandable that a human being would want to know "how he may best sustain his body."[28] The problem is when such seeking of knowledge is deemed ultimate or becomes excessive. In a follow-up question, where he contends temperance is needed for studiousness so that it doesn't become the vice of curiosity, he quotes Augustine: "On the contrary, Augustine says (*De Morib. Eccl.* 21): 'We are forbidden to be curious: and this is a great gift that temperance bestows.' Now curiosity is prevented by moderate studiousness. Therefore studiousness is a part of temperance."[29]

Notice Aquinas only tempers Augustine's stark claim that all curiosity is forbidden. He contends studiousness avoids such sinfulness because it is aligned with other virtues like temperance. Aquinas also relies upon—and slightly tweaks—Augustine in the two articles of the next question (167). He first asks: "Can the vice of curiosity regard intellective knowledge?" At stake here is whether knowledge in itself is wrong. Aquinas dismisses such a claim, as knowledge and truth are goods that come from God, who is ultimate Truth, and so are "essentially good." We are also called to be like God, and such a path involves a quest for knowledge and truth. However, Aquinas distinguishes between knowledge itself, which is good, and the desire for that knowledge. He clarifies that studiousness, within which is a desire and pursuit of study, can be good, but such knowledge can also be used for sinful ends or result in ownership and pride. He again quotes Augustine to rebuke those who see and claim to own a knowledge of the world as if they now "dwelt in the very heavens about which they argue." Like Augustine's warning against inordinate desires, Aquinas sees sinfulness in curiosity through four ways. The first is forsaking learning higher things for lower things (what is deemed "less profitable"). The second is seeking to learn through unlawful teachers, like desiring to know "the future through demons," and here, Aquinas cites Augustine to condemn "superstitious curiosity." The third way is seeking knowledge without clear links to God as the creator of

26. Pappin, "Directing Philosophy," 343.

27. Aquinas, *Summa Theologica*, 2.2.166.1.

28. Aquinas, *Summa Theologica*, 2.2.166.1.

29. Aquinas, *Summa Theologica*, 2.2.166.2.

all and the right end of all knowledge. The fourth way is studying beyond an individual's "capacity of his own intelligence."[30]

While Aquinas provides some justification for study, there are limits and dangers. Curiosity remains a vice.

From Religious Vice to Secular Virtue

Curiosity was rehabilitated and then elevated in the Enlightenment, as the call to question, investigate, and examine became, for many, a new religion and way of life. Peter Harrison, for example, highlights the influence of Francis Bacon in the transformation of curiosity from a religious vice to a secular virtue: "For Bacon, knowledge of the world is neither forbidden nor exceeds our capacities. God has fitted the world to human capabilities."[31] Such a view became part of the social imaginary of a growing cohort of European intellectuals. As Harrison writes: "In short, if for Aristotle wonder was the beginning of knowledge, for Hume and his contemporaries that honor now fell to curiosity."[32] The call to discover and test everything seemed limitless.

From Galileo to Darwin, and from Darwin to Freud, Einstein, Hawking, Sagan, and Watson and Crick, human beings have since penetrated the inner workings of the mind and of the unconscious; the language of DNA; the elasticity of the time-space continuum; the origins and future of an expanding universe; and the life-worlds within subatomic particles; debunking many miracle claims and pushing the boundaries of what seemed impossible or unknowable. Many of these discoveries were often painted, however, as part of a war of attrition between science and religion, or knowledge and faith.[33] Some God-believers tried to fight back, even as their political power to silence or condemn such discoveries was diminished. I would allege few theists, though, celebrate the discoveries as signs or proofs of God's majesty. Even if, contrary to creationists, they acknowledge the depth and reach of scientific truths, most probably live as if these discoveries do not impact faith claims.

Where then does this leave curiosity today for a religious believer, or in my context, a Catholic? A general distaste and rebuking of curiosity

30. Aquinas, *Summa Theologica*, 2.2.167.1–2. A follow up article on "whether the vice of curiosity is about sensitive knowledge" highlights the role of the senses in learning and how sight is the main sense of knowledge. Aquinas again stresses how much depends on the intent and aim of the knowledge sought. Is care for a neighbor, for example, really idle curiosity and gossip or a genuine desire for charity?

31. Harrison, "Curiosity, Forbidden Knowledge," 279.

32. Harrison, "Curiosity, Forbidden Knowledge," 287.

33. See, for example, Watson, *Age of Atheists*.

continued in the Catholic Church up to at least the Second Vatican Council,[34] and continue in many statements from Pope Francis. In a meditation on the book of Wisdom (7:22–8:1) on November 14, 2013, Francis highlights how "the spirit of wisdom triumphs over worldly curiosity." Humans are called to respond to the Spirit of God and the wisdom that comes from the Spirit. Turning to Luke (17:20–25), he cautions: "We find ourselves confronted by another spirit, which is opposed to the spirit of God: the spirit of curiosity. It leads us to want to become masters of God's plans, of the future, of things, to know everything, to seize hold of everything." The pope adds: "The spirit of curiosity is not a good spirit; it is the spirit of dissipation, of drawing away from God, of talking too much."[35]

In addition to Augustine and Aquinas, we can see the influence of *The Spiritual Exercises* of St. Ignatius. So crucial to Pope Francis's Jesuit formation, curiosity there arises in mostly negative terms, from the curiosity of Herod (who didn't really want to inquire who Jesus was for salvation) or is portrayed merely as a counter to what should be desired by and through knowledge, namely as piety or compassion.[36]

The pope continues: "Jesus tells us something quite interesting in this regard: this spirit of curiosity, which is worldly, leads us into confusion." After again turning to the Gospel passages about those looking for signs of the end of the world—about which it is worthwhile to note, Jesus said only the Father knows—Francis claims curiosity makes us listen to empty conjectures. Of those who may claim they had a vision of Mary purporting the end times, Francis quips: "Look, Our Lady is a Mother and she loves us all. But she is not a post woman who sends messages every day."

He then highlights Thérèse of Lisieux as a saintly example of someone who had "to stop herself when faced with the spirit of curiosity." Fearing she was straying into idle news from a fellow sister's narrative, "she sensed

34. Boyd, for example, traces curiosity in Augustine, Aquinas, and J. R. R. Tolkien, writing of Tolkien that he, "like his theological predecessors, saw curiosity as a tendency to go beyond what is appropriate and as an unhealthy fixation with an object that consumes us." He has in mind three characters from *The Lord of the Rings* who have contact with the Palantiri, magical objects used to see distant objects, and the moral danger that befalls them (Boyd, "Augustine, Aquinas, and Tolkien," 222). Interestingly unlike Saruman, Denathor, and Pippin, Boyd notes that "Aragorn as the owner of the Palantír, has the right to use it. Yet, he does not succumb to the power of Sauron since his intent is not a curious interest in knowledge or power, but to deceive Sauron into turning the gaze of the great eye away from the true threat to Mordor. Aragorn thus uses Sauron's own curiosity against him" (Boyd, "Augustine, Aquinas, and Tolkien," 233fn54).

35. Francis, "Spirit of Wisdom."

36. On Herod, see Ignatius Loyola, *Spiritual Exercises*, 195.

that this was not of the spirit of God, since it was a spirit of dissipation, of curiosity."[37]

Here again we have a division of knowledge that is profitable and of God or knowledge that opposes and undermines such knowledge. He concludes the homily by saying: "The kingdom of God is in our midst. Do not seek strange things, do not look for novelties with worldly curiosity."[38]

A tweet a few years later in August 2016 provided a positive path for curiosity: "The secret to joy: never suppress positive curiosity; get involved, because life is meant to be lived."[39] Connecting the 2013 meditation and the 2016 tweet, I would contend the reign[40] of God, especially as promoted in the Beatitudes, a vision of justice and peace for all, brings joy. A positive curiosity could be linked with this compassionate vision. However, while a 2018 homily acknowledges a "healthy curiosity" can open us up to new discoveries, the pope again condemns excessive curiosity that can lead to paths which harm the soul. As an example he mentions children accessing the internet and driven by a curiosity "without discipline," and so stumbling upon things they should not see.[41] Finally, in a Lenten meditation in February 2020 he warns against "an empty and superficial curiosity"[42] and contends we must place our trust in the Holy Spirit who "doesn't come with a package full of certainty." Limits, warnings, and boundaries regarding curiosity remain.

Towards a Holy Curiosity

In *An Instinct for Truth: Curiosity and the Moral Character of Science*, Robert T. Pennock, reflecting on Darwin, inquires whether curiosity is actually an "evolved instinct" or a "Darwinian predisposition." He writes that evolution would have closed off curiosity as a "disposition" if it were only harmful to survival and adaptation—when clearly curiosity at times "provides a selective advantage in many environments."[43] He also examines curiosity as a moral virtue. We see a similar argument on why altruism or cooperation

37. Francis, "Spirit of Wisdom."

38. Francis, "Spirit of Wisdom."

39. Francis, "Secret to Jjoy."

40. Feminist, liberation, and postcolonial theologies challenge the ethics of kingship ideology and its link to war and patriarchy and so prefer words like "reign" and not "kingdom."

41. Esteves, "Curiosity Can Lead to Dangerous Paths."

42. Francis, "Message for Lent 2020."

43. Pennock, *Instinct for Truth*, 13.

make more sense from an evolutionary standpoint, too. Cooperation builds trust with others and provides additional protection.[44]

In *The Penultimate Curiosity*, cowritten by an artist and writer, Roger Wagner, and a professor of nanomaterials at Oxford, Andrew Briggs, the authors examine the historical relationship of science and religion and see curiosity as a driving factor in the intertwined development of both. They describe metaphysical questions, especially regarding any search for the divine and ultimate meaning, as ultimate curiosity, while penultimate curiosity is "what has shaped and motivated the kind of interest that human societies manifest in the physical world around them."[45] Applying the image of a slipstream from the V formation of geese, or simply of one person walking behind another, the authors argue that "the penultimate curiosity of science has throughout human history swum in the slipstream of an ultimate metaphysical curiosity."[46] As a theologian, I would add how theology more and more swims (or should swim) in the slipstream of science, too.

I am also persuaded by curiosity's higher standing in Rabbinic, and especially much of contemporary Jewish, thought. Rabbi Bradley Shavit Artson, quoting Einstein, calls on theists to keep questioning and to "never lose a holy curiosity."[47] So, too, Rabbi Adin Steinsaltz highlights how the sustained celebration of study and curiosity in learning the Tanach and Talmud is not only ordained by God but is perhaps a unique human trait.[48] As he writes: "Our interest in irrelevant things—in things that have no immediate, and maybe even no remote, relevance to our existence—is part of our uniqueness as human beings."[49]

Intrigued by holy curiosity, but still needing some tie-breaker, I turned to my wife, Kelly. "What is curiosity?" I asked her, as she sat on the couch, petting the dog.

"Imperative to human life," she immediately said. "Without it, we are mere animals. It's a defining characteristic of humanity—though also what a lot of people lack."

I told her my initial pull towards wonder instead, but she added: "Wonder is passive; curiosity is action-seeking." Going deeper, she reminded me how growing up I was not encouraged to question—and it was

44. See, for example, Norenzayan, *Big Gods*.

45. Wagner and Briggs, *Penultimate Curiosity*, 52.

46. Wagner and Briggs, *Penultimate Curiosity*, 411.

47. Artson, "Holy Curiosity."

48. Steinsaltz, "Curious Jews."

49. Steinsaltz, "Curious Jews." Note that uniqueness should not be construed as superior.

a painful process once I started questioning everything. She went back to petting the dog. I ruminated some more, somewhat annoyed how easy such insights came to her (!).

Returning to the Counting Crows song that began my section, it ends with a call for change, interspersed with the light of the sun and of the moon (the latter in the image of a feather) descending upon us. The mixture connotes a sense of healing and warmth—of exploration and adventure; perhaps of starting over.

Such attempts to restart and renew also resonate with holy curiosity, another key pillar of theist-atheist dialogue

---

*

Response

Andrew Fiala

In Peter's contribution to this chapter, I more clearly see the connection between curiosity and desire. I described curiosity in my contribution as a desire to know and a desire to make meaning. I also connected this with a desire for power, including a desire for power over others. It is the desire for power that is linked to the ideological critique of the evangelical urge of religion and the desire to convert. Religious and philosophical traditions have often taught that desire is a problem. Peter recognizes this in quoting Augustine's critique of disordered desires and in Aquinas's critique of prideful desire for knowledge. He also notes that desire is a problem for Judaism and for Buddhism.

In my response, I want to dig a little deeper into desire and try to clarify the kind of desire found in virtuous curiosity. With Buddhist teaching in mind, I note that desire can be the source of great suffering. Greed, envy, and lust are the kinds of desires that can disrupt tranquility and corrupt the soul. We see this in Christian texts (such as in Augustine). We also see it in the Buddhist idea that suffering comes from desire or craving (*tanha*). A similar idea is also found in the ancient Greek and Roman philosophical tradition. Plato was critical of disordered desire, as were the Stoics. Even Epicureanism, which is a kind of hedonism, instructed people to understand and control desire.

Indeed, the idea of philosophy involves a kind of desire. The term *philo-sophia* is understood as "love of wisdom." But the kind of love involved here is not the craving of eros. Philo is more elevated than eros. It is not interested in selfish possession of the thing it desires. It is not interested in gaining power over that thing and using it to satisfy selfish need. Rather, philo is a kind of disinterested love. It is a desire for the good, the true, and the beautiful, which involves respect and self-control. In the Greek tradition it is connected to moderation, continence, and the kind of mature development of the soul, which helps to bring the body and its unruly desires under the control of the mind.

When we are thinking of curiosity as a virtue of dialogue that can help us find common ground, it is useful to characterize it in terms of this kind of love—the moderate and disinterested love that is associated with philosophical speculation. Admittedly, this is different from the kind of zealous love that is sometimes associated with fervent religious belief. There is a place for ardor and passion in human life. Sometimes this occurs in erotic relationships. Sometimes it occurs in the ambition of art, science, and business. Sometimes it occurs in religion. But philosophers have often cautioned us to keep a wary eye on the fires of passion: sometimes they burn out of control. Buddhists, Stoics, and others have taught the wisdom of moderating desire.

Curiosity of the sort that can help promote dialogue and find common ground would have to be understood as a moderate passion. Perhaps it can be understood in relation to the concept of *Gelassenheit*. This term is associated with Anabaptist religious traditions, with the mysticism of Meister Eckhart, and with the work of Martin Heidegger. Gelassenheit means letting things be or letting things go. In Heidegger's thought it involves allowing things to reveal themselves as they are. My friend Bret Davis—who is an expert on Heidegger and on Japanese Zen—has offered an account of Gelassenheit that opens a window onto psychology, theology, and ontology. Gelassenheit involves allowing things to be revealed. It involves a kind of obedience (in Eckhart) to the will of God. It may also be compared to the Taoist concept of *wu wei*, which can be translated as non-action. Perhaps this is something like what Peter is aiming at in his account of "holy curiosity." Gelassenheit involves a way of seeing that transforms self-will into something more open, welcoming, and receptive. At one point Bret Davis asks: "Would the profoundest meaning of 'God' then be: 'letting beings be'?"[1] The idea is that God is the being, or source of beings, who throws things into existence, reveals things to us, and allows things to be. In this abstract, Heideggerian way of speaking, we get a glimpse of a possible common ground. Religious faith is focused on connecting to that ontological source of things that is called God. But this is also what science and philosophy are focused on—at least when the scientist and philosopher look up from concrete and specific problems and attempt to figure out what it all means and how it all fits together. Everyone should look up from time to time and ask the big

1. Davis, *Heidegger and the Will*, 132. I discuss this and Gelassenheit in more detail in Fiala, *Transformative Pacifism*.

questions. Where did all of this come from? What is it here for? And how are we to live? Theists will answer these questions differently than atheists. But curiosity is contained in the questions themselves.

Let me conclude by turning to another problem. While questioning and Gelassenheit can offer a way of entering into a kind of mystical vision of being and beings, often this kind of wondering openness remains passive. There is virtue in passivity, especially when understood as a response to the incessant movement of the modern world and the suffering caused by craving and desire. But passivity cannot cure disease or feed the hungry. We also need activity, technology, and scientific inquiry. The task of life is to find a way to integrate passivity and activity, to link the peaceful respite of Gelassenheit with something more assertive, analytical, and creative.

Peter's wife seemed to see this when she explained to him that wonder is passive, while curiosity is action-oriented. I think we need both wonder and curiosity. We benefit from moments of aesthetic contemplation, when we see the world feathered in moonlight, as Peter suggests. But we also benefit from the productive activity of science, technology, and art itself. Songs must be written, after all. They are created by passion, ambition, and a kind of curiosity. A dialogue must also be written, spoken, and enacted. It is not enough merely to let things be. Mystical vision and serene acceptance are only part of life. The other part of life involves curiosity, which drives our attempt to live well with diverse others, our need to understand self and other, and our desire to create a social and political world that can contain the multitude.

6

Being Honest about Our Differences

ANDREW FIALA, PRIMARY AUTHOR

CURIOSITY, WHICH WE DISCUSSED in the previous chapter, must be connected to honesty about one's own beliefs. Differences must be admitted and explored. The point of dialogue is not simply to produce bland agreement about vague generalities; it should also elucidate differences. In this chapter, Fiala begins by pointing out areas of honest disagreement with theism. These disagreements are about metaphysics and epistemology: about the existence of God, the reality of the soul, and the kind of knowledge provided by faith and by religious texts and traditions. The differences explored here are profound. But the hope is that the shared value of honesty allows for common ground. When we are honest about our differences, we can develop mutual respect and understanding—much more so than if we fail to articulate what we disagree about.

Honest Dialogue

Dialogue depends upon honesty. We ought to disclose what we believe and admit when we disagree. But absolute honesty is impossible. It is not possible to fully disclose yourself. And it is often not wise to say all that you believe. Human life is in motion. New ideas and interpretations are discovered or invented. And there are secret corners and hidden reserves within us that we can never fully uncover. Dialogue is not a simple process through which I divulge everything and you respond in kind. There are necessary gaps and silences in dialogue, as well as ambiguities and open questions. There are also discoveries and the creation of new ideas and points of view. From my perspective, honesty is best understood in terms of an aspiration for authenticity as well as openness. We should say what we mean and mean what we say. We should also listen openly and respond generously.

Honesty is usually understood in terms of speech. We speak honestly and tell the truth. But gestures and actions also matter in dialogue and in life, since we are embodied beings. Honesty depends on what you *do* as well as on what you *say*. The hypocrite says one thing but behaves differently. Accusations of dishonesty and hypocrisy occur frequently in the typical theist-atheist discussion. These accusations often serve as conversation stoppers. To accuse another of dishonesty and hypocrisy is to make an ad hominem claim to the effect that the other cannot be trusted as a reliable partner in dialogue.

Atheists have often accused religious believers of dishonesty and hypocrisy, while focusing on the moral and political failures of religious organizations. When the Roman Catholic Church knows about pedophilia and covers it up, that's dishonest and hypocritical. Similar accusations can be mounted against a church that has banned books, engaged in the Inquisition, and participated in anti-Semitic pogroms. Similar problems occur when religious folks dismiss science while turning to modern medicine. A related problem is created when religious believers dismiss other people's religions as cultish or superstitious, without considering the superstitiousness of their own belief system. And then, of course, there is the question of money and the way that some clergy and churches enrich themselves while preaching about charity and care for the poor. I do not raise these issues here because I believe that all theists are dishonest hypocrites. Rather, I raise these accusations because they are well-known and have been made both by atheists and by religious people themselves. It would be dishonest to ignore them.

Let me also stipulate that there are honest and sincere theists—just as there are honest and sincere atheists. Honesty is not a function of theological belief (or disbelief). Rather, it is a function of ethics and character. However, one obstacle for theist-atheist dialogue is the fact that the theological tradition has tended to link honesty to belief in God. Atheists were often presumed to be incapable of honesty. John Locke's "Letter on Toleration" called for extensive toleration, except for atheists. He explained: "Those are not at all to be tolerated who deny the being of a God. Promises, covenants, and oaths, which are the bonds of human society, can have no hold upon an atheist. The taking away of God, though but even in thought, dissolves all."[1] Even today, there is a prevailing view among the general population that atheists cannot be trusted, that they are liars, deceivers, cheats, and hypocrites. Polling data shows that atheists are among the least trusted members of society.[2] In some American states, there are still residual laws

1. Locke, "Letter Concerning Toleration," 425.
2. See "Atheists Tend to Be Seen as Immoral."

on the books prohibiting atheists from holding public office.[3] These laws are not enforced—and likely violate the First Amendment. But the fact that they exist shows us the depth of the accusation against atheism. In Western secular democracies, the laws against atheism have changed. But in twelve countries apostasy is punishable by death.[4]

As a result, atheists often learn to keep their mouths shut. It is socially unacceptable to affirm atheism in many communities. And even for me, as an atheist philosophy professor, I often would rather change the subject than get into a debate with a religious person about my lack of faith. Sometimes, my taciturnity is a matter of tact and humility. When I attend religious ceremonies, rituals, and events I remain silent. When my students ask me what I believe about religion, I know better than to tell them all that I am thinking. And even in interfaith meetings and philosophical dialogues about religion, I find that it is wise to keep quiet to one degree or another.

This may seem dishonest. But honesty must be balanced with other virtues. In the case of religious services, it would be rude to say all that you are thinking. No one wants to enter into a dialogue about religion at a funeral or a wedding. With regard to my students, my awareness of the power differential is a crucial part of my taciturnity. It would be wrong to foist my views upon students or to engage in critical questioning of their deeply held beliefs. And in dialogues about religion, the point is not simply to put everything you believe (or don't believe) on the table—as if that were possible. The goal is not simply to confess but also to seek common ground. We can't find common ground if we are not honest. But it is difficult to be honest in a debate between atheists and theists, when there is so much historical and social baggage accompanying this debate.

Honesty, Authenticity, and Community

Honesty is a social virtue. It is not merely about our relationship with the truth: it also involves a relationship with "the other." If a person were alone in the world, the question of honesty would not come up. It is only when some other person appears that the issue of honesty arises, in connection with what we divulge to the other. There are, of course, problems of self-deception and lying to yourself. To say that we need to be honest with ourselves implies an internal "other"—a self that is estranged from itself or that has parts that are in conflict.

3. See Mehta, "Why Do Seven States' Constitutions."

4. See Humanists International, "Right to Apostasy in the World."

To be honest is to live authentically or with integrity. This includes saying and doing things that you believe to be true, while representing yourself honestly either to another or to yourself. There is a close relationship between honesty and other virtues such as authenticity, sincerity, and integrity. To be honest is to be true to yourself. But this is still one-sided. To be honest is also to be true to (and with and for) the others with whom we share social space. To be true to your friends, for example, is to keep your promises. Honesty is thus related to loyalty and fidelity.

Josiah Royce explained this in detail in his *Philosophy of Loyalty*. He said: "Truth seeking and loyalty are therefore essentially the same process of life merely viewed in two different aspects."[5] Royce has a deeply social view of the self. The self, Royce suggests, finds itself in the midst of various communities, which create competing demands for loyalty. We are members of families, social groups, business groups, states—and of humanity as a whole. We also belong to religious groups. One of the difficulties of life is to find a way to integrate all of our competing loyalties: to live authentically and truthfully as we circulate among this diversity. This becomes quite challenging when there are competing values and truths among these groups. The task of integrating our beliefs requires us to be honest with ourselves and to think carefully about what we believe and are faithful to. This is a process of interpretation and dialogue. It involves the process of reviewing ideas within the various communities of interpretation in which we dwell. The idea of a community of interpretation was explored by Royce in *The Problem of Christianity*. Royce offered a reconstruction of Christianity that pushed beyond theology toward a social and pragmatically grounded experience of community. As Royce explained:

> No one who loves mankind can find a worthier and more significant way to express his love than by increasing and expressing among men the will to interpret. . . . When Christianity teaches us to hope for the community of all mankind, we can readily see that the beloved community, whatever else it is, will be when it comes, a community of interpretation.[6]

Royce's notion of the beloved community would go on to influence Martin Luther King Jr. Royce's idea, as well as King's, is that through honest and open dialogue we can create justice and build community.

This reference to King reminds us that silence and hypocrisy remain significant problems. King said, in his "Letter from Birmingham Jail," that one of the great impediments to social justice is the "appalling silence of

5. Royce, *Philosophy of Loyalty*, 314.

6. Royce, *Problem of Christianity*, 218–19.

the good people."[7] King made special mention of the hypocrisy of his fellow Christians who remained silent "behind the anesthetizing security of stained glass windows." By dishonestly remaining silent in the face of racism, "good" people become hypocritical and end up in complicity with evil and injustice. A genuine community of interpretation requires that we overcome silence and speak out against hypocrisy, injustice, and untruth. But this is not easy, as the history of King and the American civil rights movement shows.

It often seems easier to ignore injustice and hypocrisy. This has occurred in dealing with racism and injustice in society—and in dealing with some of the failings of religious organizations mentioned above. It can also occur in interfaith discussions and in dialogues and debates between religious and nonreligious people. In an effort to find common ground, we sometimes set honesty and truth aside. Sometimes this is prudent. But other times it is unwise. And, when silent hypocrites remain complicit with injustice, it is morally wrong. The difficulty is knowing how much to say, when to say it, and whom to say it to. This way of putting things hearkens to the virtue tradition, which is focused on questions about the right time, right amount, and right way of doing things. We must be wise about our honesty. Wisdom consists in finding ways to be true to ourselves while also seeking to build up genuine and inclusive communities of interpretation.

We ought to strive to cultivate a social and political world in which honesty and authenticity are possible. In the history of religion, this has often been lacking. Atheists have often dissembled and hid their ideas out of fear of persecution. And while things are better in secular democracies that protect freedom of religion and freedom of speech, there is still a lot of dishonesty in discussions of religion. For example, the Catholic Church has been involved in substantial dishonesty about the abuse of children by priests. And LGBTQI persons have often been forced by religious authorities to be less than fully honest about their identities. This mention of LGBTQI issues gives us a metaphor for honesty in the idea of coming out of the closet. Secret beliefs and suppressed identities are kept in the closet. For an open dialogue to take place, the closet doors must be opened, the skeletons aired out, and the light of transparency must be directed toward the shadows.

In this broadly social way of understanding honesty, it is not merely a one-sided virtue of the person who speaks. Rather, it is a relational concept that also involves openness to the other in an effort to build a more inclusive community of interpretation. There is, after all, such a thing as "honest listening."[8] Dishonest or disingenuous listening occurs when I encounter

7. King, "Letter from Birmingham Jail."

8. See Shanks, *Faith in Honesty*.

the other in a superficial way. If I am "honestly listening" to you, I am open to you, receiving what you are sending without impediment or ulterior motive. This means that honesty is not only about talking and expressing yourself but also about how you receive the other. Honesty is about us and our relationship. When we have an honest relationship, we feel at home; there is trust and a sense of mutuality. We share the goal of interpretation, seeking honestly to understand our differences while also searching for common ground. A dishonest relationship involves dissembling, deception, and lack of openness. Dishonesty also occurs when the interpretive effort is one-sided: when we merely seek to pontificate and convert without also seeking to learn and understand. In an honest dialogue each partner is empowered to express him- or herself while each partner also seeks to understand the point of view of the other.

The philosophical tradition has often viewed honesty as a self-regarding virtue and not as a feature of the dialogical or social situation. Honesty is often understood as a cardinal virtue.[9] This traditional view of honesty looks at it as a motivational or dispositional state associated with truth. Honest persons do not willfully distort the facts. To be honest is to respect truth and truthfulness. Sometimes honesty is reactive: honest people are willing to disclose truths and facts when asked. But honesty is also proactive: it also seems to involve a desire to seek out truth—not merely in response to a query but for the sake of truth itself. Is someone really honest who believes something, while avoiding counter-evidence for fear of losing faith? It is easy to see that honesty and curiosity are linked. If curiosity is understood as a desire or motivation to learn more, then honesty adds that this desire for knowledge also ought to be guided by a concern for truth. A curious person could, for example, simply be curious about all of the things that confirm what they already believe. The combination of curiosity and honesty implies that there is an interest in learning more and also in learning what is true.

We might also add that honesty is constrained and defined by other virtues such as justice, loyalty, courage, concern for the common good, and care for the well-being of others. There are also obligations of confidentiality, promise-keeping, and so on that make honesty complicated and difficult. If I promise not to tell a secret you have shared with me, and someone asks me to share it, am I dishonest for keeping the promise? Or perhaps I have an obligation of honesty, at least, to divulge that I have made a promise of keeping such a secret. The complexities here have been explored in practical

9. See: Wilson, "Honesty as a Virtue"; Roberts and West, "Virtue of Honesty"; and Miller, "Honesty."

and applied ethics. There are related issues such as whistleblowing, white lies, the obligation to pursue truth (vs. negligent disregard), and so on. The sphere of practical ethics reminds us that honesty can have a vocational aspect: doctors and journalists have different obligations with regard to honesty than lawyers and cops do. Applied ethics also shows that care and concern for the well-being of others may lead us to be less than honest (as in the case of a white lie). In general, as with almost every virtue, the virtue of honesty must be balanced with our other values. This returns us to the social definition of honesty. An honest dialogue links willingness to disclose the truth with other virtues that are necessary ingredients of genuine dialogue, including care, loyalty, justice, and compassion.

An Atheist's Honest Assessment of Theism

Now let's turn to some of the honest differences that atheists have with theists. We mentioned a few of the typical kinds of accusations that atheists make against religion above—with regard to hypocrisy and dishonesty in the church, for example. But those accusations are not about theism itself. Pedophile priests are not the best representatives of religious belief. Nor are racist white churches the only churches worthy of consideration. Christians have also led the way in working against child abuse, sexual predation, gender equality, and racism. It is dishonest to dump all religions and all religious people into the dustbin of history because of the moral failure of some Christians. It is not reasonable to indict a set of theological principles based upon the hypocrisy and misbehavior of those who supposedly affirm those principles. Such an approach is known as the fallacy of the ad hominem argument. Dishonest and hypocritical people can believe things that are actually true.

With this warning in mind, let's leave the ad hominem accusations aside and turn to some of the basic issues in metaphysics and epistemology that form the core of the disagreement between theists and atheists. The most obvious disagreement is about the existence of God. Atheists deny that there is a god. In previous chapters, I have claimed that the sky-god of the revealed religions obviously does not exist. About the abstract God of theology, things are not as obvious, even though skepticism remains. Let's consider each of these points in turn.

1. The sky-god of revealed religion. By "sky-god" I mean a notion of God as a being who lives in the heavens above us and who controls things like the weather and the movement of the stars. The sky-god interacts with human beings as their creator and judge. He floods the earth, sends rainbows, and intervenes in battles. The cosmology of sky-god religion simply does not work today. The idea of heaven as above us and hell below is destroyed by modern cosmology, which tells us that the earth is not a fixed ground around which the stars and planets revolve. We have known since the time of Copernicus and Galileo that there is no heaven above us. Nor is there any hell below. The earth is a small planet in a solar system and galaxy that is a minuscule part of a universe that contains billions of stars, planets, and galaxies. The weather is determined by ocean currents, the jet stream, atmospheric chemistry, and the input of solar energy. Rainbows are caused by light refracting through water. And so on.

It should come as no surprise that a number of atheists have pointed out the problem of the sky-god theology. But these problems have also been pointed out by sympathetic Christian theologians who offer a different vision of religion and theology. For example, Bishop John Shelby Spong states this argument bluntly, showing how the Copernican and Newtonian worldview undermines much of the Christian scriptures:

> The fact that we know today that the earth is not the center of the universe, with heaven above the sky, renders the worldview of the biblical writers seriously inaccurate. Was God ill-informed or did God choose not to reveal such truth to the authors of the biblical books? Yet an earth-centered, three-tiered universe underlies such biblical stories as the Tower of Babel (Gen 11), manna falling from heaven (Exod 16:4ff), the wise men following the star of Bethlehem (Matt. 2) and even the cosmic ascension of Jesus (Luke 24; Acts 1). The Bible tells us that the Israelites wandered nomadically in the wilderness between Egypt and the Promised Land for forty years, guided by the magic signs of a pillar of cloud by day and a pillar of fire by night, which connected them with the God who lived just above the sky (Exod 13 and Exod 16:35). The Bible makes assumptions that most of us who live in a post-Newtonian world of "natural law" could never make.[10]

Some theists do not take the sky-god scriptures literally. But some do. There continue to be flat-earthers out there. Some theists continue to believe that the earth is only a few thousand years old. Some theists deny that evolution exists, since the Bible says that God created humans and animals as discrete beings in the garden of Eden. Some theists believe that God would never permit climate change to destroy the ecosystem because

10. Spong, *Sins of Scripture*, 20–21.

God promised Noah, under the sign of the rainbow, that he would never flood the earth again. And so on.

This reference to Noah and the rainbow points us toward two other problems of the sky-god religion: the problem of the wrathful God and the problem of miracles. The Noah story is terrifying in what it says about God, who basically kills everyone in order to start over. This is a God who created a botched humanity at the outset, who gets angry, and who destroys his creation. This is far away from the omniscient and benevolent God of abstract theology. Perhaps the flood points toward God's omnipotence; but the God of Noah does not seem all-knowing or all-good. Furthermore, there is something odd about a God who intervenes in nature by miracle. The notion of miracles involves us in a number of absurdities that undermine our understanding of the natural world and its natural laws. This critique of miracles and defense of natural law was articulated by David Hume and the deists during the Enlightenment. Today it is even harder to believe in miracles as our understanding of the intricacies of the natural world deepens. The same is true as our sense of morality deepens. It seems morally problematic to believe in a sky-god who desires obedience and sacrifice, who gets angry, who punishes, and who saves us through his miraculous power.

But notice that if we reject this idea of God, then much of Christian dogma falls with it: the idea of the incarnation of Christ, his resurrection, and our thinking about sin, grace, and the power of prayer. There are profound metaphysical problems here. Even if we move beyond a simplistic sky-god theology, Christian theology appears to rely upon the idea that there are two substances or two realms: the spiritual and the material. This idea was made famous by Descartes. This dualistic view was thought to help explain a variety of conundrums in Christianity, including for example, what happens in the mystery of Eucharist and how the soul is related to the body. But the methodology and assumptions of empirical science rejects dualism. The worldview of empirical science is not dualistic: it affirms that there is only one substance, the material substance of this universe.

Christian dualism comes, in part, from a literal reading of certain biblical texts, including those that speak of the ritual of Holy Communion. The Gospel of John says that eternal life comes from eating the flesh and drinking the blood of Christ (John 5:54–57). And Jesus says in Matthew 26:26–28 that the bread is his body and the wine is his blood. A nonliteral reading of these texts would see this merely as a poetic metaphor. And in fact, this is how many Protestants understand this sort of thing. But transubstantiation is Catholic dogma. As the catechism explains:

> That in this sacrament are the true Body of Christ and his true Blood is something that "cannot be apprehended by the senses," says St. Thomas, "but only by faith, which relies on divine authority."[11]

There is a longer story to be told here of how Thomistic metaphysics (based upon Aristotle) gave way to Cartesian dualism. But the key point for a skeptic is underlined by this appeal to St. Thomas. The empirical method of humanists and naturalists is grounded in the senses: it only sees bread and wine in the Eucharist. But the religious understanding of the Eucharist is not grounded in the senses, it is based upon an appeal to divine authority—and thus in an appeal to some kind of literal interpretation of the scriptural passages used as the basis for the communion ritual.

Further examples show us the challenge of scripture and interpretation. Some beliefs of a literal sky-god Christianity lead to pernicious outcomes. To deny the threat of climate change, for example, because God promised Noah that he would not flood the earth again is both dumb and dangerous.[12] Other examples of the problem of biblical literalism will be discussed in chapter 8. The fact is that the Bible's story contradicts what natural science tells us. We might also note that there are also contradictions among the world's other sky-god religions. In Hindu cosmology, for example, the universe is cyclical (unlike the linear model of time we see in the Bible) and there are multiple deities and avatars of the gods. We could go on to include details from the Greeks, the Celts, pre-Columbian America, Africa, Asia and so on. This diversity of ancient cosmologies makes the skeptical point more obvious: the revealed religions of the ancient world were all developed in a prescientific era, without access to telescopes and microscopes, advanced mathematics, and computers. Modern scientific techniques are simply better at explaining the natural world. If religious people still maintain faith in ancient sky-god cosmology, that's because they have not taken seriously the diversity of alternative cosmologies or because they do not understand the power and accuracy of the modern scientific method.

11. *Catechism of the Catholic Church*, 1381.

12. I wrote about this in Fiala, "Moral Imperative of Hope." In 2009, Republic Rep. John Shimkus said in a congressional hearing that the story of Noah and the flood shows that the earth will not be destroyed in a flood: "The earth will end only when God declares it's time to be over. Man will not destroy the earth. This earth will not be destroyed by a flood" (Goodenough, "Is the Good Book"); also see Right Wing Watch Staff, "'Green Dragon' Slayers." Joe Barton and James Inhofe have made similar arguments. See Goldenberg, "Texas Congressman Cites Noah's Ark"; and Bruenig, "Why Do Evangelicals."

In chapter 8 I will consider how biblical literalism has produced patriarchy, homophobia, and other pernicious outcomes. Let's push this critique a bit further toward a critique of ideology and power, asking whether the priests, prophets, and politicians who propagated the sky-god religions were more interested in power than in truth. The concern here is that those priests and politicians who disseminated and defended the sky-god religions did so because they personally had something to gain from it. While such an argument takes us in the direction of the ad hominem argument I am trying to avoid, there is no denying that the history of religion includes a serious effort to consolidate power under a central authority and defend the power of the patriarchy against heretical voices, foreigners, apostates, and revolutionaries. The history of Christianity provides a prime example: the Roman and Jewish authorities were opposed to the new cult of Jesus. Jesus was crucified by those authorities and his followers were persecuted. Over time, power fell into the hands of the Christians, who then used their power to persecute minority voices. A similar story could be told about other religions. Islam, for example, was eventually disseminated along with political power as Muslim warriors fanned out around the ancient world. And indeed, the Muslim world came into direct conflict with Christendom throughout the medieval and early modern periods. The patriarchal and authoritarian power of religion was, for many long centuries, connected to militant and antidemocratic social and political power. Much of this can be traced to claims made in the name of the sky-god of the primary texts. The Bible was used to justify slavery, the Crusades, colonial wars of conquest, and anti-Semitism. This patriarchal authoritarianism was grounded upon a kind of literalism connected to sky-god theology: we can trace the authority of the popes, the hierarchical understanding of races and genders, and even the "divine right of kings" back to biblical texts. The divine right of kings, for example, was modeled on Adam's rule over creation and Paul's letter to the Romans, which said that the monarch is empowered to execute God's wrath on wrongdoers (Romans 13).[13] Atheists will find all of this to be absurd: both the pernicious moral, social, and political consequences of sky-god religion and the way that these consequences are grounded in ancient texts that modern science demonstrates to be false.

2. The abstract God of theology. Now that I have offered an honest assessment of the God of biblical literalism, let's turn to a consideration of the God of theology. This is the God who is omniscient, omnipotent, and omnibenevolent. I have discussed this already in a previous chapter

13. One source for the divine right of kings argument is Robert Filmer, *Patriarcha: Or the Natural Power of Kings*. Filmer was the foil for John Locke's more liberal and democratic argument in Locke's *Two Treatises on Government*.

(chapter 4), where we considered the problem of evil. The sky-god of ancient religion does in fact appear to be the cause of much mischief in the world, as seen in the case of God's supposedly wrathful destruction of the human beings who existed before Noah, which we discussed above. But the God of abstract theology is not thought to be the cause of evil. Rather, he is said to permit evil, as a foreseen but necessary feature of his benevolent creation. Evil is permitted to exist, according to what is called "theodicy" (accounts that justify or "vindicate" God) because, for example, freedom of the will is a great good. If God had created humans with wills that were not free, something of great value would be lacking in the world. So even though freedom of the will means that there will be sin and evil, God permits these evils. Furthermore, God provides a remedy or cure for those who suffer evil through his grace and mercy. There is much more to be said here about theodicy. I have offered some critical remarks in chapter 4. But let me reiterate that atheists simply do not find the typical Christian theodicy to be compelling. To be honest, this seems like a kind of defensive and rearguard action, designed to shore up the ideal of the philosophical God, a way of making it possible for him to be omniscient, omnipotent, and omnibenevolent, even though this does not seem plausible.

To push this a bit further, it's worth considering whether a slightly less elevated notion of God isn't more plausible. Maybe God is not omnipotent. Or maybe he is not omniscient. Or maybe he is not omnibenevolent. The problem of evil becomes a problem only if we assume these three predicates of God. But if we give up one (or all) of them, then evil is not a contradiction. The view of God that results has been explored in a number of ways by theologians and described in various ways.[14] Among these possibilities are:

- deism (where God is an abstract prime mover who is either indifferent to human happiness or who is unable to intervene through miracle)
- process theology (where God changes and suffers with human beings)
- pantheism (where God is everything, in which case God actually includes evil, suffering, and loss)
- dualism (where there is a great struggle between equally powerful good and evil gods)
- Gnosticism (of the sort that views this as a fallen universe that is the plaything or creation of a defective god)

14. For a useful recent discussion, see Patterson, "Problem of Evil."

These possibilities for thinking about God and the problem of evil leave us with a skeptical problem, however. Each has its problems. The classical image of the omnipotent, omniscient, and omnibenevolent God seems conceptually superior—and has appeared so to the mainstream of theology. But this classical theology leaves us with the challenge of the problem of evil. Furthermore—and here is my main point: how would we know which of these theologies to accept? To be honest (here in a chapter on honesty), I have to admit that it is not easy to decide among these theologies. In fact, it is more honest, from my perspective, to admit that none of these is any more persuasive than atheism itself.

Let's push deeper into the thickets of theology and turn to arguments for the existence of God. We will consider two traditional arguments here: the cosmological argument (including the argument from design) and the argument from morality and meaning. I will mostly ignore the ontological argument here, since to my mind, as an empirically-minded thinker, it is simply a nonstarter. My quick rejection of the ontological argument is based upon criticism of the argument found in Hume (who said: "There is no being, therefore, whose non-existence implies a contradiction. Consequently there is no being, whose existence is demonstrable") and in Kant (who said that "existence is not a real predicate").[15]

The cosmological argument holds that the universe must have a cause—and that the cause is God. The related **argument from design** holds that the complex structures of the universe give us evidence of a designer. These are powerful empirical and logical arguments, which can be persuasive. Everything appears to have a cause that precedes it. This means that the universe itself must have a cause. And it does seem as if human beings were created for some special purpose. This sense of specialness and the apparent need for a first cause leads us to suppose that God is the cause and that God created us in our specialness. But during the past few centuries an alternative explanation of all of this has emerged. Big bang cosmology provides one explanation. The proposal of the big bang is that the universe emerged from some original singularity and that the laws of physics guided the inflation and expansion of the universe. Admittedly, there are complexities here and disagreements among cosmologists. Perhaps there is an oscillating series of universes. Or maybe this universe emerged as a bubble out of some other larger structure of multiverses. To make sense of this, we would need to dig into the details and complexity of physics, relativity theory, and quantum mechanics, while coming to terms with new measurements of

15. See Hume, *Dialogues Concerning Natural Religion*, 478; and Kant, *Critique of Pure Reason*, B626–27.

the universe and its forces. It is simpler, in a sense, to postulate God as the first cause. But this turn to simplicity replaces powerful physical science with a mystery. The question remains as to why God created the universe. One kind of answer points toward the creation of humanity in the image of God. But again, the natural sciences have offered an alternative story: the theory of evolution. Evolutionary explanations require us, again, to delve into complexity. The evolutionary theory requires us to understand genetics and DNA, the vast scales of geological and phylogenetic time, the fossil record, comparative anatomy, and so on. It is certainly simpler to say that God created the species as distinct and human beings in his own image. But this biblical account flies in the face of modern biology. And in fact, modern biology provides us with a powerful set of tools that are employed in medicine, agriculture, and so on.

A further problem comes from deism. It might be that God started the universe, along with its laws and evolutionary processes. But the laws of nature appear to be such that the first cause of the universe can no longer intervene in the flow of nature, which is why deists tended to reject the idea of miracles. Furthermore, there is no real proof one way or another about this first cause. Nor can we say much about it other than that it exists. Deism points toward a crucial different between a rational religion (based upon the cosmological argument) and revealed religion (which tells us about God's will and the content of his plans for his creation). A deistic reconstruction of the cosmological argument leaves us agnostic about the cosmological first cause: we can't know one way or another about it in sufficient detail for it to really matter much to us. Thus, I have argued elsewhere in favor of an atheistic rejection of the sky-god theology that remains agnostic about the abstract god of cosmological theology.[16]

The argument from meaning and morality holds that God gives us moral law and meaning in life. Said differently, without God, there would be no meaning and no morality. This claim is an old one. In the Old Testament, the Psalms (14) say that the fool says that there is no God—and from that appears to flow evil and corruption. Dostoevsky suggested that if there were no God, then everything would be permitted. This idea is connected with the idea of what is sometimes called "divine command" ethics. The divine command story holds that God gives us commandments that we must fulfill. These commands provide a source of morality as well as the motivation to follow those commandments. The motivation comes from the threat of punishment and the promise of reward for ethical behavior. Let's consider two difficulties for the divine command account:

16. See Fiala, *Against Religions, Wars, and States.*

1. regarding the content of these commands; and
2. regarding their motivational power.

First, God's commands are not as clear (or as benevolent) as they could be. The biblical texts contain lots of commandments. Some of these appear to conflict with each other and with common sense ideas about right and wrong. We'll discuss this in more detail in chapter 8. But let's consider one obvious problem here to make my point: the issue of slavery. The Bible appears to condone slavery (for example, in Leviticus 25 or in Paul's letters to the Ephesians and the Colossians). But the idea of keeping a person as a slave who is created in the image of God seems wrong. The point here is that an appeal to divine command does not really help us decide about many ethical issues. We also need independent moral judgment, informed by science, philosophy, and reason.

Finally, we turn to the question of motivation. There is certainly some power to the idea that goodness will be rewarded with eternal life (and that evil will be punished). But it is not clear that this is necessary for us to be motivated by morality. There is ample evidence that morality is its own reward. Aristotle and the Greeks provide one source: they taught that happiness and flourishing (*eudaimonia*) was inherently linked to virtue. We are happiest when we do right and live well. This continues to be true today. Ethical behavior helps us succeed in business, professional life, and friendships and families. Of course, a theist may respond by pointing out that some good people end up unhappy and that some evil people succeed. The idea of judgment and reward after death can help to rectify the apparent injustice of the universe—and to keep us on the straight and narrow path when things seem bleak. This makes sense. It is undeniable that good people can end up unhappy. But an empirical and naturalistic account of ethics and the good life does not promise a panacea. The point is merely this—that ordinarily and for the most part goodness and happiness are connected. And yet, a theist may respond that this is insufficient. Furthermore, a theist may point out that death remains a problem. And here we get to an important difference of opinion about life and its value. For a naturalistically inclined humanist, death is simply part of life. We must accept its inevitability and learn to live with its presence. The promise of eternal life is simply not of interest for atheists. One problem is that there are metaphysical mysteries in eternal life that seem to lead to absurdities. But a further problem is that there is a kind of hubris involved in the aspiration for eternity. All things die. And through our dying we make way for new things to be born. This seems obvious, natural, humble, and well . . . honest.

Conclusion: Honesty, Envy, and Admiration

To ask for more than this short lifetime seems rude and wrongheaded. We are guests on this earth for some seventy or eighty years. We ought to be thankful for what we receive. We ought to leave the place better than when we found it. And when our time is over, we ought to step aside and let history move on without us. During our time here, we struggle to make meaning, find joy, and do the right thing.

I suspect that Peter would agree with the spirit of my conclusion here, even if we both arrive at a kind of humble acceptance of life (and death) from different directions. As I conclude my contribution here, let me return to the importance of dialogue. My remarks here have laid bare some serious points of divergence between atheism and theism. But I don't offer these remarks in order to belittle or denigrate my theistic friends and colleagues. The fact of the matter is that we simply disagree about some important ideas.

Now let me offer a caution to my atheistic friends and colleagues. Sometimes in discussions such as this, atheists become incensed and outraged at the absurdity of theistic belief. I can feel that way sometimes myself. But here is where an honest appraisal of one's own emotions and thinking can help. I suspect that some of the outrage experienced by atheists is connected to a kind of envy or jealousy. It often seems that the theist has an easier and simpler time of it. The theist can go along with the flow of tradition, can enjoy the pageantry and ritual of religion, and can be content with his or her place in a universe imbued with meaning, purpose, and a promise of eternal life. If we are being totally honest, there is something nice about all that. The atheist's universe can sometimes appear to be a bleak and unwelcoming place. I don't think this is necessarily true. There are joys and wonders in the natural world. But atheists can resent the seemingly complacent life of the faithful.

The challenge of dialogue is for envy and resentment to transform itself into admiration and companionship, while also remaining authentic and honest. One wonders whether there is any room for admiration and appreciation of theism, when considered from an atheist's point of view. I think there is, especially if we understand that the mysteries of theology and the rituals of religion are human creations. Theists will obviously have another interpretation of all of this. But if atheists are being honest, we must admit that theism itself is a human product, something that can be admired as a creation of the human spirit, even if it is not accepted as true.

---- * ----

Response: Reckoning and a Surrender

PETER ADMIRAND

> Woe to you who have lost your nerve! What will you do when the Lord's reckoning comes? —Sirach 2:14

> Then Jeremiah said to Zedekiah, "Thus says the Lord, the God of hosts, the God of Israel, 'If you will only surrender to the officials of the king of Babylon, then your life shall be spared, and this city shall not be burned with fire, and you and your house shall live.'" —Jeremiah 38:17

IT CAN SOMETIMES FEEL we theists are left defending an exposed and near-defenseless castle, and the king, if such a royal being ever really existed, seems long, long gone. Assaults of doubt, never-ending calamity, and our own needlessly started fires and self-destruction encroach often and almost everywhere. The call to surrender seems the only reasonable option. If there are weapons still available, are they not all blunted by now? And who wants to use weapons anymore, anyway? Either way, mere survival is not enough. Is there another choice?

The quote above from Sirach, canonical only in the Catholic tradition, is typically read as a believer lacking faith or resolve and to remember vindication is at hand.[1] The call is to be steadfast. In the Tanach, any reckoning by such a deity often has violent consequences. The threat is palpable. The quote from Jeremiah is in the context of his giving advice to the besieged (and weak) Israelite king Zedekiah. Jeremiah is counseling the king to surrender to the Babylonians, as God has already decided to use the Babylonians as an instrument to punish Judah. If Zedekiah does not surrender, the city will be burned and all its captives taken.[2] This, indeed, is what happens.

1. For commentary, see Corley, *Sirach*.
2. On Jeremiah, see for example, Lundbom et al., *Book of Jeremiah*.

Surrender and reckoning seem far from appealing. Can we theists instead see these apparent "attacks" as something else, perhaps as gifts and opportunities for growth and expansion through stripping down and cleansing?

One problem is most of us don't really like to hear the truth. We do if it's good news (for us) or supports or reinforces our value and beauty. But what about when it stings or burns, undermining our conceptions or beliefs?

Usually, a volley of truths from an atheist position on the fallacy of belief in God is met by a counter volley. I apologize to readers of all parties, but here I finally surrender. Here I open the gates, and not only let the "attackers" in, but seem to hear in a voice, perhaps within, perhaps far, far away: "Quickly, bring out a robe—the best one—and put it on him; put a ring on his finger and sandals on his feet. And get the fatted calf and kill it, and let us eat and celebrate; for this son of mine was dead and is alive again; he was lost and is found!'" (Luke 15:22–24).

Such a feast, of course, is not (mainly) for these new guests. They, too, may be lost in their own ways, but it is theists like me who are lost. It is we who need to acknowledge our failures and to seek forgiveness, and try to make amends.

It is time to surrender.

It is time to face more difficult truths.

To start: I again am grateful for Andy's honesty and the challenges he raises here and will expand on in chapter 8. If a response beyond "thank you" is demanded, it would include the following truths from a theist:

1. The world is a better place because of many atheists—and religions are better-off because of many atheist positions and arguments. Why? Because they can challenge, humble, and purify religious positions and beliefs. They help the religious avoid complacency and self-righteousness, and promote questioning, seeking, and introspection. As for the virtue of honesty, we read: "One who gives an honest answer gives a kiss on the lips" (Prov 24:26).

2. Ongoing self-conversion should be the priority. Andy raises the truth of religious hypocrisy, though he also generously notes such individuals don't reflect core religious beliefs or how religions also produce moral exemplars of integrity. Theists need to be even more honest with themselves. Extending the metaphor above, is the castle even worth saving? It is so much easier to focus on the failures of others. "Why do you see the speck in your neighbor's eye, but do not notice the log in your own eye? Or how can you say to your neighbor, 'Let me take the

speck out of your eye,' while the log is in your own eye? You hypocrite, first take the log out of your own eye, and then you will see clearly to take the speck out of your neighbor's eye" (Matt 7:3–5).

3. Religions are mostly human-constructed with all their rituals, words, laws, and claims. Andy contends religions are only human-constructed. Theists may bicker over the percentage that is human-based or my word "mostly," but like a tiny drop of blue dye that turns the water blue, humanity plays a major role in the religion produced and practiced. And thus we too often reflect our needs and visions and not any divine power or source. The Bible repeatedly stresses mercy over acts of ritual or sacrifice (Hos 6:6). While such claims may scapegoat human beings, they at least speak to the truth of the failure and hypocrisies of religions and we who claim some religious identity or affiliation.
4. Too many theists have created and facilitated senseless and needless suffering on others—and such acts have often been blessed by aspects of our holy books or so-called holy leaders, or met with general silence or resignation. There is no shortage of hypocritical theists, from a Catholic hierarchy concealing sexual abuse of children by clerics to theists serving as corrupt judges, politicians, property speculators, hedge fund managers, and CEOs destroying our environment, pummeling the poor, reaping profit from war and weapons, and maintaining structural injustice. Add also theists who abuse their wives, partners, or children. Perhaps a reckoning should be coming: "If any of you put a stumbling block before one of these little ones who believe in me, it would be better for you if a great millstone were fastened around your neck and you were drowned in the depths of the sea" (Matt 18:6).
5. Theists should read their holy books with the other as the victim and the oppressed and ask why and how it is theists who are the persecutors. Such reading could further enhance the beauty of the Sermon on the Mount, for example, especially when we read: "Blessed are you when people hate you, and when they exclude you, revile you, and defame you on account of the Son of Man. Rejoice in that day and leap for joy, for surely your reward is great in heaven; for that is what their ancestors did to the prophets" (Luke 6:22–23). Instead of a complacency from victimhood, what if we actually see and face those we imprison or leave hungry, destitute, and unconsoled? What if we actually look upon those we (really) hate, exclude, revile, and defame; those we smother with indifference or false kindness—often from supposed zeal for Jesus?

6. Faith is both a gift and a burden. Andy writes: "But atheists can resent the seemingly complacent life of the faithful." Complacency is part of the problem noted above, yet theists should recognize at least two main points perhaps implied in the statement. First, faith is a gift. Despite my doubts and worries, most arguments against God, whether from a Hume, Russell, or Dawkins, leave me unmoved. So, too, do theist responses and counter-syllogisms. At a fundamental level, I believe the world is not simply material. Going further, I believe in the moral and spiritual revolution of love, compassion, and nonviolence represented (or incarnate) in Jesus. Let me again state, though, that I have no need or desire for Christianity to be seen as the only or best viable spiritual or religious path for everyone. I see religious diversity—in which I also include ethical humanist positions—as holy, good, and interconnected,[3] even amidst their differences and distinctive priorities, strengths, and weaknesses. I can't embrace, though, the call to place all my trust in empirical science, verification, and homo sapiens, which seems as mistaken as putting all claims of truth into only one religion. Yet faith as a gift can bring a certain level of comforting peace, joy, connection, and hope.

   But it is also a burden. As Elie Wiesel writes: "It would be within my rights to give it up. I could invoke six million reasons to justify my decision, but I don't. I am incapable of straying from the path chartered by my ancestors. Without this faith in God, the faith of my fathers and forefathers, my faith in Israel and in humanity would be diminished. And so I choose to preserve the faith of my childhood. . . . Yes, my faith was wounded and still is today . . . but it is because I still believe in God that I argue with him."[4]

7. The problem of theodicy, the existence of useless, extensive mass atrocity in this world, should be met by theists with silence or, at best, with what David Burrell (referring to my approach) describes as a "fractured faith built on a fractured theodicy."[5] This means we and our religions are broken.

Such is my response: part self-reckoning, part surrender, and hopefully, all honesty, in what Andy rightly calls "an aspiration for authenticity as well as openness."

3. See, for example, Thatamanil, *Circling the Elephant*.

4. Wiesel, *And the Sea Is Never Full*, 70; see also Admirand, *Amidst Mass Atrocity*, ch. 8–9.

5. Burrell, "Foreword," x.

Chapter 7

Compassion (of God and Outlaws)

Peter Admirand, Primary Author

Arthur Morgan is a fictional, late-nineteenth-century, American outlaw in the video game *Red Dead Redemption 2*. Like the cowboys John Grady Cole and Billy Parham in Cormac McCarthy's *Border Trilogy*, he is quick with a gun. Even if you play him with high honor, Arthur leaves many dead bodies in his wake. While it may be strange to first think of him in a chapter on compassion, it is his encounters with Mother Superior Calderón that I have in mind. An otherwise minor figure in a game exploding with scope, details, and abundant characters, she is an African-American Catholic nun devoted to the poor of the St. Denis slums. Is it too much to say I found her words some of the most theologically beautiful and moving on compassion? I'll explain why at the close of this chapter.

First, though, I'll define compassion by disentangling it from Nietzschean pity. I also want to examine whether we should draw a clear line between compassion and empathy as Paul Bloom and Rutger Bregman contend. This mostly apophatic approach is fitting as I then explore how I envision the compassion of God. Here no deity smites enemies, unleashes floods of destruction, or hurls fire and brimstone to burn and flay. Yet there may be something of Arthur Morgan in my God, too. For the cries of the forsaken need to be heard and the atrocities of their perpetrators condemned. Can compassion heal even the most bedraggled and darkened of sinners? Can both justice and compassion be fairly deployed?

Noting a general dearth of compassion in many atheist-theist dialogues, I next focus on the Dalai Lama, both for his elevation of compassion as a foundational universal virtue and his promotion of secular ethics. I will also highlight the Charter for Compassion. My final subsection will be looking at compassion within nature and the deep need for us to practice compassion towards all living things. I will then return to the conversation of a gunslinger and a nun in a wimple.

A Severe or Rational Compassion? On Pity and Empathy

Norman Mailer, in his preface of the fiftieth anniversary of *The Naked and the Dead*, invokes the greatness of Tolstoy, who shows us that "compassion is of value and enriches our life only when compassion is severe, which is to say that we can perceive everything that is good and bad about a character but are still able to feel that the sum of us as human beings is probably a little more good than awful."[1] It's a startling and somewhat off-putting connection. Mailer adds that "compassion is valueless without severity (for otherwise it cannot defend itself against sentimentality)." First, note compassion, like humility, another virtue often misunderstood for passivity and weakness, is rooted in reality. While tinged with optimism and hope, it is not blind to what is broken. Going further, this virtue is dependent on seeing (and often experiencing) such darkness and pain. Mailer says it must be severe, a word that connotes something harsh or strict, but also intense, while sentimentality denotes a false feeling, inflated by an excessive and self-indulgent pathos.

Mailer's analysis drips with Nietzsche's often-quoted scorn of pity.[2] Like humility, pity for Nietzsche was a tool of so-called Christians controlled and orchestrated by bitter priests. They hindered the possibility of greatness for the deserving few by claiming some responsibility and need to help and succor all—especially the most vulnerable and defenseless.[3] Such pity was only a means really to assert false power that would either diminish the vitality of the pitier or degrade the one pitied.[4]

The compassion advocated here does not whither or emasculate. It does not shame its recipient with guilt or a debt to repay, nor then gild the giver with some expectant celestial boon. True compassion seeks no reward, but empowers the other while also accepting our mutual frailty. Contra Nietzsche, compassion sees our interconnectedness, dignity, and equality, and this seeing is a source and foundation for our moral growth and vitality.

What about empathy? While compassion and empathy can seem synonymous, some recent works argue the former is more praiseworthy than

1. Mailer, *Naked and the Dead*.

2. On Mailer's reading of Nietzsche, see Lennon, *Norman Mailer*, 318.

3. The writing on this topic is immense, but see for example, Frazer, "Compassion of Zarathustra."

4. Nietzsche, *Anti-Christ*, 7 (130). For an article that contends Nietzsche does not systematically condemn all acts of compassion, "but only when such concern erases any vantage point on our situation that might lend suffering significance," see Harris, "Compassion and Affirmation in Nietzsche," 17.

the latter. In *Against Empathy: The Call for Rational Compassion*, as the title contends, philosopher Paul Bloom advocates a clear distinction for moral flourishing. He sees empathy as easily manipulative, too often playing on unreliable emotional desires. It blocks sober judgment and so jeopardizes attempts to minimize overall suffering. Empathy is not only used for ill-intent (confer child predators who feign genuine understanding and sympathy with their victims to elicit positive connections) but too often plays on our immediate desires for self-satisfaction. It does so through a hyper-focus on the image of pain we are immediately witnessing and so want to heal. This otherwise well-meaning bias "focuses you on certain people at the expense of others." Bloom states empathy is "the problem, a source of prejudice, not kindness." He contends it would be more effective to employ a more reasoned approach to such suffering. He calls this "rational compassion."[5]

This approach is also advocated by historian Rutger Bregman in *Humankind: A Hopeful History*. One of his "ten rules to live by" includes Rule IV: "Temper your empathy, train your compassion."[6] When it comes to the suffering of others, we need "feeling not *with* them, but *for* them."[7] He takes his guidance from neuroscientist Tania Singer's work with Buddhist monk Matthieu Ricard. They realized a strong feeling of co-suffering with victims left most individuals more pessimistic and weakened of resolve. Drawing on his extensive meditation practice, Ricard was asked to contemplate on others' suffering with "feelings of warmth, concern, and care." They found that healthy detachment coupled with controlled reason enables individuals to be more effective in planning how to heal such suffering.[8]

The Other as Mirror

Is the difference so clear between empathy and compassion? Ecologist Carl Safina contends that "feeling with another, feeling for another, and acting to help . . . are three levels of empathy." He includes showing compassion under the third level of empathy.[9] His definitions also stress the importance of feelings in our aim to understand beyond the self.[10] Likewise, in the opening chapter of *The Oxford Handbook of Compassion Science*, Jennifer L. Goetz and Emiliana Simon-Thomas frame compassion "as a discrete

5. See Bloom, *Against Empathy*.

6. Bregman, *Humankind*, 386.

7. Bregman, *Humankind*, 387 (italics in original).

8. Bregman, *Humankind*, 387.

9. Safina, *Becoming Wild*, ch. 7. See also any of the great books by Loren Eiseley. For my writing on Eiseley, see Admirand, *Humbling Faith*, ch. 5.

10. Goetz and Simon-Thomas, "Landscape of Compassion," 3.

and evolved emotional experience." They define it as "a state of concern for the suffering or unmet needs of another, coupled with a desire to alleviate that suffering." They also differentiate compassion and empathy by contending the latter is more broad while compassion is "a specific emotional response to suffering." They write: "Empathy alone lacks a specific social urge, while compassion expressly involves feeling concerned and wanting to do something to reduce another's suffering."[11]

In the context of racial injustice, James Baldwin contends compassion (or empathy) starts with really seeing the other as in a mirror. Regarding the white man looking at the dark-skinned man, Baldwin writes: "This color seems to operate as a most disagreeable mirror, and a great deal of one's energy is expended in reassuring white Americans that they do not see what they see."[12]

In a 1986 essay, one hundred and twenty-three years after the Emancipation Proclamation, and twenty-two years after the (supposed) end of racial segregation and American Jim Crow laws, Baldwin proclaimed: "There was not, then, nor is there now, a single American institution which is not a racist institution." He adds: "white power remains white."[13] As I reflect on his words in the summer of 2020, thirty-four years after their publication, there is, finally, perhaps real talk of trying to face such truths and rectify such wrongs. With the murder of George Floyd and the mass protests against racism that have followed, hopefully something has finally shifted among white people. Maybe, finally, we are ready to see what has been plain for so long and to listen with compassion and without defensiveness.

"It Is Time for Reparations," Nikole Hannah-Jones writes in the June 26th, 2020, cover article of *The Sunday New York Times*.[14] Most white people usually dismiss the idea. Will now be different—or will there have been other crises and other murders and so a return to the status quo? Without both empathy and rational compassion, it is difficult to hope for any overturning of systemic racial and economic injustice.

Regarding the 2001 earthquake that struck El Salvador, liberation theologian Jon Sobrino writes it was like an x-ray on the country's stark inequality. It revealed the growing and shameful gulf between the desperately poor and the economically comfortable and privileged. The latter had hill-top homes equipped to withstand most shocks, had more resources

11. Goetz and Simon-Thomas, "Landscape of Compassion," 6.

12. Baldwin, "White Man's Guilt," 41.

13. Baldwin, "Price of the Ticket," 34. See also Alexander, *New Jim Crow*; Ralph, *Torture Letters*; and Wilkerson, *Caste*.

14. Hannah-Jones, "It Is Time for Reparations."

for better medical care, and the means to leave for safer lands.[15] We see similar disparities with the onslaught of COVID-19. War-torn countries like Yemen are especially vulnerable; so, too, are destitute communities and minority ethnic groups.[16]

Compassion not only involves looking into that mirror of the other and seeing oneself, but asking painful questions of why. Why is Yemen war-torn?[17] Why are its people more vulnerable to the virus right now? And why are certain communities in our own countries suffering more than others?

From gender injustice to discrimination against LGBTQI individuals and communities, to ongoing marginalization of Indigenous peoples, it can seem a lack of compassion is the real common ground.

As a theologian, how does my conception of God influence or mediate such crises and moral failures?

A Compassionate God of Justice

How atheists imagine God matters. Often overlooked, a common ground for atheists and theists is to move towards some agreement or understanding on the God theists should envision, worship, and seek. Admittedly I am wading into an indispensable but immense topic, so here I can only sketch a picture of my compassionate God of justice. In this section, after noting the value of this discussion for atheist-theist dialogue, I explain my moral criteria in reading the Bible and the Jesus I follow. While guidance is needed to interpret any purported holy texts rife with unholy ideas or stories, I believe there can be, or should be, deep consensus on core theological matters among theists, especially if we bear in mind the growing reach of global human rights. Such rights, rooted in the value and dignity of all human beings, and balanced by core moral obligations towards others, should be reflected by (or founded in) a God of compassion and justice.[18]

Of course, this combination is tenuous and fraught and will again return us to the ubiquitous problem of theodicy and especially the question of a compassionate God in the face of mass murderers or plague victims. This also raises postmortem issues, especially of hell.[19]

15. See Sobrino, *Where Is God?*

16. "Impacts of COVID-19."

17. See, for example, Yee, "Yemen Aid Falls Short."

18. See, for example, Regan, *Theology and the Boundary Discourse.*

19. For an extended examination of these topics, see Admirand, *Amidst Mass Atrocity.*

As noted in my reply to Andy in the honesty chapter, queries, questions, challenges, and doubts of atheists, nontheists, and agnostics should push theists to be clearer, more refined, and humble in their God-conceptions. Theist-atheist dialogue can:

1. uncover blind spots, unseemly contradictions, excessive paradoxes, and moral or logical inconsistencies in God belief;
2. provide the means for theological growth and development; and
3. help shape a more humane, cosmopolitan, and pluralist image of God.

Such a conception can then be reflected back in actions, doctrine, and rituals. Faith and doubt, and the mutual shaping of believer and nonbeliever, continue, but at a sharper level. As Alec Ryrie writes in *Unbelievers: An Emotional History of Doubt*, atheists and theists have "intertwined fates," and faith and doubt are partners who "have both shaped each other more than they would like to admit."[20]

For theists, this process is more than simply claiming God will be a better projection of our own inner or outer drives, fears, or dreams—though visions of God often reflect mundane and finite origins. An angry, racist, homophobic, and elitist individual or organization is not likely to enshrine a cuddly, omnibenevolent, and expansive deity. Human beings are, though, fraught with self-contradictions. A loving conception of God is still weaponized in various ways, and we know troubled, bitter artists and visionaries who fashion sublime notions, ideas, and works of art.[21] But here is also where a theist may speak of grace, the call and flow of the Spirit working within and through creation for healing, love, nonviolence, and, to use a Buddhist term, interbeing—the connectedness of all life. Whatever reflects or manifests as such goods touches on or traces God's presence. When these foundations are undermined, absent, or denied, then how can we coherently hint at God's echo or voice?

In searching for an imago dei (image of God), the above is my general rule for the Bible and when assessing the moral value of holy book passages and decrees. Ultimately, I seek a God of unconditional love but one who promotes what liberation theologians call a preferential option for the poor and oppressed, the abused and murdered, the forgotten and despairing.[22] Such a God of the forsaken is essential in a world of injustice and useless suffering. So, too, is a God of justice, as I'll repeat below.

20. Ryrie, *Unbelievers*, 12.

21. See Admirand, "Should We Still Teach."

22. See, for example, Groody and Gutierrez, *Preferential Option for the Poor*.

But I also seek a God of unbounded beauty and joy, and even humor. The natural world may contain violence, but it is also steeped in majesty, mirth, laughter, and general weirdness, from sea creatures like the pink see-through fantasia to porcupines mating, or the existence of dark matter and black holes. God is not boring.

My yearning for God is also filtered through my reading of Jesus based on the guidelines above. Such a reading entails response and imitation, rooted in the idea that we are made in God's image and likeness (Gen 1:27) and so meant to seek and be like God. Pope Francis proclaims that "compassion is the language of God."[23] The utterance is reflected in Jesus' words: "Be compassionate as your Father is compassionate" (Luke 6:36). As Henri Nouwen, Donald McNeil, and Douglass Morrison explain, a God of compassion, a God who suffers with us, is a God of solidarity. Such a God "is willing to enter with us into our problems, confusions, and questions."[24] As they note, the biblical phrase "to be moved with compassion" comes from the Greek verb *splangchnizomai*. It occurs twelve times in the Gospels and draws upon the *splangchna* as "the entrails of the body . . . the guts" (or bowels). It is a deeply felt and potent expression.[25] Consider one example, Mark 6:34: "And Jesus, when he came out, saw much people, and was moved with compassion toward them, because they were as sheep not having a shepherd: and he began to teach them many things."

Similarly, we witness our own calling and purpose when Jesus cures a leper (Matt 8:1–4); praises the faith of prostitutes (Matt 21:31); inspires or insures everyone is fed (Luke 9:12–17); challenges political, religious, and colonial oppression and occupation (Matt 5:38–42, Mark 5:1–20, and Matt 22:21); forgives corrupt tax-collectors (while also nudging restitution, Luke 19:1–10); praises a woman for seeking discipleship (Mary sitting at his feet, Luke 10:38–42); equates discipleship with serving the most lost and destitute (Mark 10:31); celebrates the beauty and joy of life (Luke 10:21 and John 2:1–12); cautions us on false attachments (Mark 10:17–31 and Matt 4:1–10); and challenges us to "take up our cross" (Matt 16:24), believe that "whoever is not against us is for us" (Mark 9:40), that "no one has greater love than this, to lay down one's life for one's friends" (John 15:13), and is open to ongoing learning and correction (even) by a Syrophoenician or Canaanite woman (Mark 7:29 and Matt 15:28). Our restless hearts, as Augustine intoned, are shown a way home.

23. Bordoni, "Pope at Mass." See also Smith, *Radical Compassion*, 188.

24. Nouwen et al., *Compassion*, 12.

25. Nouwen et al., *Compassion*, 14.

Whatever elevates humanity to strive in love for peace and justice, especially of the most vulnerable and forgotten, is, for me, holy, and so of God. Potential sources of the holy are wide and deep, from the Vedas to the Qur'an, Guru Granth Sahib, the Talmud, an atheist manifesto, Indigenous spiritual wisdom, or the writings of a Francis of Assisi, Dorothy Day, or Thich Nhat Hanh. Again, this does not mean all are equally proficient and clear in every area of such ideals. This is where dialogue, comparative study, learning, and practice are all required—but the field is expansive and richly pluralist.[26]

Religious texts, rituals, doctrines, and practices that do not reflect such values must be discredited. Such must also be taught to the youth. Would acknowledging that our religious faith systems are broken and flawed—but also potential havens and schools for enlightenment and salvation—form and fashion believers who search and question, dialogue and learn from other ways, and who seek to heal and not slander another? Such remains my hope.

Of course, I am not blind to the heated views of my fellow theists, especially Christians, on many of these matters. My pull towards embracing religious pluralism is not currently an orthodox Catholic position, though what I write is rooted in Catholic Social Teaching.[27] As I often say, though, Christian ecumenical dialogue can sometimes be the most challenging dialogue. Consider, for example, the case of sexual ethics, an area often prioritized, to the consternation of many like Pope Francis, in a world rife with genocides, wars, filthy and depredating mass poverty, systemic racial, ethnic, class, and gender injustice, and growing environmental catastrophes.[28] Of course, sexual ethics do matter. They highlight the importance of balancing freedom of the self and obligation to others. We don't have carte blanche to do whatever we want because our actions affect the dignity and values of other lives. Boundaries of some kind will still be needed, even as setting such boundaries, through human rights law, remains divisive.[29] To me, the most difficult moral issue in this area remains abortion[30] because it affects more than one life yet also involves a pernicious history of men

26. For an interfaith book on compassion in the Abrahamic faiths, see Clark et al., *Strangers, Neighbors, Friends*.

27. See, for example, Himes et al., *Modern Catholic Social Teaching*.

28. See, for example, Lynch, "Can Pope Francis"; and Ivereigh, *Wounded Shepherd*.

29. On the disparity of sexual consent and age laws in various countries, see Richards, "Why the Age of Sexual Consent."

30. Here is not the context to try to discern, if one conclusively can, at what point after a sperm and egg join, human life exists. For two helpful books on sexual ethics and Catholic theology, see King and Rubio, *Sex, Love, and Families*; and Farley, *Just Love*.

controlling women's bodies (often through religious decrees), the detestable and horrid reality of rape, including mass rape as a means of genocide, of societies who shame women for having an abortion, but offer limited or no resources to help nurture and sustain the lives of all its citizens, or respond to a pregnancy outside marriage with shame and moral chiding rather than a celebration of expectant life.[31] One can also raise questions of the rights of the partner (typically a father) in the context of a pregnancy; the role of sexual responsibility and choices; discrimination against those born (or believed to be born) with defects; and a deeper examination of not only the spiritual after-effects of abortion on some women, but what it means in a society to say all life is valuable and precious, from the unborn to the disabled, the elderly and sick, the refugee, and the prisoner. The challenge is to be compassionate to all life.

What, then, of the mass murderer or mass rapist—aren't they beyond compassion? Always we can devise some trolley-car scenario where decrees of loving everyone are tested with impossible choices—and we may again be back to just wars and other means of claiming how a desire for love, healing, and interbeing requires dividing lines between us and them, killing to defend an individual, family, group, or nation. "So it goes."[32]

As I have argued elsewhere, a God of compassion must also be a God of justice, especially when we turn to difficult cases like the Shoah or examples of child prostitution or child soldiers. Rage is understandable when confronting such evils, but if we really want to embrace a God of compassion, then forgiveness and unconditional love also become inseparable. While life and murder just roll on without purpose in Vonnegut's novel, alluded to above, my conception of God means somehow, someway, God loves every being—which includes those who have committed heinous and seemingly unforgiveable crimes. It also means God has a moral responsibility to heal those whose lives have been drenched in misery and agony. Such healing, if not in this life, must occur in some postmortem context.[33] Without such healing, theodicy fails and so then does any hope of a meaningful or viable religious faith or belief in God.

While a compassionate God yearns even for perpetrators to repent, it is difficult to fathom how compassion and justice operate at such a level by such a being. As I have argued elsewhere, we need to prioritize a

31. In the context of Nigerian girls raped and impregnated by Boko Haram, see Lamb, *Our Bodies, Their Battlefield*, 59–62.

32. Vonnegut, *Slaughterhouse Five*.

33. For the claim that eternity would make our life "meaningless," and that "what I do and what I love can matter only to me because I understand myself as mortal," see Hägglund, *This Life*, 5.

victim-centered approach of restorative justice. Such includes, though, the desperate pleas of victims like Aisha Khode Bhanu: "I would like my rapists to be killed for what they did. Let them be hanged."[34]

While I am not an advocate for universal salvation (the idea that everyone must be saved), and am deeply pulled by accounts of witnesses of mass atrocity, it is also difficult to hold together a God of compassion and the idea of souls tormented eternally. Even with restorative justice, the quagmire of individual free will and responsibility remains. So, too, does the fact of abandonment and suffering in this world. Elie Wiesel, for example, while trying to be sympathetic to the idea of a suffering God in some kind of solidarity with Holocaust victims, also stated he could never theologically understand or justify the existence of Auschwitz. As he writes: "Perhaps someday someone will explain how, on the level of man, Auschwitz was possible, but on the level of God, it will forever remain the most disturbing of mysteries."[35]

Andy has rebuked postponing final judgment of the God question or theodicy until we are already dead. I empathize with such a claim and have previously stated atheism founded on the existence of useless, mass atrocities is not only rational, but moral. Nevertheless, I believe there is reason to hope in a God of compassion, not only in the stories of Jesus mentioned above but, as importantly, in the lives that embody and mirror such stories. In the meantime, religious individuals and institutions can strive to never be used as a means or excuse for violence and oppression against another; for wars; patriarchal abuse and lording; economic exploitation and denial of basic human rights; and environmental destruction.

Ultimately, the God theists believe in should matter to atheists because it affects them regardless, as history can attest. Greater partnership and dialogue can also develop between atheists and theists if the God theists promote is truly liberating and compassionate. Atheists can at least see such a being as potentially deserving of worship or as a useful, though ultimately human-created, source of moral renewal and kindness.

Compassion in Dialogue

To reach any understanding in God-thought, compassion will be needed by all sides. Within theist-atheist dialogues, though, too often the focus has

34. Lamb, *Our Bodies, Their Battlefield*, 109. Bhanu is one of many rape victims during Pakistan's brutal crackdown in what was East Pakistan (now Bangladesh) to suppress and end the Bengali nationalist movement in 1971.

35. Wiesel, *Legends of Our Time*, 6.

been proving why the other is wrong, whether philosophically or theologically, and minimizing common concerns, shared doubts, and similar hopes. Always presented as a negative-sum game and antagonistic pairing, theists and atheists have also often failed to show ample compassion towards one another. A contemporary helpful figure in bridging this divide through compassion is the Dalai Lama. For him, compassion—especially as rooted in the golden rule—is the foundational virtue. More importantly, it is accessible to everyone. As he writes, compassion "constitutes a basic aspect of our nature shared by all human beings."[36] For the Dalai Lama, compassion can be divided into at least two levels. The biological sphere is what we all share as human beings, and he often illustrates this idea through the compassion a mother exhibits towards her child. The second level has to be cultivated, and here is where religions and ethical systems can play an essential role.[37] Such cultivation entails being taught to be compassionate and then to practice this virtue. As an aside, while many of us have to be prodded and reminded to show kindness to the stranger, especially one living far away, how difficult it also is to be tolerant and loving on a daily basis towards those we live with or often encounter. Once-off acts of compassion to someone needy can feel good, but daily compassion can be a chore and drudgery. Such has been particularly challenging during COVID-19, especially for those already living in cramped or precarious conditions.

The Dalai Lama is the first to note that his own isolation quarters in "a palace high in the Himalayas" are "cushy," but his life, especially witnessing the Chinese government's oppression of the Tibetan people, bears the mark of great suffering.[38] And yet his outlook remains hopeful. As he wrote in an April 2020 article on compassion and COVID:

> We Buddhists believe that the entire world is interdependent. That is why I often speak about universal responsibility. The outbreak of this terrible coronavirus has shown that what happens to one person can soon affect every other being. But it also reminds us that a compassionate or constructive act—whether working in hospitals or just observing social distancing—has the potential to help many.[39]

We thus can all play a role in alleviating the suffering of others. While his way is through the Geluk School of Tibetan Buddhism, the Dalai Lama stresses that the resources of compassion and love can be found in all the

36. Dalai Lama, *Toward a True Kinship of Faiths*, 109.

37. Dalai Lama, *Beyond Religion*, 50.

38. Rowlatt, "Dalai Lama."

39. Dalai Lama, "'Prayer Is Not Enough.'"

world's faiths.[40] As he remarks in *The Book of Joy*: "Different medicine, but same aim: to cure our pain, our illness."[41] Going further, he advocates secular ethics so as to include every human being in this call and responsibility. He is adamant that one need not have God as a source to stress the importance of this virtue. Noting that over a billion people in the world are nonbelievers, he asserts it is more effective to spread compassion "beyond religion." As he remarks: "They also have the right to become happier human beings and to be good members of the human family. So one need not depend on religious faith to educate our inner values."[42] Prominently, his Buddhist practice of loving-kindness meditation is a key feature of achieving and maintaining active compassion towards all life—and even towards one's persecutors. Through years of meditation, he breathes in the ills of the world, including the pain caused to his fellow Tibetans by the Chinese government. He exhales thoughts of loving-kindness and compassion, extending it even to so-called enemies.

Such compassion, he contends, is also a form of self-love. Without the love of self, you cannot help others as effectively. While excessive self-centeredness can lead to suffering,[43] compassion for others brings joy.[44] As he maintains: "Ten minutes on the well-being of others can help one to feel joyful for the whole day—even before coffee" (!).[45] Beyond the benefits to the self, compassion can inform justice and peacefully confront injustice.[46]

Endorsed by the Dalai Lama, among other luminaries—and signed by over two million people—the Charter for Compassion was initially invoked by Karen Armstrong in February of 2008. She sought to use the money from her TED Prize to work in collaboration with scholars of many faiths to construct the charter.[47] Resonant with much of the Dalai Lama's work above, the charter concludes: "Born of our deep interdependence, compassion is essential to human relationships and to a fulfilled humanity. It is the path to enlightenment, and indispensable to the creation of a just economy and a peaceful global community."[48]

40. Dalai Lama, *Toward a True Kinship of Faiths*, 157–58.

41. Dalai Lama and Tutu, *Book of Joy*, 252. See also Dalai Lama, *Toward a True Kinship of Faiths*, ix.

42. Dalai Lama and Tutu, *Book of Joy*, 31.

43. Dalai Lama and Tutu, *Book of Joy*, 251.

44. Dalai Lama, *Beyond Religion*, 28.

45. Dalai Lama and Tutu, *Book of Joy*, 261.

46. Dalai Lama, *Beyond Religion*, 70.

47. See, for example, Armstrong, *Twelve Steps*.

48. "Charter for Compassion," https://www.charterforcompassion.org/english. For a balanced evaluation of the aims and impact of the charter, see Marsden, "Golden Rule."

Such a hope and aim are especially intertwined with our care and compassion of not only the marginalized of our world, but nonhuman animals.

Compassion and the Natural World

"Mother Nature is a bitch," Ellie tells her companion Dina in the video game *The Last of Us Part II*.[49] Her comment is understandable in the midst of a worldwide virus that has killed billions and morphs the dead into grotesque zombies. If we don't feel similarly after COVID, we can also highlight earlier plagues and the untold millions of deaths caused in their wake. While Ellie's brash comment may be spoken more delicately in other circles, the idea is the same. There's an efficient ruthlessness in nature where weakness is not tolerated. Without adaptive and proper defenses, survival, let along flourishing, is unlikely. Compassion, unless rooted in a practical altruism linked with species survival or some kind of quid pro quo, is rarely rewarded. Exceptions are often simply YouTube exceptions—funny or heartfelt videos of a lion in a zoo adopting a feral cat, or a humpback whale protecting a seal. The thriving of one life, though, usually involves the taking of another. Nature is bounteous, insanely diverse, electrically colorful, awe-inspiring, and quirky—but also profusely bloody and violent. It is a reality that renders talk of a pacifist Jesus as God Incarnate more than problematic. Astrotheology may swoon at images of our solar system and speak of a God of creativity, expansiveness, and fluidity. Upholding a compassionate Creator-God, however, takes a lot of theological tightrope walking,[50] especially if we want to sing of beauty in a cheetah killing a young gazelle or rove beetles mimicking the look and smell of ants to not only invade an ant colony but "devour the young of their unsuspecting companions."[51]

The other day (please don't judge) I saw something scurry in our living room/kids' toy room. It was a mouse. My first thought was to lock both doors and get one of the cats. My wife, though, is more efficient under such pressure, so she grabbed the right cat and dropped him in the mouse's vicinity. A bite, shake, and snap, and the mouse was dead. A small trail of red blood glistened on the floor near Barbie dolls, Legos, and stuffed animals. As I write these words in a chapter on compassion, I can still see the spot where the dead mouse had lain. Regardless of my own role as an accomplice in that killing, the cat did not have to be prodded or convinced.

49. *The Last of Us Part II* is a 2020 PS4 game created by Naughty Dog and written by Neil Druckmann and Halley Gross. Ellie is voiced by Ashley Johnson.

50. For a helpful and challenging resource, see Haight, *Faith and Evolution*.

51. Coghlan, "Sneaky Beetles."

While killing in proportion and for sustenance cannot be equated with senseless, wasteful culling, let alone cruelty and torture in killing, our world is not lions laying down with lambs. It is not the sweet, slumbering scene in John Milton's *Paradise Lost*, when Adam whispers to Eve to arise and

> to mark how spring
> Our tended Plants, how blows the Citron Grove,
> What drops the Myrrhe, and what the balmie Reed,
> How Nature paints her colours, how the Bee
> Sits on the Bloom extracting liquid sweet.[52]

Nevertheless, without compassion towards the world around us and to the young and future beings of this planet, we know the verdict and repercussions will be catastrophic. As Pope Francis writes in *Laudato Si'*: "A sense of deep communion with the rest of nature cannot be real if our hearts lack tenderness, compassion and concern for our fellow human beings."[53] The care for the least of human beings is also reflected in the care of nonhuman animals. Betrayal of either is inevitably linked to the betrayal of all.

In Hope Ferdowsian's *Phoenix Zones*, she depicts programs and stories of human beings and animals who experienced horrific trauma but were able to be reborn, not only through their own resilience, but in the care and compassion of others.[54] Her book not only points to how compassion can help those scarred by injustice, but expands the need to practice this virtue to the nonhuman world, especially to those animals whom human beings have tortured or slaughtered with seeming impunity. Compassion for the environment, nonhuman animals, the broken in this world, and our future progeny is crucial to our physical, let alone moral, survival. While many of these social justice causes often operate in independence, Ferdowsian highlights the strengths of a more inclusive focus. She cites, for example, the Warrior and Wolves project, where the founders, Lorin and Michael, practice a "loving commitment to veterans and animals," while another program in Oklahoma cares for both homeless and abused children and their companion animals.[55] As she writes: "The guardians of Phoenix Zones aren't victim to the optical delusion of separation; to them, the principles of sanctuary are ubiquitous. They are generous with their empathy."[56]

52. Milton, *Paradise Lost* (Milton Reading Room), 5:20–25.

53. Francis, *Laudato Si'*, §96. For further theological commentary, see Roewe, "Five Years Ago"; and Lane, *Theology and Ecology in Dialogue*.

54. Ferdowsian, *Phoenix Zones*, 8.

55. Ferdowsian, *Phoenix Zones*, 155.

56. Ferdowsian, *Phoenix Zones*, 155.

Referring back to the Dalai Lama's Buddhist term of interbeing or interdependence, we are all connected—humans and nonhumans. The loss of habitats, the endangerment and extinction of species, and the failure to address climate change and global warming will need more than compassion—but without that virtue as a guide, ecological prospects will remain bleak. Perhaps we can also take some comfort in scientific accounts that praise compassion as part of our human hardwiring. Showing compassion, it is said, was a useful and more effective means to insure group solidarity and cooperation. Such increased the likelihood of survival. Can it spur us to act more cooperatively now?

Conclusion: A Gunslinger and a Nun Sit on a Train Bench

The virtue of compassion does a lot of heavy lifting in this book, in solidarity with love, kindness, empathy, generosity, hospitality, forgiveness, and tolerance. For our context, this virtue overflows with hope for how the believer/nonbeliever dialogue and partnership can flourish. Rooted in a deep and piercing recognition of suffering in our world and the need to allay these cries, compassion is the wellspring for future harmony and moral growth. In areas of social justice, cognizant of racial and gender inequality, economic disparities, human rights denial and destruction, and the refugee crisis, humanist and religious declarations of words and deeds often overlap, in near unison. We sometimes take this truth for granted, both a comforting and ho-hum proclamation. Nevertheless, this is another foundational element of common ground. It shows the universal pull of many ethical aims and the need for partnership.

While there are many other examples of compassion I could cite, the most recent one to deeply move me, as noted above, came within a violent video game. Compassion can often surprise.

Red Dead Redemption 2 is an open-world video game of many choices. Decisions you make not only determine which plotlines go forward but the kinds of interactions you will have with other characters. Much of the decisions involve an honor system, so you can build towards high honor if you accept or perform random good deeds and avoid blatant wrongdoing like robbing or shooting innocent people—though you play as an outlaw looking for a big score, so you are no saint.

The player (as Arthur Morgan) only encounters Sister Calderón if he first assists her colleague, Brother Dorkins. Arthur meets him when the friar is asking passersby for money for the poor of St. Denis. He then asks Arthur for aid in rescuing local children being held as slaves. If the player completes the quest, he then meets Sister Calderón. She subsequently requests Arthur's help when a street urchin she was tutoring steals her crucifix (a precious gift from her mother before she died). "Don't hurt him, please!" she pleads.

If the player restores the cross to her, the choice opens up further interactions. The nun constantly praises Arthurs as "the most wonderful man," while he continually demurs. He does not see or cannot see himself as a good man. In their next encounter, Arthur sees the nun by her church requesting support for the needy. She again thanks him and they sit and talk on a nearby bench. She asks how he is doing and says he reminds her of herself when she was younger. This really gets his attention. She tells him she kept doing "terrible things" because "I did not believe that goodness existed." But once she did see that love was real, "doing bad things became not impossible, but ridiculous." Arthur admits he just wants a dignified end, so Sister Calderón expresses she will pray for him. He clarifies he is not a religious man and admits he's an outlaw. Always speaking with kindness and compassion, she smiles and replies: "What fun. Religion is just a word. Hearts are rarely pure but equally they are rarely impure either." Arthur is again moved. She continues: "To me, God is people and people are God, so we must all do what we can." Connecting faith with social justice, she adds: "These people are starving. Go find them some food. Don't worry so much about your heart. The actions will lead and the heart follows." As Arthur insists he is a bad man, she also plays on this idea, but always with compassion: "I will still think of you in nasty terms, as you wish." But she knows better.

If the player gives a donation, she again calls Arthur "wonderful." He will again demur, so she'll joke: "I meant wonderful but so very frightening . . . exactly." The compassionate and loving person sees the real individual before them, or as importantly, the person he or she aspires to become.

Their final encounter only happens if the player has done the good deeds above, along with similar actions to be of high honor. Otherwise, a more sobering interaction occurs with a different character (Reverend Swanson). In the high honor version, Sister Calderón is about to take a departing train for Mexico to leave for the missions. As Arthur greets her and she asks if he's okay, he coughs violently and tells her: "I'm dying, Sister. Yeah, I got T.B. . . . I got it . . . beating a man to death . . . for a few bucks." He sighs and adds: "I've lived a bad life, Sister." Her expression remains open and nonjudgmental. She replies: "We've all lived bad lives, Mr. Morgan. We all sin. But I know you." The outlaw shakes his head and interrupts, "You don't know me," but she continues: "Forgive me, but that's the problem. You don't know you." He is curious and asks: "What do you mean?" She describes how whenever they meet, he is always smiling and trying to help people. After Arthur mentions some of the tragic events in his life, Sister Calderón shares her own loss, warmly saying: "Life is full of pain, but there is also love and beauty."

When Arthur asks, "What am I gonna do now?" she answers: "Be grateful that for the first time, you see your life clearly." Like the Dalai Lama, Sister Calderón suggests he help someone, as "helping makes you really happy." Arthur sighs and hesitates: "But . . . I still don't believe in nothing."

The nun, chuckling, says: "Often, neither do I." Arthur, too, chuckles. She adds: "But then, I meet someone like you and everything makes sense." He laughs. "You're too smart for me, Sister." She has reached his deeper self, though. The outlaw admits: "I guess, I'm afraid." She is adamant: "There is nothing to be afraid of, Mr. Morgan. Take a gamble that love exists and do a loving act." As the conductor shouts all aboard, they walk to the train. Arthur, carrying her bags, says: "I shall try." Her voice rising, she chirps: "I know you will."[57]

57. *Red Dead Redemption 2* was created by Rockstar Games in 2018. It was written by Dan Houser, Michael Unsworth, and Rupert Humphries. Full credits can be found here: https://www.rockstargames.com/reddeadredemption2/credits. The voice actor for Arthur is Roger Clark, while Irene Debari performs the voice of Sister Calderón. I played the game on PS4. YouTube clips of the scenes with Sister Calderón can be found here: https://www.youtube.com/watch?v=5Q5r6-NQqNM.

*

Response

ANDREW FIALA

ONCE AGAIN, PETER SURPRISES me with the breadth of his interests. His account of compassion ranges from the Dalai Lama and Pope Francis to a cat killing a mouse in the playroom. The sources of his reflections include theology, literature, and video games. This reminds me of a general truth about human beings: we are often surprisingly diverse in our interests and influences; we are not narrowly defined or constrained by a small number of values and interests. Theologians play video games. And atheists listen to Bach and read religious scriptures.

One of the most important scriptures from the Christian tradition, for my response, shares the name of my dialogue partner. Peter the apostle exhorts his followers (1 Peter 3:8) to have "unity of spirit, sympathy, love of the brethren, a tender heart and a humble mind." The term translated as "tender heart" (*eusplagchnos*) is connected to the term for compassion that Peter Admirand discusses above, *splangchnizomai*. These terms point toward a kind of visceral movement.[1] The term is connected to the involuntary movement of the bowels or guts—a feeling in the pit of the stomach or some kind of response related to breath and heartbeat. In the most famous biblical passage where this term occurs—the parable of the good Samaritan in Luke chapter 10—the point is that we ought to be physically and spiritually moved by the suffering of others. The Samaritan was so moved and, says Jesus, we ought to go and do likewise. This is a powerful and important moral idea. The Epistle of Peter links tender-heartedness to unity, harmony, sympathy (*sympathes*), brotherly love (*philadelphia*), and humility.

In my response, I will also emphasize the importance of surprise, wonder, reverence, and awe in relation to compassion and dialogue. I will

1. I discuss this and the parable of the good Samaritan in Fiala, *Secular Cosmopolitanism*.

consider a serious problem for compassion, which is that since it is often about an inward experience (that movement of the guts and heart) it often remains subjective. And I will offer a lesson learned about the problem of God and holy scripture.

Let's begin with the challenge of defining compassion. There are complexities and complications about the topic of compassion that have kept scholars busy for centuries. Aristotle, David Hume, Adam Smith, and Martha Nussbaum (along with many others) have discussed the various differences between sympathy, pity, compassion, love, empathy, and other related emotions.[2] These complexities become even more complicated when we engage in cross-cultural and interreligious study. I wonder, for example, whether Christian *splangchnizomai* is indeed what we see in Buddhist compassion, where key concepts include *karuna* (a kind of pity related to the suffering of others) and *metta* (a kind of loving-kindness related to sharing joy with others). There is a difference between a positive affirmation of the value of others and suffering with others. We see this in the difference between brotherly love (*philadelphia*), disinterested love (*agape*), and the sense of suffering with the other that is found in *splangchnizomai*. We do not have time to dig deeply here into linguistic and religious differences.[3] Instead, let's contrast two kinds of compassion: one that is focused on the suffering other in a way that makes the bowels quiver and the heart move; and another kind of disinterested sympathy or love that spreads toward all suffering beings and which participates in joy as well as suffering. We might identify these two possibilities as follows:

1. as a negative/visceral kind of suffering with the other; and
2. as a positive/spiritual experiencing with the other.

Both of these types of compassion are important in dialogue. We need to attend to the suffering of the other: we should be responsive to the uncomfortableness and suffering of the other, even attending to body language and expressions of visceral discomfort. If we say something offensive, we need to gauge how the other feels and respond appropriately. We also need to put ourselves, in a disinterested way, into the mind or thought processes of the other and try our best to understand what moves them spiritually, in a positive way in terms of what they believe and value.

2. See Aristotle, *Rhetoric*; Hume, *Treatise of Human Nature*; Hume, *Enquiry Concerning the Principles of Morals*; Smith, *Theory of Moral Sentiments*; and Nussbaum, *Upheavals of Thought*.

3. See Davidson and Harrington, *Visions of Compassion*; and Bein, *Compassion and Moral Guidance*.

In a dialogue between an atheist and a theist, the first (negative) kind of compassion is easy: as human beings we can see what others are experiencing and feel along with them. The second kind of compassion is more difficult: to find a way to relate positively to what the other believes and values.

Here is where wonder and surprise come in. To experience spiritual compassion, as I want to call it, is to be open to wondering at what the other finds to be wonderful. Abraham Heschel once explained that wonder is essential to the experience of religion. He said: "Wonder or radical amazement is the chief characteristic of the religious man's attitude toward history and nature."[4] Heschel distinguishes wonder from curiosity by explaining that wonder comes to us from without, overwhelms, and asks questions of us, while curiosity is more subjective and is related to pride, ambition, and other self-regarding attitudes. There are a number of emotions, attitudes, and experiences that are related to surprise and wonder, including also reverence, awe, and vexation. These emotions are related to the second sort of compassion: the compassion of positive affirmation that takes in or feels along with the spiritual experience of the other. To feel with the other (to have "passion with" as compassion and sympathy might be interpreted) in this spiritual sense is to take their experience seriously enough to be moved by it—or for it to make a demand upon us that is not merely selfish, prideful, or subjectively motivated. One need not agree with the cognitive dimension and truth claims connected to the experience. But one might be moved nonetheless. In order to be so moved, one must be open to the other and (for the moment at least) free of judgment. This is easier, perhaps, when the other's experience is so significantly different from my own that I am genuinely surprised by it (or vexed or in awe). The opposite of surprise and wonder is indifference, callousness, or disregard. To be surprised requires us to be open to things that are novel and different. To wonder is to be open to new experiences. This is closely related to curiosity, which we discussed above. And it is essential for spiritual compassion.

This leads us to think about compassion and wonder and their role in our dialogue. Through compassion and wonder, atheists can find themselves in a deeper relationship with theists (and vice versa). This idea has been emphasized in ecumenical, interfaith, and interreligious dialogue. One typical approach shows that compassion is an important value in all of the world's diverse traditions. But often this stops at the border between religion and nonreligion.

Compassion—along with reverence, awe, and wonder—has even created an impediment to discussion across the religious/nonreligious divide.

4. Heschel, *God in Search of Man*, 45.

What theists find to be wonderful, atheists mock and ridicule. When atheists speak of compassion growing out of wonder at the natural world, theists malign this as insufficient. When humanists who ground their thinking in science (including the theory of evolution) claim that there is a natural basis for compassion found in mammalian life (and in processes such as kin/group selection), theists will complain that this is a kind of relativism.[5] William Lane Craig, the Christian apologist, may be among the most prominent to make this argument. He equates atheism with moral relativism and nihilism. He states: "The absence of moral accountability from the philosophy of atheism thus makes an ethic of compassion and self-sacrifice a hollow abstraction."[6] He then quotes R. Z. Friedman, who says: "Without religion the coherence of an ethic of compassion cannot be established."[7] This criticism reminds us that religious and nonreligious ethical frameworks involving compassion may remain quite far apart.

But let's leave this substantial dispute about divine command ethics, naturalistic accounts of ethics, and the religious basis of morality aside. I'll discuss it further in my contribution to the next chapter. Instead let's focus here on the question of spiritual compassion: the ability to imagine oneself into the spiritual life of the other—to relate to what they find wonderful and worthy of reverence. In this regard, what matters most is what people value when they choose the God they worship. Peter's vision of God is admirable (from my point of view). He thinks of God as compassionate. He pictures a God of solidarity, justice, and love. He says that the God he seeks is "a God of unbounded beauty and joy, and even humor." This is inspiring. If I were looking for God, I would also be searching for such a God. We can agree, I think, about the values we aspire to see in the divinity. And even though I think that there is no such divine being (and I worry that religious traditions often do not portray God in this positive light), I am sympathetic to Peter's vision and his values. I might even say that Peter and I share a view of the holy. But I suspect that my own atheistic interpretation of the holy will be quite different from a theistic idea of the holy. The holy is (following Rudolf Otto) that which is wonderful in Heschel's sense, awe-inspiring, numinous, transcendent, and more than merely psychological.[8] It comes to us from without and overwhelms, while making some demand upon us.

5. For compassion in animals and natural selection processes, see de Waal, *Bonobo and the Atheist*; and Wilson, *On Human Nature*.

6. Craig, "Kurtz/Craig Debate," 33.

7. Craig quotes Friedman, "Does the 'Death of God' Really Matter?," 322.

8. Otto, *Idea of the Holy*.

Otto gives us a number of examples. One worth considering is Bach's Mass in B Minor. It is possible to get a sense of something wonderful, holy, and beautiful in listening to Bach. And in fact, this is related to compassion: to be moved by music (or by poetry, drama, painting, literature, and even by nature) is to experience a kind of spiritual compassion.[9] But my own view of how and why this happens is grounded in a naturalistic psychology. For me, compassion, holiness, beauty, and wonder are grounded in psychosocial and physiological processes that are less elevated and numinous than what we find in Otto, Heschel, or Admirand. I think that wonder and compassion remain merely psychological and physiological and can be explained by way of natural processes in the body, the brain, culture, and our relation to the natural world.

The risk of my account is that compassion (like wonder and surprise) is merely then "in the eye of the beholder." There is some truth to this risk of subjectivism. Sometimes we feel compassion (for the mouse we kill) and sometimes we do not. Sometimes a storm or a mountainous landscape evokes a sense of the sublime. Other times, we respond with indifference. Some people are moved by Bach; others find Bach boring. Compassion (and related emotions) remains somewhat too psychological and culturally relative. It begs to be supplemented by something more concrete: a moral law, a rule, or a principle of justice. I'll explore this more in the next chapter.

Before concluding here, let me reiterate that Peter and I seem to agree about the ideal vision of God as a compassionate being. Peter suggests that atheists and theists should seek agreement about the ideal image of God. He writes:

> Ultimately, the God theists believe in should matter to atheists because it affects them regardless, as history can attest. Greater partnership and dialogue can also develop between atheists and theists if the God theists promote is truly liberative and compassionate. Atheists can at least see such a being as potentially deserving of worship or as a useful, though ultimately human-created, source of moral renewal and kindness.

This is very important. If theists and atheists could agree about the ideal of God as a compassionate being, this might alleviate some of the dispute between them. Atheists typically complain (as Ivan Karamazov, Nietzsche, and a variety of others have) that the God of theism is capricious, cruel, narrow, and vindictive. This complaint is often directed at the sky-god, as I've called it, of old-time (Old Testament) religion. But this indicates the remaining problem. Is God really compassionate? Well, that depends upon

9. See Johnson-Laird and Oatley, "Emotions, Music, and Literature."

whom you ask (and which tradition you consult). And one wonders who has to do what with regard to this issue. Is it up to the atheist to remind the theist of the need to reconstruct God in more compassionate light (and to ask that such a reconstruction make room for solidarity with atheists)? This seems to ask too much of the atheist, who has very little power over the way that theists imagine God. It would seem, instead, that it is up to theists to continue the reform and reconstruction of God, i.e., to criticize those versions of theism that fail to acknowledge the importance of compassion, even compassion for atheists. But what ought atheists do to further the dialogue? I propose in conclusion that atheists who value compassion ought to continue to remain open to the genuine and complicated humanity of their theistic colleagues. We ought to dwell in a space that is sensitive to the first (visceral/negative) kind of compassion: we ought to be aware of the suffering of others, including our dialogue partners. We ought also to seek common ground in the second (spiritual/affirmative) kind of compassion: we should search for common joys and wonders in music, art, literature, nature . . . and even in video games.

Chapter 8

Honor and the Holy

ANDREW FIALA, PRIMARY AUTHOR

THE SOURCES OF VALUE are many: there are many things worthy of wonder, honor, and respect. This is true for both Christians and non-Christians. This chapter examines the depth of conflicting ideas about what ought to be honored—with discussions of moral disagreements. At issue in moral disputes are disagreements about what counts as an authoritative source of value. Common ground is found in acknowledging that these disputes are honorable in intention. For example, pro-life opposition to abortion values the life of unborn fetuses, while pro-choice permission for abortion values the autonomy of women. Such disagreement runs deep. But there are honorable motives on each side. The challenge in dialogue is to honor the sincerity (rationality and goodwill) of the other's beliefs while also remaining committed to one's own values and moral commitments.

One significant stumbling block for discussions between theists and atheists is the interpretation of key texts and the very question of which texts, ideas, commandments, and laws we ought to honor. In chapter 6, I outlined some of the problems of biblical literalism, including especially the problem of how sky-god cosmology conflicts with the modern scientific worldview. Scriptural interpretation creates further difficulties for discussing contentious ethical issues. Homosexuality, for example, has been criticized based upon biblical texts that condemn same-sex relations. It has also been criticized in light of what some theists view as the gendered structure of God-created reality and the teleology of human sexuality. But on the other hand, defenders of homosexuality will argue that such interpretations are anachronistic and based upon a faulty account of human sexuality and a denial of a kind of innate longing of sexual desire. In Leviticus 20, for example, homosexuality is condemned along with adultery. The punishment for both is death. But we no longer punish adultery or homosexuality by death. Indeed, as we have reevaluated our views of homosexuality, we have also reevaluated our views of the death penalty, divorce, the status of women, reproductive ethics, and a whole bunch of other issues.

This example shows that there are larger hermeneutical issues here about which texts are taken seriously and how they are to be interpreted. These issues are related to the question of what we honor or what we take as holy or sacred. While Christians believe that the Bible is holy, atheists do not share that view and may indeed be skeptical of the idea of the holy (as I explained in part in my response to chapter 7). Atheists do not believe that any text is holy, the Bible included. So when theists use scripture to find answers to ethical questions, atheists will not honor that method. It is worth noting here at the outset that not all theists look to holy scriptures for ethical commandments. The natural law theory of ethics has a time-honored place in Christian ethics. Some secular ethicists are critical of the natural law theory, claiming that this theory usually assumes quite a bit about what it takes for granted as "natural." But the theory is grounded in claims about reason that can open the door to conversations about ethics that are not grounded in scripture. The natural law theory may provide a place to find common ground for discussions of ethics between theists and atheists.[1] But even this approach risks running aground when theistic language is introduced about what is "sacred" or "holy." When someone claims that human life is "sacred," for example, this seems connected to a religious account. But some secularly-minded ethicists have claimed that it is possible to reinterpret the sacred in a way that is not

1. For discussion of natural law see Fiala and MacKinnon, *Ethics*, ch. 7. Natural Law has roots in ancient Greek/Roman thought and in medieval Christian tradition associated in particular with Thomas Aquinas. The idea had an impact on modern thinkers such as Hobbes, Locke, Rousseau, and others. More recently there have been a few scholars who have been described as "new natural law" thinkers. Important texts in new natural law include: Grisez, "First Principle of Practical Reason"; Grisez, "Natural Law, God"; Finnis, *Natural Law and Natural Rights*; and essays collected in George, *Natural Law and Moral Inquiry*. Critics of the new natural law will build upon a concern expressed by Hume about the "is-ought" distinction and what has come to be known as the "naturalistic fallacy." The problem is that nature is subject to many interpretations and there is no easy, obvious, or clear way of deriving moral principles from descriptive accounts of the natural world. Nor is it clear that there is some fixed and permanent "human nature" to which we could appeal—especially in light of cultural diversity and evolution. For discussion see: Chappell, "Challenges Facing Natural Law Ethics"; and Nielsen, "Thomistic Theory of Natural Moral Law." Discussions of natural law often occur in the context of applied ethics discussions, where critics will complain that usage of the term "natural" is merely an expression of preference. For example see Corvino, *What's Wrong with Homosexuality?* On the other hand, Lloyd Steffen has argued that something like natural law can provide a kind of "common agreement" about applied issues. See Steffen, *Ethics and Experience*.

theological but which is rather understood as a claim about what has ultimate value, has intrinsic value, or is held as inviolable.[2]

The question of what is holy, sacred, or worthy of honor strikes to the heart of many disagreements between theism and atheism. There are at least two levels of this dispute: an ethical level and an ontological one. I'll discuss both here, making two related points. First, with regard to ethics, while theists may appeal to a holy text or sacred writ for moral guidance, atheists reject this approach, along with the divine command theory of ethics. Second, with regard to ontology, while theists understand self and world as creations of the divinity having a kind of "natural" value established by the fiat of the Creator, atheists do not agree. Atheists do believe that human life is worthy of reverence, care, and honor. But this is understood in secular and humanist terms. What is worthy of honor in human beings—from the atheist's point of view—is our capacity to feel, think, reason, and understand. While theists will claim that human beings are created in the image of God (and ground ethical commandments in the idea of the *imago dei*), atheists reject this idea and ground ethical commandments in the need to honor life, especially human life, as unique and irreplaceable. In the end, theists and atheists might agree about much with regard to ethics. But disagreements will remain that can be traced back to differing methodologies, disagreements about authoritative evidence, and disagreements about metaphysical, psychological, and epistemological questions.

The Ten Commandments

Let's begin by considering the ongoing dispute about the text known as the Ten Commandments. This is actually two related texts (Exod 20 and Deut 5), which include significant claims about what ought to be honored and what ought to be respected as holy. We are told that we ought to keep the sabbath holy and that we ought to honor our mothers and fathers. The text begins with a declaration of God's sovereignty and identity: God says "I am the Lord, thy God." God further declares that we should not worship other gods or take God's name in vain. And then there is a list of basic ethical prohibitions: we should refrain from murder, adultery, theft, bearing false witness, and coveting our neighbor's things. The fact that this seminal text in the Western tradition combines holiness and honor in one place shows us a clear link between religion and ethics. This link is often understood according to what scholars call divine command ethics. This approach to ethics grounds ethical ontology, moral epistemology, and moral psychology in God's will. The

2. This is Ronald Dworkin's claim in *Life's Dominion*.

ontological idea is that God is the source of ethical value: in his role as the Creator, he also creates ethics and gives things their value. The epistemological point often made in defense of divine command ethics is that if there were no divine commandments, human beings would not know anything about what to honor or what to value. The psychological point is this: God provides a motivating force for ethical behavior, in his role as the Judge who distributes punishments for sin and rewards for good behavior.

The divine command approach to ethics has often been criticized by philosophers, even those who are religious. But atheists have a particular bone to pick with the divine command account of ethics, since it seems to imply that those who do not believe in God are ethically deficient (since they cannot know the good and are not motivated to do good). As I mentioned in chapter 6, one famous way of putting this is to appeal to Dostoevsky, who suggested that if there were no God, then everything would be permitted. Atheists reject this claim. Instead they argue that morality can be grounded in the natural world, in culture, and in reason. When atheists focus on ethics without God, they affirm an account of what is to be honored that is divorced from an account of the holy. It turns out that atheist ethics honors much that is very similar to what is found in theological ethics. In fact, there is significant overlap among all of the world's ethical thinking and traditions, that also overlaps with secular and humanistic approaches to ethics. Something like the Golden Rule ("love your neighbor" and "do unto others as you would have them do unto you") is important. Murder, adultery, lying, and theft are wrong. And we ought to honor our promises, as well as our parents. Atheists differ from divine command theorists in maintaining that these basic moral ideas can be derived without appeal to God.

If it is true that there is common ground between atheists and theists with regard to much of the content of ethics, then we might wonder why there is so much turmoil about the Ten Commandments. But the text—and public monuments that celebrate it—is problematic for nonreligious people. The basic problem is that the text implies the divine command argument—since it begins with the monotheistic declaration and contains a number of specifically religious commandments—and it thereby excludes atheists as well as religious people who are not adherents of Judeo-Christian monotheism. A text that begins with a declaration about holiness and monotheism is a problematic source of ethics in the secular world. For this reason, the Ten Commandments has become a site of contention in contemporary culture wars. American states such as Arkansas and Alabama have constructed monuments to the Ten Commandments. In response, defenders of secularism have filed suit to have these monuments removed as violations of the First Amendment to the US Constitution. In Alabama, for example, in 2001, the chief justice of the State Supreme Court, Roy Moore, installed a monument to the Ten Commandments in the State Supreme Court building. Justice Moore argued that God was the foundation of the law who has "sovereignty" over the state.[3] The Federal Appeals Court found this to be a violation of the "establishment clause" of the First Amendment and ordered that the monument be removed. Chief Justice Moore refused to comply with the court's order. He was subsequently removed from office—and the Ten Commandments monument was also removed. More than a decade later, when a Ten Commandments monument was erected in Little Rock, Arkansas, in 2017, a state senator said, "We have many monuments on our Capitol grounds that honor many various different things, but we did not have a monument that gave honor to the historical, moral foundation of law. The Ten Commandments is one of the first written codes of law ever. That's why we chose to build that particular monument."[4] The senator stated clearly that the monument was erected to honor a sectarian account of the foundation of law.

But there are difficult questions about what we choose to honor and view as the basis of value in a pluralistic, secular democracy. A statue at a courthouse or on the grounds of a state capitol makes a public declaration of value. In this context it is worth considering that in Arkansas, among the other statues at the capitol in Little Rock are two monuments that honor the Confederacy: a Confederate Soldiers Monument and a Monument to Confederate Women. As Black Lives Matter protests erupted across the United States in the summer of 2020, one of the focal points was the Confederate flag and monuments to the Confederacy. There was a wave of change that brought down monuments and flags, representing a significant shift with regard to what we honor in public. The State of Mississippi agreed to remove the Confederate flag symbol from its state flag. And the Governor of Arkansas indicated in an interview that he was open to the idea of removing the monuments to the Confederacy in Little Rock.[5] As I am writing this, there is a remaining open complaint focused on removing the Ten Commandments monument in Little Rock. At issue in these related controversies is the question of what we honor, what we hold as holy, and how we can deal with these questions in a pluralistic and secular context.

There is a web of concepts to consider here: holiness is connected to what should be honored, which is connected to what is good. This idea is

3. Glassroth v. Moore, 335 F.3d 1282 (11th Cir. 2003). https://law.justia.com/cases/federal/appellate-courts/F3/335/1282/515631/.

4. Fanney and Pettit, "Ten Commandments in at Capitol."

5. Brantley, "Gov. Hutchinson Appears to Support Removal."

not merely a Christian one. We see the link between honor, holiness, and ethics also in Plato. In Plato's *Euthyphro*, Socrates and Euthyphro ask the fundamental question of religious ethics. As Socrates puts it: "Is that which is holy loved by the gods because it is holy, or is it holy because it is loved by the gods?"[6] We might put this in more colloquial terms: is something good because God loves it and makes it good through his love; or are good things good independent of God's love, which is why God loves them? Religious people often answer by saying that things are holy, honorable, and good *because* they are loved by God. This is the basic idea of divine command ethics. Atheists obviously have a different idea about the source of ethics and the motivation to be ethical. For atheists, the things we honor are either valuable in themselves or are valuable because we imbue them with value. What motivates us to be ethical is not an external threat of punishment or the promise of reward. Rather, there are forces and sources within physiology, psychology, culture, and society that encourage goodness. Atheists also tend to avoid the language of *holiness* (and related terms such as *sacred*) since this seems to imply something about a divine source of value. And as should be obvious, atheists will reject the idea that things become good, honorable, or holy because of God's will, love, or creative power. For the atheist, if something is good or honorable, this is either because it has innate value or because it is viewed as valuable for us.

This dispute about the sources of honor and value can lead to a dead end for dialogue. In the case of the dispute about Confederate flags and monuments, this dead end has become clear. Defenders of these flags and monuments claim that these are expressions of their identity as Southern Americans, who are descended from sons and daughters of the Confederacy. But Black Americans see these symbols as expressions of racism. There is no denying that White Supremacists have adopted these symbols and employed them in racist ways. But is it possible for Southern Americans to honor the Confederacy as a heritage that is not also racist? Questions about heritage, tradition, identity, power, and change can provoke profound disputes. Similar disputes arise with regard to monuments to the Ten Commandments and other religious icons, statues, and symbols (for example, Christmas displays or public displays of the Christian cross). Christians who defend such symbols think that they are honoring their tradition, which they also see as fundamental to the American tradition. Some may be Christian nationalists and Christian exclusivists who support such symbols as weapons used against non-Christians. But others may

6. Plato, *Euthyphro*, 10a. In Plato's text, the Greek term for holy is *hosion*. In the material in Exodus, the term for holiness is *hagios*.

think that there is nothing offensive about a cross or a crèche and find it hard to believe that a simple text such as the Ten Commandments could be offensive. And yet, non-Christians will find these texts, symbols, and monuments to be exclusionary, oppressive, and offensive.

Struggles for Honor and Human Rights

This dispute shows us the general problem of honor. In some cases, what one person honors will be viewed by others as rude, belligerent, absurd, and so on. In upholding symbols and advocating for their dissemination, certain values are prioritized and certain ideas are put forward. This can occur as a kind of zero-sum game or struggle for power and supremacy. In the history of philosophy, this has been understood in terms of the struggle for recognition described by Hegel.[7] This has both psychological and world-historical effects, as people and nations are willing to fight to the death in defense of what they honor and hold as holy. Pini Efergan offers an interpretation of Hegel's notion of honor that makes this clear. He explains:

> Honor is a primordial human phenomenon, whereby injury to honor, or the individual's sense of self-worth, is not just injury to one of the component elements of her self-identity. . . . Injury to honor is perceived as injury to the very core of the individual's identity, and can be righted only by restoring that sense of self-worth by physically endangering one's life, that is, engaging in a life-and-death struggle.[8]

Honor in this sense is not only about what I value or possess as an individual (or about what we value as a community); it also involves the demand or quest to have what you honor be honored by the other. In struggles for recognition of this sort, I don't merely want to establish my physical superiority over the other or protect my possessions, I also want the other to recognize me as a being who is worthy of being honored.

This idea of the fundamental nature of struggles for honor helps explain quite a bit about social and political life. It also helps to explain much about the history of religion and religious struggle. Disputes about the holy and about what is to be honored become life-and-death struggles involving fundamental questions about identity and value. We see a hint

7. The classic statement of Hegel's Lord-Bondsman dialectic is found in Hegel, *Phenomenology of Spirit*. This idea had an impact on Marx. It can also be found in a different form in Nietzsche's Master-Slave dialectic. An influential interpretation of Hegel is found in Kojève, *Study of Hegel*. I discuss this in Fiala, *Public War, Private Conscience*.

8. Ifergan, *Hegel's Philosophy of Spirit*, 89.

about this in the declaration of monotheism and the theological commands found in the Ten Commandments. The God of the Ten Commandments declares himself to be a jealous God (Exod 20:5). This God wants all of the honor and recognition. He wants to be worshiped as the ontological basis of value—all that is holy and worthy of honor. For religious people who take this seriously, a denial of honor to God is an egregious affront that shatters the basis of value and identity.

Atheists see things differently. Humanists like myself have a less elevated idea of honor and of "holiness" (if that word even makes sense in a nonreligious context). I do not feel the need to worship an ontological source of being and value. Nor do I feel the need for others to recognize this. But I am suspicious of the totalizing claim made by the jealous God of the Old Testament, since I am much more attuned to a pluralistic account of value. But this does not mean that I am not moved by a sense of honor. There are things that I honor and value and which give me a sense of identity and worth. However, from my perspective these sources of honor are less metaphysical. For me what is worthy of honor is human dignity, freedom, rationality, and love. I also believe that individual human rights ought to be honored.

But even that way of putting it leads us back into a dispute. There is, in fact, a substantial dispute about the language of human rights that occurs in discussions across the religious/nonreligious divide. The American Declaration of Independence contains this inspiring phrase: "We hold these truths to be self-evident, that all men are created equal, that they are endowed by their Creator with certain unalienable Rights." The American founders based this idea on that kind of natural law thinking that was typical of the Enlightenment and which could be traced back through John Locke to Aquinas and Augustine. The claim is that there is a Creator who gives value to his creatures and endows them with their rights. Some of the founders interpreted this in a very abstract and philosophical way known as Deism, which holds only that there is a Creator (the Supreme Being) who puts value into the universe and who then disengages from the universe, allowing nature to take its course. Others likely agreed with a much more dogmatic and stringent interpretation of divine command ethics, such as is found in the moral theology of Jonathan Edwards, who was an important figure during the generation or so before the American Revolution. Edwards explained, for example, that moral obligations that are focused on human happiness or some other principle are inferior to an ethics based on the love of God. Edwards explained: "Nothing is of the nature of true virtue, in which God is not the first and the last; or which, with regard to their exercises in general, have not their first foundation and source in apprehensions of God's supreme dignity and glory, and in answerable esteem and love of him, and have not respect to God as the supreme end."[9] To put this more simply, we might note that Edwards offers an interpretation of Jesus's two commandments (love God and love your neighbor—as in Matthew 22:37–38), which puts the first commandment as primary and superior. First we must love God; and it is through the love of God that all other love finds its focus, meaning, and value. A related idea is what has been called the *imago dei* argument for human rights.[10] This theocentric argument holds that humans have value and rights insofar as they are created in the image of God. On this view, we ought to value our fellow human beings (and love our neighbors as ourselves) because human beings are godlike, contain a spark of the divine, or are representations of God. A related idea holds that we ought to love, value, and respect human beings because God loves human beings. It is God's love for humanity that gives humanity its value.

Atheists will, of course, reject all of this because they reject the idea that there is a God who is the source of value. This means that atheists will also be puzzled about what it means to love God and what it means to claim that human beings are created in the image of God or are loved by God. Atheists will instead contend that all of this can be understood merely as a metaphor. To bring in God and the holy in discussions of ethics and value is simply to point out that this discussion is very, very important. To claim that human beings are created in the image of God or are loved by God is to say that human beings are very, very special and worthy of respect. And to stress that we are endowed by our Creator with inalienable rights is merely to reiterate that these rights are fundamental. A deflationary and humanistic strategy of interpretation such as this is found in the work of Immanuel Kant. Kant cannot be considered an atheist in any straightforward understanding of the term. He was an agnostic whose view of God pushed the divinity beyond the phenomenal reality and into the noumenal realm. Kant discussed the connection between ethics and love of God in his book *Religion within the Bounds of Reason Alone* in discussing the Sermon on the Mount. Kant writes:

> Finally, he [Jesus] combines all duties (1) in one *universal* rule (which includes within itself both the inner and the outer moral relations of men), namely: Perform your duty for no motive

9. Edwards, "Nature of True Virtue," 560.

10. I discuss this in Fiala, *Secular Cosmopolitanism*, ch. 9. Sources discussed there include Kraynak, *Christian Faith and Modern Democracy*; Wolterstorff, *Justice*; Perry, *Idea of Human Rights*; O'Donovan, "Rights, Law, and Political Community"; O'Donovan and O'Donovan, *Bonds of Imperfection*; Adams, *Finite and Infinite Goods*; and Adams, *Virtue of Faith*.

> other than unconditioned esteem for duty itself, i.e., love God (the Legislator of all duties) above all else; and (2) in a *particular* rule, that, namely, which concerns man's external relation to other men as universal duty: Love everyone as yourself, i.e., further his welfare from good-will that is immediate and not derived from motives of self-advantage. These commands are not mere laws of virtue but precepts of holiness which we ought to pursue, and the very pursuit of them is called virtue.[11]

Kant says here that the quality of these commands as universal and unconditioned makes them "precepts of holiness." These commands are not about what makes us happy; rather, they are absolute stipulations about human behavior. On Kant's view, ethical behavior is not undertaken in order to achieve happiness. Rather, ethics is obedience to the moral law which comes from understanding that the moral law has a kind of dignity and worth that makes it honorable. An atheist or humanist would interpret this to mean that these commands are of utmost importance—not that they are grounded in or come from God. Kant himself maintains that holiness is merely a kind of guiding idea of what is good, pure, and worthy. In his *Critique of Practical Reason*, Kant discusses "the holy will" in a number of places. In these discussions it is clear that the holy will is an ideal toward which we aspire (but which is beyond the capacity of a human being to actualize). Kant says, "This holiness of will is, however, a practical idea, which must necessarily serve as a type to which finite rational beings can only approximate indefinitely, and which the pure moral law, which is itself on this account called holy, constantly and rightly holds before their eyes. The utmost that finite practical reason can effect is to be certain of this indefinite progress of one's maxims and of their steady disposition to advance."[12] On this view, holiness is not the source of value; rather, it is the ideal toward which we aspire to advance.

The religious and nonreligious points of view about ethics—about what is worthy of honor and what is holy—remain at odds. On the one hand, is the view that God is the source of value; on the other, is the denial of this. This way of putting it makes the dispute extreme. A source of the divide can be found in Kant and post-Kantian ethics and philosophy. Of course, as we've seen, this dispute can be traced back to Socrates and his dialogue with Euthyphro. But after Kant, in the nineteenth and twentieth centuries the problem became acute. Most philosophers turned away from divine command and religious ethics. Marx, Nietzsche, and Freud pushed

11. Kant, *Religion within the Limits*, 148.

12. Kant, *Critique of Practical Reason*, bk. 1, ch.1, para. 80, p. 121.

humanistic ethics even further away from religion, since they tended to view the source of what we honor and value as found in social, cultural, and psychological forces—and not in the divinity. This dispute is stated succinctly by Abraham Heschel, who recounts the problem in discussing his attempt to weave together the study of philosophy with the development of his Jewish faith. Heschel explains:

> The problem to my professors was how to be good. In my ears rang: how to be holy. At the time I realized: there is much that philosophy could learn from Jewish life. To the philosophers: the idea of the good was the most exalted idea, the ultimate idea. To Judaism the idea of the good is penultimate. It cannot exist without the holy. The good is the base, the holy is the summit. Man cannot be good unless he strives to be holy.[13]

Heschel seems to agree with Kant about the need to struggle up the mountain toward the holy. But he also points out (in the rest of this particular essay) that the mountain and the holy itself is a lived experience. To be Jewish (or, one presumes, to be committed to any other religious tradition) is to try to live well, to orient one's life around a set of values, principles, ideas, and traditions with God at the center. It is to honor these traditions, to keep track of the holy days, to participate in sacred ceremonies, and so on.

Nonreligious people may seem to lack this idea of a holy summit to be visited and a holy tradition to be honored. There is certainly more freedom and creativity enjoyed by nonreligion, when the calendar of holy days and sabbaths, commandments, prohibitions, and the like do not constrain our behavior. To religious people this kind of freedom may look like relativism or nihilism. But an ethically grounded, nonreligious life does not consist of unbridled license. It involves obligations to others (some freely given, some demanded by society). It involves responsibility and accountability to self and others (and to career, country, and social group). And in the long run, it involves finding something to love, honor, and serve.

The Common Ground of Honor

Indeed, a substantial source of common ground here is found in the very idea that things are worthy of honor. Atheists and theists both honor, value, and revere things. Some atheists may even agree with theists that some things are worthy of the highest kind of honor available (which might be called the holy, the sacred, or simply that which is absolutely or innately

13. Heschel, "Meaning of Observance," 95.

good). But some atheists are reluctant to affirm such a hierarchical view of value, which holds that some things are absolutely valuable. The question of absolute value remains a difficult point of contention here. Some theists will dig in here and argue that if the atheist's scheme of values lacks a source in God and is not able to ground a claim about absolute value, then the atheist is a kind of relativist and even a moral nihilist. In response we might point out that even theists find it difficult to figure out exactly what counts as an absolute value. Life consists, instead, of conflicts of value and competing objects of love, care, and attention. For example, the Ten Commandments stipulates that the sabbath must be kept holy, which implies that the sabbath is of infinite worth. But most Christians will compromise with regard to sabbath-keeping. If we are being honest, we should admit that we honor and value many different things in many different ways. And for the most part, we struggle to live a morally coherent life.

Now a Puritan like Jonathan Edwards might rise up here and talk about sin. Sin is intimately related to our failure to live well. And while some Christians will speak of utterly fallen depravity and the power of the devil to lure us away from righteousness, in reality most people strive to be good most of the time. Sometimes we fail to live well, out of ignorance or carelessness. Other times, we find ourselves in dilemma situations where there are fundamental conflicts of value. But a less judgmental account of moral failure will not focus on utter moral depravity. Instead, it is useful to admit that we are trying to live better and improve. This holds whether one is a theist or an atheist. We can find common ground in the idea that we are striving to be more honorable and working to better honor the things we love.

This melioristic approach fits better, I think, with an account of moral philosophy, moral development, and moral psychology that is grounded in a humanistic worldview. Humanists are interested in the physiological, psychological, cultural, and social conditions in which moral development occurs. And they are skeptical of those kinds of religious approaches to ethics that focus on sin, irredeemable fallenness, and the need for forgiveness and grace. Certainly forgiveness is an important value in social life. But humanists do not tend to think that human beings are fundamentally broken and incapable of learning and making progress.

Conflicts of Morals

With these issues in moral psychology and divine command ethics in mind, let's turn to the problem of moral conflict. Some of the critics of atheism seem to think that moral conflict would fade away if people were more religious. They will blame moral decay on secularism and the turn away from biblical ethics. In response, it is important to note that there are conflicts of morals even within the biblical tradition. I wrote a book about this a while ago called *What Would Jesus Really Do?* where I attempted to figure out what biblical and theological ethics would tell us about some of the hot-button ethical issues: poverty and economic/racial injustice, sexual ethics, abortion, euthanasia, the death penalty, and war. What I discovered in my research was that conflicts remain even within a biblically based approach to ethics. The Golden Rule and the Ten Commandments only provide a general outline of ethical principles. But they do not really provide an adequate guide for thinking about something as complex as genetic engineering or euthanasia at the end of invasive and futile medical procedures. One approach to these issues seeks to find guiding texts within the Bible. But even here there are very few clear answers. The Bible does not, for example, speak about medical abortion. There are more passages about the death penalty and giving to the poor. There are also a few passages condemning homosexuality. And one of the very clear things that Jesus says is that it is wrong to get divorced. But all of this needs to be interpreted in context. Safe medical abortion was unknown to the ancient world. Women were viewed as inferior to men. Sexuality was subject to strict codes of hygiene and purity that included rules about miscegenation with members of enemy tribes and rival religious groups. Biblical texts take slavery for granted. And systems of punishment were quite different in an era when corporal and capital punishment were pretty much the only possible form of punishment. Would we really want to derive moral insight from a text written thousands of years ago, when diseases were thought to be caused by demonic possession, when menstruating women were viewed as impure, when slavery was common, when crucifixion was a common punishment, and when the political structure was undemocratic?

Consider, for example, the issue of sex and gender and the challenge for Biblical literalism created by feminism and by LGBTQI issues. A literal reading of the Bible tells us that God created Adam and Eve (and not "Adam and Steve" as some religious critics of homosexuality put it). This story maintains that the distinction between the genders is fixed by divine creation—which simply runs counter to the factual reality of intersex people (those who have non-typical genitalia or non-typical sex and gender chromosomes). A literal reading of the biblical account also stipulates that the female is subordinate to the male, while also ruling out homosexuality. The literalists will claim that the female is subordinate—created from Adam's rib and responsible for original sin. And in the New Testament Paul explains: "For man was not made from woman, but woman from man. Neither was man created for woman, but woman for man" (1 Cor 11:8–9). This kind of thing is at the root of the patriarchal culture of Western Christendom. It continues to influence debates about social equality and about women and the priesthood. This cosmological account of sex and gender is also supplemented by biblical proscriptions against homosexuality. For example, Leviticus 20:13 says: "If a man lies with a male as with a woman, both of them have committed an abomination; they shall be put to death, their blood is upon them." This clearly prescribes the death penalty for male homosexuality. And the condemnation of homosexuality continues in the New Testament with Paul explicitly condemning male-male relations (under the term *arsenokoites*) in 1 Corinthians 6:9 and in 1 Timothy 1:10.

We have evolved quite a bit since the time of the Bible. Today in the United States it is possible for same-sex couples to be married. Same-sex couples can reproduce through biotechnological interventions. And it makes sense to speak of a man's husband or a woman's wife. Social relations, political structures, and sexual/reproductive technologies have changed along with our understanding of the social, economic, and psychological function of marriage and the family. Much of this evolution has involved a conversation within and among religious people about the meaning of all of this. Atheists did not force these changes upon society. They were the result of ongoing conversations among the religious majority of society!

One very important fact is this: Christians disagree among themselves about sex and the family, as well as about a variety of other ethical issues. In fact, one significant factor in the proliferation of Christian denominations has to do with disputes about ethics. Luther's Reformation included questions about ethics (such as whether priests should marry). And more recent disputes among congregations also follow a similar trajectory (for example, churches and denominations have split when forced to confront issues such as gay marriage, abortion, and the like). Two further facts are equally important:

1. the Christian world has opened up to include robust dialogue with religious people who are not Christian—Jews, Muslims, Hindus, Buddhists, Indigenous traditions, and so on; and
2. the past few centuries have seen the rise of secular political systems as well as the growth of nonreligious ethical thought.

At one point it may have been easy to pretend that the Bible was the sole source of ethical insight or that the Church in Rome was the primary source of moral guidance. But today with growing diversity among Christians, the presence of deep diversity in the interreligious field, and the reality of what

Charles Taylor calls "the secular age," there is no going back to a simple and homogeneous account of what is good, honorable, and holy.

Two Examples: Abortion and the Death Penalty

Let's consider two further examples that have resulted in some interesting convergences and divergences: abortion and the death penalty. What I hope to show here is that it is not possible to draw clear lines between atheists and theists with regard to these kinds of issues and that intelligent people can reasonably disagree.

Abortion is often viewed as representing a clear divide between atheists and theists in applied ethics. On the one side we are supposed to find secular feminists who maintain that women have an absolute right to control their own reproductive lives. On the other side we are supposed to see theists who argue that life begins at conception and that abortion is murder. In fact, abortion, reproductive ethics, and women's rights are issues that span the religious/nonreligious divide in many ways.

But let's consider two crucial points of dispute: the rights of women and the ontological status of the fetus. A secular argument that permits abortion emphasizes the right of women to decide for themselves. This argument digs deep into claims about religious liberty and freedom of conscience. And it is connected to a historical critique of male dominance and patriarchy. The history of religion has often been oppressive of women. For many long centuries, it was not possible for a husband to rape his wife, for example, since marriage was thought to provide a husband with an absolute right to use his wife's body for reproductive purposes. We have progressed beyond this idea in Western democracies. But this history has unfolded slowly and also includes repeated denials of religious liberty. In the old days, when women were subject to patriarchal power, minority religious beliefs, including atheism, were also denied, ostracized, and persecuted. One connection worth mentioning here is the accusation of witchcraft against women, which was both a way of policing women's bodies and a way of excluding heretical belief.

But we have made progress. The good news is that many religious organizations have responded to feminism and have developed greater respect for women. In some denominations, women are allowed to serve as priests and ministers. Women's experience is now given more credence when it comes to issues such as domestic abuse, the need for divorce, and the need for reproductive and sexual health. This story is not perfect. Some churches have more work to do. There are even a few feminists who will argue in favor of atheism as a response to the patriarchal problem of religion.[14] But the connection between atheism and feminism is complicated, especially in light of the fact that atheism is typically gendered as male. Prominent atheists are usually male. More men affirm atheism than women do: in the United States, 70 percent of atheists are men and only 30 percent of atheists are female.[15] And religiosity is typically associated with femininity: even among people who claim a religious belief, women tend to be more "religious" than men.[16] Despite this, common ground can be found in affirming a kind of feminism: religious people and nonreligious people ought to seek ways to better honor women.

The history of abortion rights in the United States parallels the growth of women's rights and the development of more extensive religious liberty (it also parallels the expansion of civil rights and racial equality). This progress with regard to women's liberty should be viewed as a good thing, especially among religious people who understand the importance of religious liberty. It is important to recall that the expansion of religious liberty in the United States was not driven by atheists. Rather, it was minority religions (including Christian minorities) who championed the call for greater religious liberty. The colonization of America involved developments that can be traced to the Reformation, including the development of the Anglican Church. Some colonists came to America as Protestant reformers seeking to escape religious intolerance, including both the Puritans of New England and the Quakers of Pennsylvania. In the United States there was a proliferation of alternative Christianities (including Christian Science, Mormonism, and so on). This history includes the subsequent arrival of Roman Catholic immigrants (from Ireland, Italy, and other places) and growing tolerance for Catholicism. Along the way there has also been a growing number of non-Christian religious people, including Jews, Buddhists, Hindus, Muslims, Sikhs, and so on. With all of this in mind in the background it is easy to understand how the kinds of claims about freedom of conscience and the right to privacy that are made in discussions of abortion connect to claims about freedom of religion.

And yet, many religious organizations are opposed to abortion—including diverse Christian denominations as well as non-Christians. One reason for this opposition is the kind of *imago dei* argument we discussed above, focused on the claim that life begins at conception and that a fetus is

14. See Overall, "Feminism and Atheism"; also see Mahlamäki, "Religion and Atheism from a Gender Perspective."

15. Pew Research Center, "Demographic Profiles"; more detail in Lipka, "10 Facts about Atheists."

16. Pew Research Center, "Gender Gap in Religion."

an ensouled being that is created in the image of God. Such a claim might appeal to natural law arguments about the purpose and function of reproduction. But these claims are ultimately metaphysical, declaring something about the ontological status of the fetus that is grounded in claims about souls and the work of the divinity in conception, gestation, and birth. Of course, not every religious person agrees with this account. Some Christian denominations defend a woman's right to choose an abortion; and there are no clear guidelines in scripture.[17] There are a couple of passages in the Old Testament that touch upon something like abortion, but these are nothing like what we have in mind today with regard to medical abortion; and Jesus is silent on the topic.[18] There has even been evolution in thinking about abortion within traditions. The Catholic tradition had a different view in earlier times when, under the influence of Aquinas, ensoulment was not thought to occur until "quickening" (a point weeks or months after conception, when the fetus gains the capacity to move on its own).[19] It was not until the nineteenth and twentieth centuries that Catholicism became focused on the idea that life begins at conception.

The fact that there is diversity even within religious traditions opens the possibility of finding common ground. This may seem impossible, since scientifically-minded atheists have a quite different account of personhood and the ontological status of the fetus. Often such a humanistic approach focuses on psychological capacity as a criterion for personhood. From this point of view, a conceptus or early fetus is simply not a person because there is not enough brain activity for anything resembling psychological personhood to exist. But there is room for agreement here, as well, that is grounded in what we know about human conception and gestation. There is no denying, for example, that a fertilized ovum is a new kind of being—with a unique set of DNA composed by a combination of contributions from father and mother. Knowledge of this was not available to Thomas Aquinas. But this advance in scientific knowledge has proved useful in the abortion debate. Some pro-life arguments do in fact focus on the uniqueness of the genetic material in a conceptus as a marker of individuality and personhood. This kind of claim prompts defenders of abortion to clarify their own thinking about the ontological status of a fetus. If genetic uniqueness is not taken as fundamental, then it becomes clearer that psychological capacity is more important.

17. I discuss some of these denominational differences in Fiala, *What Would Jesus Really Do?*, ch. 6.

18. I discuss scriptural references in Fiala, *What Would Jesus Really Do?*, ch. 6.

19. See Singer, *Rethinking Life and Death*, 85–88.

This way of describing the evolution of the debate about abortion helps us understand that there are reasonable claims on all sides. People on both sides seek to honor women, to honor the dignity of life, and to honor the "miracle" of birth (in scare quotes here to indicate that atheists will interpret this "miracle" differently than theists will). People on both sides might also agree that there is something wrong with abortion when it is used by authoritarian states to control population (as it was in China), when abortion is connected to a patriarchal system that results in systematic use of abortion to eliminate female fetuses (as in China and India) or disguise the results of incest (as happens in the US and elsewhere), and when abortion is connected to eugenic projects. These issues are themselves complicated. But by connecting abortion to these larger moral and political topics, it is possible to find common ground. Rather than viewing the abortion debate as an intractable one, we might view it as an evolving conversation in which reasonable people might disagree, while respecting the rationality and good intentions of those on the other side. One possible frame for such rational disagreement is to broaden the conversation to one that is about women's health and reproductive ethics in general. I have contributed to this idea in a discussion of the idea that abortion should be "legal but rare."[20] This moderate position encourages us to think about abortion in relation to sexual ethics and birth control—with the goal of encouraging men and women to better understand and regulate sexual behavior. Admittedly this is not a panacea and disagreements will remain. But my point here is that there are ways that we can find common ground even with regard to the abortion debate.

Views of the death penalty involve a similar narrative of competing and overlapping values. The scriptures reveal a kind of ambiguity about the death penalty. In the Old Testament, the death penalty is clearly prescribed for a number of crimes (including things that we do not think of as capital crimes today): adultery, incest, bestiality, blasphemy, sorcery, idolatry, and failing to keep the sabbath day holy.[21] The death penalty (stoning to death) is even prescribed for sons who are rebellious against their fathers (Deut 21:18–21). The New Testament offers a revaluation of some of those Old Testament values. Jesus suggests forgiveness and mercy as key values. He teaches his followers not to return evil for evil. He questions the entire retributive scheme of the *lex talionis*, which demands eye for eye, life for life (see Matt 5:38–39). The New Testament also shows Jesus willingly submit to the death penalty in his

20. Fiala, "Legal but Rare."

21. See Recinella, *Biblical Truth about America's Death Penalty*. I discuss biblical views of the death penalty in Fiala, *What Would Jesus Really Do?*, ch. 8.

own crucifixion. And Paul appears to offer a defense of the death penalty in Romans 13 (or at least a defense of Christians submitting to the punitive power of the Roman authorities).

This brief account of biblical teaching on the death penalty shows us that there are disputes within the biblical tradition itself. There are also divergences among Christian denominations about this issue, and Christian thinking about the death penalty has evolved. At one point, Christians burned heretics and witches. But today Christian denominations, including Catholicism, are among those advocating for the abolition of the death penalty. What is furthermore of interest to me here is that secular philosophers have disagreed about the death penalty. Kant and Mill both support it. Kant's deontological argument in defense of the death penalty is grounded in a strict kind of retributivism connected to his understanding of the categorical imperative of the moral law. Mill's utilitarian defense of the death penalty focuses on the deterrent power of capital punishment. But other secular ethicists have argued against the death penalty, claiming either that the state does not have the right to kill (and worrying about extending state power in a way that allows it to kill) or that the state's job is ensuring public safety and not dispensing retributive justice to the wicked.[22] Religious abolitionists have argued along similar lines, claiming that since life and death belong to God, it is not up to the state to kill. In the last couple of years, Pope Francis has argued that human life has inherent dignity (another version of the *imago dei* argument) and that even murderers do not lose that dignity and so ought not be executed.[23] The catechism of the church has been changed to reflect the new idea that the death penalty should be abolished.[24]

The question of the death penalty is significant because it directs our attention back to the question of what is worthy of honor and how we honor those things we value. Do we honor the value of human life when we kill those who murder? Kant and Mill both seem to claim that this is the case: by executing a murderer, we honor him by giving him what he deserves, while also conveying a message about how much we value the life of the innocent victims of murder. Or should we express honor for human life by refraining from all killing, even refusing to execute murderers? This is the kind of thinking found among Catholic abolitionists who claim that the *imago dei* argument extends even to murderers.

My point here is that good people will disagree about these things. I am not offering a kind of relativism that undermines all moral discourse.

22. See Nathanson, *Eye for an Eye*.

23. Francis, "Address of October 11, 2017."

24. Revision to #2267 of the *Catechism of the Catholic Church*.

The common assumption of the present conversation is that murder is wrong. The wrongness of murder is grounded in the fact that it dishonors or disrespects human life. We can agree about the wrongness of murder whether we adopt a divine command approach to ethics, an *imago dei* argument, or some basic utilitarian claim about the pleasure, happiness, and value of human life. This common agreement leads, however, to a disagreement about how we ought to honor human life in those specific and limited cases of punishment for murder. Secular ethicists disagree with one another about this, as do religious people. The disagreement here is not one between religious and nonreligious people. Rather, it is a general disagreement among people of goodwill on all sides.

Conclusion

In this chapter I have discussed a range of ethical issues, pointing out that there is no clear divide between atheists and theists about these topics. We could explore a number of other issues. But we would find that ethical disagreements do not result from a fundamental split between atheism and theism. Rather, ethical disputes stem from divergent accounts of what is of value, what ought to be honored, and how we ought to apply our ethical ideas in specific cases. There is a dispute between theists and atheists about the role of "the holy" in all of this. Theists can appeal to a transcendent source of value and perhaps also a holy book containing God's commandments, while atheists will reject this. Theists may go so far as to claim that this transcendent source of value ought to supervene upon human morality and law. And here is where a clearer divide emerges. Atheists reject the idea that a set of divine commandments ought to be appealed to as the source of legal authority in society. As I argued above, however, theists may also agree about the need for a more secular approach to law, once they realize that the secular presumptions of modern legal systems have developed as a way to respect the rights of minority religious points of view. Religious people themselves have disagreed about the sources of honor and the meaning of the holy. For this reason, a secular system seems best suited for a pluralistic world. Secularism encourages us to honor our differences while respecting each individual's judgment about what is worthy of honor and what counts as holy.

Response: The Last Word

Peter Admirand

My older daughter, Kaitlyn, like many sharp and spunky teenagers, always has to have the last word, usually with a "Why?" or a phrase that starts with "Yeah, but . . . " Who has the last word also seems particularly relevant in this discussion of honor and holiness.

I must first concede, though, that like curiosity, my initial thoughts on honor were a bit muddled. My immediate associations hovered around the (US) military, the commandment towards one's parents, and signs and symbols of public recognition. All seem tinged with negative associations. In terms of honor and the military, think of Wilfred Owen's famous WWI poem, "Dulce et decorum est." "Children," as Owen writes, would not be told the "old lie" if they witnessed actual war, "the blood / Come gargling from the froth-corrupted lungs."[1] In terms of the commandment towards parents, while Exodus speaks of honoring your father and mother (20:12), Leviticus 19:3 says to revere your mother and father. At a graduate class in Boston College, Rabbi Rifat Sonsino explained how the mother was mentioned first in Leviticus as children may be more likely to look up to their father, while the father is mentioned first in terms of honoring for a similar reason. In a famous hadith in Islam, the Prophet Muhammad was asked who was most worthy of companionship, and three times, he answered: "Your mother." He only mentions the father on the fourth try.[2] Honor and reverence, though, as Rabbi Sonsino reminded me, were not love. He noted how rabbinic tradition was clear you did not have to love your parents, as some parents were not kind, supportive, or just. For me, this disassociation with love seems to tarnish honor. In terms of my third link, while external award or recognition

1. Owen, "Dulce et Decorum Est." The full Latin phrase is from an ode of Horace and means "how sweet and fitting to die for one's country."

2. *English Translation of Sahîh Muslim*, 6:413.

are not intrinsically unworthy (depending on the context), they are often fraught with unsavory and even damaging notions, or at least should only serve as instrumental ends in Aristotelian terms.

So I'm again appreciative of Andy pointing my thoughts in a more fruitful and positive direction. As he writes:

> Ethical disputes stem from divergent accounts of what is of value, what ought to be honored, and how we ought to apply our ethical ideas in specific cases. There is a dispute between theists and atheists about the role of "the holy" in all of this. Theists can appeal to a transcendent source of value and perhaps also a holy book containing God's commandments, while atheists will reject this. Theists may go so far as to claim that this transcendent source of value ought to supervene upon human morality and law. And here is where a clearer divide emerges.

I want to dwell on Andy's words above and particularly on divine command ethics. As a Catholic theologian, both the Bible and tradition are upheld. As we read in the Vatican II dogmatic constitution, *Dei Verbum*: "Therefore both sacred tradition and Sacred Scripture are to be accepted and venerated with the same sense of loyalty and reverence."[3] This is not the place for me to offer an extensive critique of the document, but let me highlight an important passage to help navigate the problem of divine command ethics and the aims of biblical study. *Dei Verbum* states:

> But, since Holy Scripture must be read and interpreted in the sacred spirit in which it was written, no less serious attention must be given to the content and unity of the whole of Scripture if the meaning of the sacred texts is to be correctly worked out. The living tradition of the whole Church must be taken into account along with the harmony which exists between elements of the faith. It is the task of exegetes to work according to these rules toward a better understanding and explanation of the meaning of Sacred Scripture, so that through preparatory study the judgment of the Church may mature. For all of what has been said about the way of interpreting Scripture is subject finally to the judgment of the Church, which carries out the divine commission and ministry of guarding and interpreting the word of God.[4]

3. Paul VI, *Dei Verbum*, §9. The document later adds: "And the teaching authority of the Church" as a third linked element with scripture and tradition (§10), though stressing it only "serves" the word of God. For commentary on *Dei Verbum*, see Witherup, *Word of God*.

4. Paul VI, *Dei Verbum*, §12.

Notice that tradition is living and ongoing, in what the document calls the work of the Holy Spirit, living among people and in the church. The aim is for greater understanding to live out God's message in scripture and as passed on from Jesus to the apostles and their successors. Now, let's put aside (if one can!) challenges to the gender limitations of the church hierarchy, and perhaps more importantly, the lack of clear learning and theological growth through engagement with other faiths.[5]

Dei Verbum stresses careful study of the context of biblical passages and the unity of scripture. In the previous chapter, I offered a moral lens to evaluate and interpret such passages and provide a way to articulate this unity amidst individually conflicting verses or morally dubious ones. Notice also the aim for biblical study is a greater understanding in aiding the maturity of the church. Remember that key hopes of the Second Vatican Council were for the church to be a greater voice, interpreter, and listener to "the signs of the times" and to engage with the modern world of the 1960s. Indeed, Vatican II helped orient the church away from its self-isolationist and triumphalist tendencies and become more humble and servant-oriented. Careful readers will note that *Dei Verbum* still places the final say of theological exegesis and interpretation within the Vatican hierarchy, "which carries out the divine commission and ministry of guarding and interpreting the word of God." Here is perhaps where it becomes self-defeating to place aside a call for women's priestly ordination and deeper interreligious learning from other faiths.

Nevertheless, the main point here is to challenge or simplify divine command ethics. As God is love, viable ethical obligations will only be rooted in love of God and neighbor. To place this in concrete terms, a God of love does not demand a father sacrifice his son or even traumatize the father and son with some test as we see in the Akedah of Isaac (Gen 20:1–19). The problem that still remains is who legitimately and convincingly has the final word? *Dei Verbum* states final authority in the Catholic Church rests with the Magisterium, but that obviously will not work for non-Catholics (and even some faithful Catholics!).

Another key issue for all theists remains how to name and discern the work of the Holy Spirit in a morally complicated world where moral priorities clash. Even some actions of otherwise good people can seem inscrutable and inconsistent. We are all frail, fallible, and marked by mortality. This reality inevitably compromises our religious, philosophical, legal, and

5. Since Vatican II, and especially *Nostra Aetate*, the church supports interreligious dialogue initiatives, but it still remains unclear how many of the dialogue topics are open to change as opposed to the church having a clear, definitive position and so seemingly walled off from any theological development, let alone alteration.

moral positions. Claims of where holiness resides should also be tempered by other virtues like humility, curiosity, and courage.

Consider Jesus' parable of the two sons in Matthew's Gospel. The father asked each son to work in the vineyard. The first son says he won't go, but does in the end, while the second son agrees to help but never does (Matt 21:29–31). While Jesus clarifies to his disciples that it was the first son who did his father's will, his subsequent words further highlight not only the importance of actions but a warning against the so-called pious alleging they have the true insights into God: "Jesus said to them, 'I tell you the truth, tax collectors and prostitutes will go ahead of you into the kingdom of God!'"

In addition to the problem of hypocrisy, how do you honor the differing values of what others honor? This is even more difficult when you believe what they honor is not worthy or is actually dishonorable. An obvious example of the latter claim is Andy's reference to the Confederate flag, rooted in the evils and bloodstains of human slavery. He also referenced differing views of the cross, which is co-opted by many Christian white supremacists, as it was during the Crusades or Inquisition. While such a co-option betrays Jesus' nonviolent platform, whereas the Confederacy's core is formed and identified by slavery, I also think of Jewish Holocaust survivors who found the cross a symbol of oppression and hatred. Because religious people differ on religious symbols and signs, and on many moral issues like abortion or capital punishment, Andy writes: "A secular system seems best suited for a pluralistic world. Secularism encourages us to honor our differences, while respecting each individual's judgment about what is worthy of honor and what counts as holy." I would agree while adding the notion that a pluralist, secular system should not just be neutral or indifferent to religious faiths, but actively support and encourage their participation and views, valuing their contributions to the common good and our understanding of human rights and obligations.

We are back to the beginning, though, and who has the final word. In our house, it's usually my wife, unless Kaitlyn is lurking around. And in a world of Kaitlyns, I think even atheists would be tempted to say: "God help us!"

Part 3

Closing Dialogues

Conclusion

Dublin and Fresno—An Epistolary Exchange

Peter Admirand and Andrew Fiala

In the past, atheists and theists might have lived in the same town while still being galaxies apart. Yesterday, Andy and I were 5,056.097 miles apart according to Google Maps and yet, through modern technology, talking easily about our kids and how the pandemic has affected them, the "return" of professional sports in America, and of course our book. Regarding the conclusion, I first suggested we each write around 1500 words on what this project has meant to us. "As in a dialogue?" Andy asked. I was outside sitting on a lawn chair in my front garden; Andy was in his office at home. "What about," I suggested, "if we each write 500 words to the other and then the other responds and we each do this three times and see how it goes? It would be like picking up a narrative thread and continuing it." Andy mentioned the idea of including a guided question as well. All agreed, we decided I would go first (as Andy opened the main introduction). As we mused further on content, he even listed a few helpful questions like what other theologians would think of a book like this, or my asking him about "those militant atheists."

Without further ado, let's start.

Dear Andy (August 5, 2020, 8:35 AM Irish Standard Time)

As this section is an epistolary one, it has me thinking of a Cicero and Atticus, but exchanging emails, not vellum or tanned leather. As I mentioned to you yesterday, I have really enjoyed this process which has offered a safe and positive space for my ideas and thoughts as well as a forum for questioning and learning. It has also provided real hope in how much common ground atheists and theists can really have even as we are under no illusions that the major difference on God's existence (or nonexistence) remains. Whenever I described the book to others, though—especially those who don't normally read theological or philosophical books—I would hear: "That's really interesting. That's a book I would get. What was your coauthor's name again?"

I think in this time, especially, of great uncertainty and fear, that there is something deeply noble and optimistic about focusing on common ground between two groups that have too often maligned or ignored one another. We need more of these projects, not less.

And as you noted yesterday in our conversation, so much has happened in the world since we first began this book, from the COVID pandemic to the murder of George Floyd that really ignited the reach of the Black Lives Matter movement, especially, it seems, among more white people. By the time this book is published, hopefully there is a cure for the virus and the momentum of the Black Lives Matter movement has continued forward. I think we can also express our common ground and hope that neither the current US president nor any member of his cabinet or family still occupy the White House.

You might not be surprised, but writing that last sentence made me slightly uncomfortable. Why? Because the space we have established and supported here to say what is on our minds is not often extended by others in the world. So many lines are drawn that seem to allow little room for mature disagreement. If you come on a different side of the divide, many will dismiss your views or respond with hostility. In this regard, many of us naturally feel more comfortable among those who think like us, or share some identity trait, whether of religion, ethnicity, race, and so on. In such a homogeneous space, we often say things we would not among mixed company.

In this regard, I am curious how an otherwise private encounter with a fellow atheist would normally address the militant atheists (see, Andy, I did take up your suggestion, after all!). Among most Christians, even if they bought the Four Horsemen's books, the general claim against Hitchens and Dawkins, in particular, is that they are anti-religious or not nuanced enough when discussing God and faith. I am asking, then, not only your experiences of how fellow atheists have viewed their works, but whether they can be allies of sorts in reaching common ground between theists and atheists.

Dear Peter (August 5, 2020, 10 AM Pacific Daylight Time)

I read your contribution to our conclusion with interest. As you mention, we are very fortunate to live in an era of global communication. I am acutely aware that in the old days (whether one hundred or one thousand years ago), someone who thinks like me would have been unable to express his views or find an ally. Our dialogue is a great example of the kind of progress that has been made in society, politics, and religion. That you are interested in our conversation says quite a lot about changes in theology. The fact that I am able to speak my mind on these topics says a lot about changes in the social world.

Some of the most important influences on my own thinking in the philosophical tradition were forced to hide their nontraditional thinking about religion. Immanuel Kant comes to mind. He published some of his critical reflections on religion in Prussia during the "enlightened" regime of Friedrich the Great. But after Friedrich died, the Prussian censors prohibited that and Kant was forced to publish his work outside of Prussia.

I remain committed to the idea of "enlightenment" that is associated with Kant (and with the American founders). I discussed this, in part, in our chapter on courage. In recent decades there has been backlash against enlightenment. There are some unsavory features of the Enlightenment that we ought to reject. Kant, like many thinkers of that era, has been justly indicted for racism, Eurocentrism, and misogyny. But enlightenment remains an admirable goal, especially when we understand it as calling for equity, inclusivity, and toleration. These enlightened values are crucially important for dialogue, especially a dialogue like ours that seeks to build a bridge across a difficult chasm.

One danger of enlightenment is that it can become aggressive, imperious, and oddly unsympathetic to lived experience. This is the problem I see among the "militant atheists," who revel in bashing religion. There is much to criticize in religion. I've included this critique in my contributions here. But we must tread carefully and be aware of how deeply religious belief is entwined with social and psychological well-being for many people.

I mentioned in chapter 1 an event that astonished me when I was giving a lecture to a group of atheists in Southern California. My slideshow included a picture of the pope. The audience booed and hissed. Part of this was the atheists having fun and feeling their oats in community with other like-minded people. I am sure that something similar happens when pastors talk with their flocks about atheists. Group psychology is such that people often love to hate.

But this makes it impossible to build bridges and find common ground. In your remarks, you hint at the polarization of the Trump era. What's missing today are the kinds of virtues and values we have discussed here: compassion, curiosity, and courage along with honesty, a sense of honor, and the desire for harmony. We have as much work to do in cultivating these virtues within our own communities as we do in trying to develop common ground across our differences. I believe that atheists should be more compassionate, curious, and humble.

And so my question for you, Peter, is whether you think that religious communities are ready and willing to do the same. Will they welcome atheists into conversation? Or is the best we can hope for a kind of secular indifference, where instead of talking to each other, we at least refrain from attacking each other?

Dear Andy (August 6, 2020, 9:47 AM Irish Standard Time)

Churches (with stipulations) were allowed to reopen in Dublin a few weeks ago, but I haven't set foot inside one in over five months since Ireland was in lockdown. This has also meant I have not received Holy Communion during this time. I first technically received Eucharist in my backyard garden in 1984 during a family mass officiated by my uncle who was a priest. Officially, it was later that year while in second grade at St. Peter of Alcantara Church in Port Washington, New York. Before the coronavirus, I rarely missed weekly Communion. Mass has always been part of my life. I find churches peaceful and love attending Catholic liturgies in different countries. It's the one time Catholic uniformity is comforting, as I can still follow the trajectory of the Mass even if I don't understand the local language.

Since the pandemic, I have the habit now every Sunday morning of watching (participating in?) live Catholic Mass from the Jesuit Institute South Africa at 8 AM. There is little singing (which is what I best enjoy about the Rathmines Folk Mass in Dublin), but the homilies are thoughtful and the video and sound are professional. It also means I can stretch and roll my calves while preparing for my mountain run or clean the kitchen so my wife doesn't wake up to another mess. The ritual also helps mark my week at a time where days can melt into one another, and even while multitasking, provides a space for me to reflect and even pray (so long as the younger kids don't wake up and start chattering away).

What scares me is that I am enjoying this ritual in part because of convenience. I don't have to get the kids dressed (or bribed!) and into the car and hope there's a parking place in the crowded church parking lot. By 8:40, Mass is over and I am soon off for my run. But am I part of any community this way? And what about the Eucharist? There's a lot for me to still reflect upon.

Andy, you asked if church communities are ready for atheists, and I wish I could say yes. Many Jewish congregations may have atheist or agnostic members—possibly even an atheist or agnostic rabbi. I am thinking, for example, of Rabbi Anson Laytner whose books taught me about Jewish protest prayer. Outside a very liberal Christian church or community, though, I could not answer with the same confidence. I think many Christians would welcome an atheist if told that was the smiling person before them, but if an atheist happened to anonymously show up at a church, would the homily speak of atheists who do good deeds or who are loved by God? Perhaps, but I can imagine other remarks, not so much the hellfire type, but subtle or off-hand comments like "Life without God has no meaning" or referencing a world without values for those who are not part of the church or have "fallen away" from God.

In the Catholic Church, so much depends upon the local pastor and bishop. While the church should be the people of God, unhealthy and unequal power concentration remains rooted in an all-male, celibate hierarchy. Being male and being celibate are not the issue, of course, but the fact that the power concentration is only among men who are supposed to be celibate.

Even as I still miss the former pastor of my church, I know you would be warmly welcomed and would also love the music; that is, if the Folk Mass Group is able again to perform at the 6 PM Mass, and it's safe for us to attend, too.

Speaking of attending mass or rituals, can you tell me what you consider to be your own (spiritual) rituals—and if I may also ask—whether, or how, such rituals were passed on to your children, and whether this passing-on matters?

Dear Peter (August 26, 2020, 5 PM Pacific Daylight Time)

Peter, I imagine that the music at your church is nice. My own taste in spiritual music tends toward Bach—but also John Coltrane and others.

Your remarks raise issues about ritual, community, and the local nature of religion. I am envious of the way you explain how family, ritual, and community function in your life. There must be something nice about participating in tradition and sharing this with your family. I simply don't have anything like that in my life. My family is close. We share inside jokes, favorite meals, and similar values. We love each other. But something of value is lost when one is not connected to a broader community or tradition.

Some friends from diverse religious communities staged a fast this year, in honor of the seventy-fifth anniversary of the bombing of Hiroshima. The fast was to last for three days—from August 6, when Hiroshima was destroyed, through August 9, when Nagasaki was bombed. I agreed to join in. There were Japanese-American Christians, Quakers, Unitarians, Catholics, and Hindus. I was the only atheist (as far as I know). I focused on a kind of spiritual practice during the fast. I read some Zen texts, sat silently, and worked on walking meditation.

But this was a lonely affair. I am not a member of a spiritual community. Zen sitting is something I experimented with years ago. But these days I don't normally meditate. So I fasted for two days. And then I gave up. Without a supporting spiritual apparatus, I had nothing to keep me going for the whole three-day fast.

This may seem like a loss and a failure. Maybe it is. But what is gained in the secular life is freedom.

The existentialists remind us that freedom can produce anxiety. I follow Camus in thinking that it is up to us to create meaning despite anxiety. But this meaning is different from what is found in the rituals of a religious community. It is thinner and less stable.

There is some benefit to traveling light in this way. Nothing is lost, for example, when a pandemic prevents church services. The secular life is open to change and experiment. If you don't like the music, change the channel. Sit and meditate, if you want. But if you get hungry, break your fast.

I know that this happy-go-lucky attitude may be viewed with suspicion by religious folks. The early Christians saw Epicureanism as a threat. One etymology of the word "religion" traces it to a Latin word (*religare*) for "binding." There is some virtue in being bound to ritual, tied to a community, and so on. But this kind of binding comes at the expense of freedom.

So my question for you is what about freedom? How much freedom is there in religion, as you practice and understand it? Is there room for Coltrane in addition to Bach?

Dear Andy (August 27, 2020, 8:41 AM Irish Standard Time)

Anxiety, guilt, freedom, and religion—with Coltrane in the background to help me riff and improvise. Let's see how it goes. Traditionally, the theological argument on freedom, religion, and God is that we are only truly free when we recognize our frailty and dependence on God. Otherwise, we are lost in ultimately false freedom and so slavery by other means. Such God-dependence entails accepting life as a gratuitous gift and our obligation and duty to live our lives seeking to reflect the love of God in our world. Paradoxically, we gain more freedom the more we focus less on our own autonomy and desires. The argument is similar to the Dalai Lama's claim that a life lived for others in compassion brings joy. Focusing on our own suffering can embitter, but thinking of the plight of others can bring solidarity, introspection, and, ideally, a call of responsibility to heal.

Again, so the traditional theological argument goes, many who break away from religious communities often seek fleeting meaning in money, status, or pleasure—or drift along without any lasting connection. Why? Because humans are material and spiritual beings.

I believe it is only in the connection to something greater than our finite and atomistic existence that freedom, and so our identity and being, can flourish. This something greater is diverse and plural, however, present through various religious, cosmological, and moral paths, sometimes in blended or even multifaith forms. There need not be one, universal way, even as all the ways are not equally transformative, and some can even be harmful and self-defeating. We usually have little say in our initial exposure to such paths and so just find ourselves living in a Hindu, Catholic, white supremacist, Agnostic, Navajo, or Jewish-Buddhist worldview. How to discern whether a path is ultimately holy and meaningful should become a life-long quest, but some worldviews don't encourage searching or questioning. More tragically, searching and questioning can be a luxury in a world with extreme poverty, disease, and sporadic or ongoing violence.

Guilt and anxiety are clearly universal. Just as I talk of Irish Catholic guilt, I hear colleagues, friends, or students talk of Jewish or Muslim guilt. We can blame the religion as the source of this guilt, but ultimately I think that's misplaced. For theists, the problem is when we substitute a healthy dependence on God with the various human structures, rituals, and practices of human religions. There also is healthy and unhealthy guilt.

Does it matter, ultimately, if I fast or go to Mass on a certain day, or do these things at all? Does my religion bring me freedom, especially amidst so many rules and obligations? One answer is in the virtues we have highlighted. I need harmony, for example, in terms of my own moderate desires and this call to heal others; or in respect for the pope but also having a healthy detachment (he's only human). I need the courage sometimes to make my own way and position, but also the humility to accept I don't have all the answers and there is great wisdom both in what has come before me and in other perspectives. Curiosity is then essential in learning about and seeking these other ways and being honest with myself about what I see and feel through these encounters and challenges. There may be some holy envy as I noted previously. But what matters is that I try to live with compassion towards myself and all other living beings, which is the greatest way to honor the Being that created us. I think these seven virtues can aid both the theist and the nontheist to find the best path for them, and with it, a balanced, healthy freedom.

Andy, what would be one other virtue you would now want to add to our list?

Chris, my fifteen-year-old son, hearing Coltrane's music from my laptop, just said: "Nice music, Dad" (and my five-year-old daughter later said: "I like it"). So, let me add gratitude—and again take the opportunity to thank you, Andy, for providing me with the gifts of your insights and graciousness and for our journey in this book together.

Dear Peter (August 28, 2020, 10 AM Pacific Daylight Time)

Peter, since we have discovered John Coltrane in common here at the end, I can't help but think of his jazz hymn "A Love Supreme." The music is challenging. And Coltrane's theology—which finds God in art and breath and music—is unconventional. But the message in the music gives me an answer to the question you posed here.

If there is a value or virtue we could add to the list, it would be love.

We included compassion among our dialogical virtues. Compassion is close to love. But love is more mysterious and transformative. Love is too much to ask for in a difficult dialogue across difference. We can have fruitful dialogues without loving each other.

And yet . . . hovering in the background is love, and the possibility of transformation.

As I look back over our book, I notice that we talked about love quite a bit, each in our own way. We've mentioned love in our families and communities. We discussed the idea that God is love and the challenge created for this by evil in the world.

You point toward love in your recent message when you discuss that which connects us to something greater than ourselves. Some may claim that atheists live a cramped, egoist existence. But this is a false caricature. Atheists are human beings. And to be human is to orient your life around the persons, places, ideas, practices, and things you love.

Understanding that we all love helps to uncover common ground. To love your neighbor as yourself is to recognize that your neighbor's loves are as important for her as yours are for you.

Theologians and philosophers can analyze this kind of thing to death. We've done our fair share of analysis in this book. But if this book succeeds, it will not only be because of the depth of our scholarship. Rather, it will be because we have put into words much of what we love: the books and authors and ideas—and even video games and music—that fill our minds and lift our spirits. I think we have shown that it is possible for theists and atheists to engage in productive dialogue—and to share what we love with one another.

And so I conclude, as well, with gratitude. Thank you, Peter, for sharing your time, energy, and your loves with me. You took a risk when you reached out to me two years ago and invited me, a stranger living thousands of miles away—an atheist from across the world—to participate with you in a dialogue. I didn't know you at all. I took a risk in responding. But dialogue always involves risk. And without risk, there is no hope for transformation.

The good news is that our little adventure has produced a powerful result in the form of this book. I've learned a lot from you. I also learned a lot about myself. I think we have shown that atheists and theists can engage in productive dialogue and that common ground can be found.

Appendix

Study Guide and Discussion Group Questions

1. **Common Ground.** This book aims to find common ground. Is it successful? Have the authors made it clear what would count as shared values and areas of agreement? Can you name three to five things that atheists and theists agree about? Is this sufficient? Is there enough common ground to allow for fruitful dialogue across the religion/nonreligion divide?

2. **Dialogue in General.** This book is about dialogue. It is written by two authors, who engage in dialogue throughout. Is it successful as an example of dialogue? Does the way it is organized and structured provide a good model? How would you organize this discussion differently? What is your vision of how a dialogue about religion would be organized?

3. **Bias and Inclusivity.** This book is written by a philosopher and a theologian who are firmly grounded in the European/American academic and religious world. Both are white, male academics. Would a dialogue about religion look different if it were written by different authors or if it included different voices and points of view? Are there biases woven into the text? What would an inclusive dialogue about religion look like?

4. **Narrative and Biography.** The authors begin the book with each offering a story about their own journey. Did anything surprise you in these stories? Do you have further questions about their stories—things you wondered about in terms of faith or non-faith? Was there anything you could relate to in their stories?

5. **The Dialogue Model.** In chapter 1 ("Dialogue: Virtues and Contexts") the authors provide a general account of dialogue, while exploring a

number of questions, resources, and issues. How does this relate to your own understanding of dialogue—either in your personal life or in public life? Do you think that dialogue is possible among those who disagree about fundamental things? Or are there some topics and issues that are "off the table"—such as religion, politics, sex, etc.? What do you think of the seven values identified in the book's model for dialogue? Would you add any values to the list?

6. **Harmony.** The second chapter focuses on Harmony. What does this mean? What is harmony? Admirand connects this with ecology. What do you think about that connection? What is your view of the way that religion (or nonreligion) promotes harmony? Are some religious (or nonreligious) ideas more "harmonious" than others?

7. **Courage.** The second chapter focuses on courage. How does courage function in your personal experience of dialogue? Fiala connects this with an "existential leap." What does that mean to you? How do you think religion (and nonreligion) supports courage—and courageous dialogue?

8. **Humility.** The third chapter focuses on humility. Is this an important value for you—and in the world today? Admirand offers an account of humility that considers a number of examples—a dog in Leningrad, Benedict, and so on. Do those examples resonate with you, and what can they teach about humility? Is humility a "religious" virtue, or does it fit with nonreligious thinking as well? Do we need more or less humility in the world today?

9. **Curiosity.** The middle chapter, chapter 4, is about curiosity. To what extent is curiosity a central value in dialogue? Admirand points out that this is not an obvious one for religious people. Is he right about that? Fiala warns that curiosity can undermine religious belief. Is he right about that? How do you think curiosity functions in the world today?

10. **Honesty.** Chapter 5 is about honesty. How much honesty is necessary for dialogue? What dangers and difficulties does honesty create? Fiala connects honesty to authenticity and to loyalty. How do these values interrelate? Do these values make more sense (are they easier—or more difficult) in a religious context or in a nonreligious context? Is it ever wise to be completely honest? Or should we hold something in reserve?

11. **Compassion.** The sixth chapter focuses on compassion. Is it possible to be compassionate to strangers and to those who have beliefs that you reject? Admirand talks about a God who is compassionate and just. How does this fit with your own understanding of God? And what

about the problem of evil? What would a more compassionate world (or religion or relationship) look like?

12. **Honor.** The seventh chapter is about honor. How do we honor our own beliefs while also listening to and learning from others? Fiala links honor to ideas about what is holy and what has value. What counts as holy and worthy of honor for you? And what should we do when other people disagree with our deepest commitments (about abortion, for example, or other moral issues)? How can we negotiate conflicts of value in the world today?

13. **Concluding dialogue.** The book concludes with a dialogue between Admirand and Fiala about a number of issues, including ritual, meaning, music, freedom, and love. What surprised you in this discussion? Were there topics that should be included but were not? Fiala and Admirand offer comments about religious communities and communities of atheists in this section. Did any of this resonate with your own experience of religious and nonreligious people? What could we do to improve dialogue?

14. **Applied Issues.** Throughout the book the authors touch upon a number of "hot button" issues. Some of this is about the tension between religion and nonreligion: religious intolerance, aggressive secularism, militant atheism, and close-minded religiosity. Some of this has to do with moral issues: abortion, sexuality, and so on. Issues related to failures within the church (pedophile priests) were discussed. And the book considered problems of inclusivity, diversity, and race/gender dynamics. Which of these issues is worthy of further consideration? Did you agree with the authors comments/conclusions about these issues? Were there issues that were not considered here that ought to be?

15. **Hope and Future Prospects.** After reading this book, are you hopeful about the possibility of dialogue across the religious/nonreligious divide? Or are there challenges and difficulties that are insurmountable? What kind of conclusion do you derive from the book about next steps in such an effort? How can you (how can each of us!) contribute to building bridges and finding common ground?

Bibliography

Adams, Robert M. *Finite and Infinite Goods: A Framework for Ethics*. Oxford: Oxford University Press, 2002.

———. *The Virtue of Faith*. Oxford: Oxford University Press, 1987.

Admirand, Peter. *Amidst Mass Atrocity and the Rubble of Theology: Searching for a Viable Theodicy*. Eugene, OR: Cascade, 2012.

———. "Atheist Critiques of the New Atheists: Advancing Atheist-Theist Dialogue." *Interreligious Studies and Intercultural Theology* 4.2 (2020).

———. "Healing the Distorted Face: Doctrinal Reinterpretation(s) and the Christian Response to the Other." *One in Christ* 42 (2008) 302–17.

———. *Humbling Faith: Brokenness, Doubt, Dialogue—What Unites Atheists, Theists, and Nontheists*. Eugene, OR: Cascade, 2019.

———. "Millstones, Stumbling Blocks, and Dog Scraps: Children in the Gospels." *Biblical Theology Bulletin* 42.4 (2012) 187–95.

———. "Should We Still Teach a Beautiful Novel by a Racist Author?" *International Journal of Ethics Education* (2017) 1–14. https://link.springer.com/article/10.1007/s40889-017-0042-2.

Alexander, Michelle. *The New Jim Crow: Mass Incarceration in the Age of Colorblindness*. Revised ed. New York: New Press, 2012.

Alexievich, Svetlana. *Last Witnesses: Unchildlike Stories*. Translated by Richard Pevear and Larissa Volokhonsky. London: Penguin Random House UK, 2019.

Ames, Roger T. "Foreword." In *The Confucian Philosophy of Harmony*, by Chenyang Li, xi–xiii. Abingdon: Routledge, 2014.

Anselm. *Dicta Anselmi*. In "The Two Guardians of the Mountain of Humility," by Gregory Sadler. May 29, 2011. http://gbsadler.blogspot.ie/2011/06/two-guardians-of-mountain-of-humility.html.

———. *Monologion and Proslogion, with the Replies of Gaunilo and Anselm*. Translated by Thomas Williams. Indianapolis: Hackett, 1995.

———. *The Prayers and Meditations of Saint Anselm, with the Proslogion*. Translated by Sister Benedicta Ward. London: Penguin, 1988.

Aquinas, Thomas. *Summa Theologiae*. 2nd and revised ed. 1920. Literally translated by Fathers of the English Dominican Province. Revised and edited by Kevin Knight. *New Advent*, 2017. https://www.newadvent.org/summa/.

Aristotle. *Metaphysics. Aristotle in Twenty-Three Volumes.* Vols. 17 and 18. Translated by Hugh Tredennick. Cambridge, MA: Harvard University Press, 1989. Retrieved from Perseus Digital Library.

———. *Rhetoric.* Translated by J. H. Freese. Loeb Classical Library 22. Cambridge, MA: Harvard University Press, 1926.

Armstrong, Karen. *Twelve Steps to a Compassionate Life.* New York: Anchor, 2012.

Artson, Bradley Shavit. "A Holy Curiosity: The Synergy of Reason and Emotion." *American Jewish University*, September 28, 2003. https://www.aju.edu/ziegler-school-rabbinic-studies/our-torah/back-issues/holy-curiosity-synergy-reason-emotion.

Atheist Ireland. "Catholic Church at UN Rejects Human Right to Freedom from Religion." March 5, 2018. https://atheist.ie/2018/03/catholic-church-un/.

"Atheists Tend to Be Seen as Immoral—Even by Other Atheists: Study." *The Guardian*, August 7, 2017. https://www.theguardian.com/world/2017/aug/07/anti-atheist-prejudice-secularity.

Augustine. *The Confessions.* Translated by Henry Chadwick. Oxford: Oxford University Press, 1992/2008.

———. "Exposition on Psalm 8." Translated by an anonymous scholar. Revised and edited by Kevin Knight. *New Advent.* http://www.newadvent.org/fathers/1801008.htm.

———. "Homily 2." Translated by H. Browne. Revised and edited by Kevin Knight. *New Advent.* http://www.newadvent.org/fathers/170202.htm.

———. "Letter 118 (A.D. 410), Augustine to Dioscorus." Translated by J. G. Cunningham. Revised and edited by Kevin Knight. *New Advent.* http://www.newadvent.org/fathers/1102118.htm.

———. "Letter 221 (A.D. 423)." Translated by J. G. Cunningham. Revised and edited for Kevin Knight. *New Advent.* http://www.newadvent.org/fathers/1102211.htm.

———. *On Christian Doctrine.* Translated by James Shaw. Revised and edited by Kevin Knight. *New Advent.* http://www.newadvent.org/fathers/12022.htm.

"Australia Fires: A Visual Guide to the Bushfire Crisis." January 31, 2020. https://www.bbc.com/news/world-australia-50951043.

Bakhtin, Mikhail. *The Problem of Dostoevsky's Poetics.* Minneapolis: University of Minnesota Press, 1984.

Baldwin, James. *Dark Days.* London: Penguin, 2018.

———. *The Fire Next Time.* New York: Vintage, 1993.

———. "The Price of the Ticket." In *Dark Days*, 19–40. London: Penguin, 2018.

———. "The White Man's Guilt." In *Dark Days*, 41–50. London: Penguin, 2018.

Barnes, Eric. *The City Where We Once Lived: A Novel.* New York: Arcade, 2018.

Baumgarten, Murray. "Seeing Double: Jewish Isolation in *Oliver Twist* and *Our Mutual Friend*." *The Dickens Project.* https://omf.ucsc.edu/scholarship/article-archive/seeing-double.html.

Bein, Steve. *Compassion and Moral Guidance.* Honolulu: University of Hawaii, 2013.

Bellah, Robert. *Religion in Human Evolution.* Cambridge, MA: Harvard University Press, 2011.

Benedict. *The Rule of St. Benedict.* Edited by Timothy Fry. New York: Vintage, 1998.

Benedict, Barbara M. *Curiosity: A Cultural History of Early Modern Inquiry.* Chicago: University of Chicago Press, 2001.

Benedictine Nuns from Holy Trinity Monastery. "Of Clowns, Killjoys and the Tenth Step of Humility." *iBenedectines*, February 7, 2014. http://www.ibenedictines.org/2014/02/07/of-clowns-killjoys-and-the-tenth-step-of-humility/.

———. "Self-Will by Bro Duncan PBGV." *iBenedectines*, January 30, 2014. http://www.ibenedictines.org/2014/01/30/self-will-by-bro-duncan-pbgv/.

Bentz, Jack. "Was Pope Francis Right to Tell a Child His Atheist Dad May Be in Heaven?" *America*, April 19, 2018. https://www.americamagazine.org/faith/2018/04/19/was-pope-francis-right-tell-child-his-atheist-dad-may-be-heaven.

Bergman, Shmuel Hugo. *Dialogical Philosophy from Kierkegaard to Buber*. Albany, NY: State University of New York Press, 1991.

Bernard of Clairvaux. *The Letters of St. Bernard of Clairvaux*. Translated by Bruno Scott James. London: Burns Oates, 1953.

———. "On the Steps of Humility and Pride." In *Bernard of Clairvaux: Selected Works*, translated by G. R. Evans, 99–143. Mahwah, NJ: Paulist, 1988.

Bloom, Paul. *Against Empathy: The Case for Rational Compassion*. New York: HarperCollins, 2017.

Bohm, David. *On Dialogue*. New York: Routledge, 1996.

Bordoni, Linda. "Pope at Mass: Compassion Is the Language of God." *Vatican News*, September 17, 2019. https://www.vaticannews.va/en/pope-francis/mass-casa-santa-marta/2019-09/pope-francis-homily-casa-santa-marta-compassion.html.

Boyd, Craig A. "Augustine, Aquinas, and Tolkien: Three Catholic Views on Curiositas." *The Heythrop Journal* 61.2 (2020) 222–33.

Boys, Mary C. *Has God Only One Blessing? Judaism as a Source of Christian Self-Understanding*. New York: Paulist, 2000.

Braiterman, Zachary. *(God) After Auschwitz: Tradition and Change in Post-Holocaust Jewish Thought*. Princeton: Princeton University Press, 1998.

Brantley, Max. "Gov. Hutchinson Appears to Support Removal of Confederate Statues from State Capitol." *Arkansas Times*, June 28, 2020. https://arktimes.com/arkansas-blog/2020/06/28/gov-hutchinson-appears-to-support-removal-of-confederate-statues-from-state-capitol.

Bregman, Rutger. *Humankind: A Hopeful History*. Translated by Elizabeth Manton and Erica Moore. London: Bloomsbury, 2020.

Brooks, David. *The Road to Character*. New York: Random House, 2016.

Brown, Peter. *Augustine of Hippo: A Biography*. New ed. Berkeley: University of California Press, 2000.

Bruenig, Elizabeth. "Why Do Evangelicals Like James Inhofe Believe That Only God Can Cause Climate Change?" *New Republic*, January 29, 2015. http://www.newrepublic.com/article/120889/evangelical-james-inhofe-says-only-god-can-cause-climate-change.

Buber, Martin. *Between Man and Man*. New York: Routledge, 2002.

———. *I and Thou*. Edinburgh: T. & T. Clark, 1937.

———. "Martin Buber to Mohandas K. Gandhi (Feb. 24, 1939)." In *The Letters of Martin Buber*, edited by Nahum Glatzer and Paul Mendes-Flohr, 476. Syracuse: Syracuse University Press, 1996.

———. *Pointing the Way*. New York: Harper, 1957.

Burge, Ryan P. "Growth and Decline in American Religion over the Last Decade." *Religion in Public* (blog), July 9, 2019. https://religioninpublic.blog/2019/07/09/growth-and-decline-in-american-religion-over-the-last-decade/.

Burrell, David B. "Foreword." In *Amidst Mass Atrocity and the Rubble of Theology: Searching for a Viable Theodicy*, by Peter Admirand, ix–x. Eugene, OR: Cascade, 2012.

Button, Mark. "'A Monkish Kind of Virtue'? For and against Humility." *Political Theory* 33.6 (2005) 840–68.

Camus, Albert. *The Myth of Sisyphus*. Translated by Justin O'Brien. New York: Vintage, 1991.

———. *The Rebel*. Translated by Anthony Bower. New York: Vintage, 1991.

Carlisle, Clare. "Humble Courage: Kierkegaard on Abraham and Mary." *Literature and Theology* 30.3 (2016) 278–92. https://doi.org/10.1093/litthe/fru066.

Cassian, John. *The Institutes*. Translated by C. S. Gibson. Revised and edited by Kevin Knight. *New Advent*. https://www.newadvent.org/fathers/3507.htm.

The Catechism of the Catholic Church. https://www.vatican.va/archive/ccc_css/archive/catechism/p2s2c1a3.htm#1373.

Catholic Bishops' Conference of the Philippines. "Dialogue towards Harmony." December 1, 2019. https://cbcponline.net/dialogue-towards-harmony/.

Catholic News Service. "Vatican Official Warns U.N. of Hostility toward Religion." *Crux*, March 6, 2018. https://cruxnow.com/vatican/2018/03/vatican-official-warns-u-n-hostility-toward-religion/.

Chappell, Sophie Grace. "Challenges Facing Natural Law Ethics." In *The Cambridge Companion to Natural Law Ethics*, edited by Tom Angier, 257–75. Cambridge: Cambridge University Press, 2019.

Charnock, Anne. *Bridge 108*. Seattle: 47North, 2020.

Chazan, Robert. "From the First Crusade to the Second: Evolving Perceptions of the Christian-Jewish Conflict." In *Jews and Christians in Twelfth-Century Europe*, edited by Michael A. Signer and John Van Engen, 46–62. Notre Dame: University of Notre Dame Press, 2001.

Chuang Tzu. *The Book of Chuang Tzu*. Translated by Martin Palmer, with Elizabeth Breuilly et al. London: Penguin, 2006.

Church, Ian, and Peter Samuelson. *Intellectual Humility: An Introduction to the Philosophy and Science*. London: Bloomsbury, 2017.

Clark, Kelly James, et al. *Strangers, Neighbors, Friends: Muslim-Christian-Jewish Reflections on Compassion and Peace*. Eugene, OR: Cascade, 2018.

Coghlan, Andy. "Sneaky Beetles Evolved Disguise to Look Like Ants, Then Eat Them." *New Scientist*, March 9, 2017. https://www.newscientist.com/article/2124050-sneaky-beetles-evolved-disguise-to-look-like-ants-then-eat-them/#ixzz6RW2IPWlh.

Cohen, Charles L., et al., eds. *The Future of Interreligious Dialogue: A Multireligious Conversation on "Nostra Aetate."* Maryknoll: Orbis, 2017.

Commission for Religious Relations with the Jews. "'The Gifts and the Calling of God Are Irrevocable' (Rom 11:29): A Reflection on the Theological Questions Pertaining to Catholic-Jewish Relations on the Occasion of the 50th Anniversary of 'Nostra Aetate' (No. 4)." December 10, 2015. http://www.vatican.va/roman_curia/pontifical_councils/chrstuni/relations-jews-docs/rc_pc_chrstuni_doc_20151210_ebraismo-nostra-aetate_en.html.

Committee on Doctrine and Committee on Ecumenical and Interreligious Affairs. "A Note on Ambiguities Contained in 'Reflections on Covenant and Mission.'" USCCB, June 18, 2009.

Cone, James H. *A Black Theology of Liberation*. Maryknoll, NY: Orbis, 2010.

Congregation for the Doctrine of the Faith. "*Dominus Iesus*: On the Unicity and Salvific Universality of Jesus Christ and the Church." http://www.vatican.va/roman_curia/congregations/cfaith/documents/rc_con_cfaith_doc_20000806_dominus-iesus_en.html.

Corley, Jeremy. *Sirach*. Collegeville, MN: Liturgical, 2013.

Cornille, Catherine. *The Im-Possibility of Inter-Religious Dialogue*. New York: Crossroads, 2008.

———. "Introduction: On Women and Interreligious Dialogue." In *Women and Interreligious Dialogue*, edited by Catherine Cornille and Jillian Maxey, 1–10. Eugene, OR: Cascade, 2013.

Corvino, John. *What's Wrong with Homosexuality?* Oxford: Oxford University Press, 2013.

Cowdrey, H. E. J. "Pope Urban II's Preaching of the First Crusade." *History* 55.184 (1970) 177–88.

Craig, William Lane. "The Kurtz/Craig Debate." In *Is Goodness without God Good Enough?*, edited by Robert Garcia and Nathan King, 25–47. Lanham, MD: Rowman & Littlefield, 2009.

Crane, Jonathan K. "Faltering Dialogue? Religious Rhetoric of Mohandas Gandhi and Martin Buber." *Anasaki Darshan* 3.1 (2007) 34–52.

Cunningham, Lawrence S. "Cassian's Hero and Discernment." In *Finding God in All Things: Essays in Honor of Michael J. Buckley, S. J.*, edited by Michael J. Himes and Stephen J. Pope, 231–43. New York: Crossroads, 1996.

Cunningham, Philip A. *Seeking Shalom: The Journey to Right Relationship between Catholics and Jews*. Grand Rapids: Eerdmans, 2015.

Dalai Lama. *Beyond Religion: Ethics for a Whole World*. Boston: Houghton Mifflin Harcourt, 2011.

———. "'Prayer Is Not Enough.' The Dalai Lama on Why We Need to Fight Coronavirus with Compassion." *Time Magazine*, April 14, 2020. https://time.com/5820613/dalai-lama-coronavirus-compassion/.

———. *Toward a True Kinship of Faiths: How the World's Religions Can Come Together*. New York: Doubleday, 2010.

Dalai Lama, and Desmond Tutu, with Douglass Abrams. *Book of Joy: Lasting Happiness in a Changing World*. London: Hutchinson, 2016.

Daley, Brian. "'To Be More Like Christ': The Background and Implications of 'Three Kinds of Humility.'" *Studies in the Spirituality of Jesuits* 27.1 (1995) 1–39.

Dalyrimple, William. *From the Holy Mountain: A Journey among the Christians of the Middle East*. New York: Henry Holt, 1999.

Daniels-Sykes, Shawnee M. "Anselm of Canterbury." In *Beyond the Pale: Reading Theology from the Margins*, edited by Miguel A. de la Torre and Stacey M. Floyd-Thomas, 37–43. Louisville: Westminster John Knox, 2011.

Davidson, Richard J., and Anne Harrington, eds. *Visions of Compassion: Western Scientists and Tibetan Buddhists Examine Human Nature*. Oxford: Oxford University Press, 2002.

Davies, Brian, ed. *Philosophy of Religion: A Guide and Anthology*. Oxford: Oxford University Press, 2000.

Davis, Bret W. *Heidegger and the Will: On the Way to Gelassenheit*. Evanston, IL: Northwestern University Press, 2007.

Dawkins, Richard. *The God Delusion*. Boston: Houghton Mifflin, 2006.

Deloria, Vine, Jr. *God Is Red: A Native View of Religion*. 30th anniversary ed. Golden, CO: Fulcrum, 2003.

Deng, Ming-Dao. *Everyday Tao: Living with Balance and Harmony*. New York: HarperOne, 1996.

de Souza, Raymond. "Israel and the Holy See Have a Unique Diplomatic Relationship." *Catholic Herald*, June 27, 2019. https://catholicherald.co.uk/magazine/israel-and-the-holy-see-have-a-unique-diplomatic-relationship/.

de Waal, Frans. *The Bonobo and the Atheist*. New York: Norton, 2013.

Dewey, John. *Democracy and Education*. New York: MacMillan, 1916.

———. *The Public and Its Problems*. Chicago: Gateway, 1946.

Diab, Khaled. "Is an Israeli Bill to Mute the Muezzin a Threat to Palestinian Identity?" *Haaretz*, November 23, 2016. https://www.haaretz.com/opinion/.premium-is-the-bill-to-mute-the-muezzin-a-threat-to-palestinian-identity-1.5465350.

Dickens, Charles. *Dombey and Son*. London: Wordsworth, 2002.

———. *Little Dorrit*. Clinton, MA: Colonial, 1947.

———. *The Old Curiosity Shop*. New York: Book of the Month Club, 1998.

———. *Oliver Twist*. London: Wordsworth, 2000.

———. *Our Mutual Friend*. London: Vintage, 2011.

Dostoevsky, Fyodor. *The Brothers Karamazov*. Translated by Constance Garnett. New York: Modern Library, 1996.

Dunbar-Ortiz, Roxanne, and Dina Gilio-Whitaker. *"All the Real Indians Died Off": And 20 Other Myths about Native Americans*. Boston: Beacon, 2016.

Dworkin, Ronald. *Life's Dominion*. New York: Random House, 1994.

———. *Religion without God*. Cambridge: Harvard University Press, 2013.

Edwards, Jonathan. "All the Graces of Christianity Connected." In *Charity and Its Fruits*, 386–409. New York: Robert Carter and Bros., 1854.

———. "The Nature of True Virtue." In *Ethical Writings* in *Works of Jonathan Edwards Online*, 8:539–627. Jonathan Edwards Center, Yale University, 2008. http://edwards.yale.edu/archive?path=aHRocDovL2Vkd2FyZHMueWFsZS5lZHUvY2dpLWJpbi9uZXdwaGlsby9nZXRvYmplY3QucGw/Yy43OjYud2plbw==).

Eilers, Franz-Josef, ed. *For All the Peoples of Asia: Federation of Asian Bishops' Conferences Documents from 1992 to 1996*. Vol. 2. Manila: Claretian, 2007.

Eiseley, Loren. *The Star Thrower*. New York: Harvest, 1978.

English Translation of Sahîh Muslim. Compiled by Imâm Abul Hussain Muslim bin al-Hajjaj. Translated by Nasiruddin al-Khattab, edited by Huda Khattab. 7 vols. Riyadh: Darussalam, 2007.

Estes, Nick. *Our History Is the Future: Standing Rock Versus the Dakota Access Pipeline, and the Long Tradition of Indigenous Resistance*. London: Verso, 2019.

Esteves, Junno Arocho. "Catechism Will Be Updated to Include Ecological Sins, Pope Says." *National Catholic Reporter*, November 15, 2019. https://www.ncronline.org/news/earthbeat/catechism-will-be-updated-include-ecological-sins-pope-says.

———. "Curiosity Can Lead to Dangerous Paths, Pope Says at Mass." *Crux*, April 30, 2018. https://cruxnow.com/vatican/2018/04/curiosity-can-lead-to-dangerous-paths-pope-says-at-mass/.

Evans, G. R. "Anselm of Canterbury." In *The Medieval Theologians*, edited by G. R. Evans, 94–101. Oxford: Blackwell, 2001.

———, ed. *The Medieval Theologians*. Oxford: Blackwell, 2001.

FABC (Federation of Asian Bishops' Conferences). Paper No. 75: "Asian Christian Perspectives on Harmony." http://www.fabc.org/fabc%20papers/fabc_paper_75.pdf.

Falzon, Christopher. *Foucault and Social Dialogue: Beyond Fragmentation*. New York: Routledge, 1998.

Fanney, Brian, and Emma Pettit. "Ten Commandments in at Capitol." *Arkansas Democratic Gazette*, June 28, 2017. https://www.arkansasonline.com/news/2017/jun/28/ten-commandments-in-at-capitol-20170628/.

Fanon, Frantz. *The Wretched of the Earth*. Translated by Richard Philcox. New York: Grove Press, 2004.

Farley, Margaret A. *Just Love: A Framework for Christian Sexual Ethics*. London: Continuum, 2012.

Ferdowsian, Hope. *Phoenix Zones: Where Strength Is Born and Resilience Lives*. Chicago: University of Chicago Press.

Fiala, Andrew. *Against Religions, Wars, and States: Enlightenment Atheism, Just War Pacifism, and Liberal-Democratic Anarchism*. Lanham, MD: Rowman & Littlefield, 2013.

———. *The Just War Myth*. Lanham, MD: Rowman & Littlefield, 2008.

———. "Legal but Rare: Toward a Transformative Critical Theory of Abortion and Unwanted Pregnancy." *International Journal of Applied Philosophy* 33.2 (2019) 203–20.

———. "Militant Atheism, Pragmatism, and the God-Shaped Hole." *International Journal for Philosophy of Religion* 65.3 (2009) 139–51.

———. "The Moral Imperative of Hope in the Age of Ecological Calamity." In *Ecology, Ethics and Hope*, edited by Andrew Brei, 29–42. Lanham, MD: Rowman & Littlefield, 2015.

———. *Public War, Private Conscience*. London: Bloomsbury, 2010.

———. *Secular Cosmopolitanism, Hospitality, and Religious Pluralism*. New York: Routledge, 2016.

———. *Transformative Pacifism*. London: Bloomsbury, 2018.

———. *What Would Jesus Really Do?* Lanham, MD: Rowman & Littlefield, 2007.

Fiala, Andrew, and Barbara MacKinnon. *Ethics: Theory and Contemporary Issues*. 9th ed. Cengage Learning, 2017.

Finkelstein, Israel, and Neil Asher Silberman. *The Bible Unearthed*. New York: Free Press, 2001.

Finley, Stephen C., and Biko Mandela Gray. "God Is a White Racist: Immanent Atheism as a Religious Response to Black Lives Matter and State-Sanctioned Anti-Black Violence." *Journal of Africana Religions* 3.4 (2015) 443–53.

Finnis, John. *Natural Law and Natural Rights*. Oxford: Oxford University Press, 2011.

Fiss, Joelle. "Anti-Blasphemy Offensives in the Digital Age: When Hard-Liners Take Over." *Brookings*, September 2016. https://www.brookings.edu/wp-content/uploads/2016/09/brookings-analysis-paper_joelle-fiss_web.pdf.

Flanagan, Richard. "Australia Is Committing Climate Suicide." *New York Times*, January 3, 2020. nytimes.com/2020/01/03/opinion/australia-fires-climate-change.html.

Fortin, John R. "Saint Augustine's Letter 211 in The Rule of the Master and The Rule of Saint Benedict." *Journal of Early Christian Studies* 14.2 (2006) 225–34.

Foucault, Michel. *The Government of Self and Others*. Edited by Frédéric Gros. Translated by Graham Burchell. New York: Palgrave MacMillan, 2010.

———. "The Meaning and Evolution of the Word Parrhesia." In *Discourse and Truth: the Problematization of Parrhesia*. Foucault Info, 1999. Etext: https://foucault.info/parrhesia/foucault.DT1.wordParrhesia.en/.

Foulcher, Jane. *Reclaiming Humility: Four Studies in the Monastic Tradition*. Collegeville: Liturgical, 2015.

Francis, Pope. *Laudato Si'*. May 24, 2015. http://w2.vatican.va/content/francesco/en/encyclicals/documents/papa-francesco_20150524_enciclica-laudato-si.html.

———. "Pope Francis Address of October 11, 2017." https://w2.vatican.va/content/francesco/en/speeches/2017/october/documents/papa-francesco_20171011_convegno-nuova-evangelizzazione.html.

———. "Pope Francis' Message for Lent 2020." *Rome Reports*, February 24, 2020. https://www.romereports.com/en/2020/02/24/pope-francis-message-for-lent-2020/.

———. "The Secret to Joy: Never Suppress Positive Curiosity; Get Involved, because Life Is Meant to Be Lived." Twitter, @Pontifex, August 2, 2016.

———. "The Spirit of Wisdom Triumphs over Worldly Curiosity." November 14, 2013. http://www.vatican.va/content/francesco/en/cotidie/2013/documents/papa-francesco-cotidie_20131114_spirit-wisdom.html.

Frazer, Michael L. "The Compassion of Zarathustra: Nietzsche on Sympathy and Strength." *The Review of Politics* 68.1 (2006) 49–78.

Fredrickson, Paula. *When Christians Were Jews: The First Generation*. New Haven: Yale University Press, 2018.

Freud, Sigmund. *The Future of an Illusion*. Translated by James Strachey. New York: Norton, 1961.

———. *Totem and Taboo*. Translated by James Strachey. London: Routledge, 2001.

Friedman, Maurice Stanley. *Martin Buber: The Life of Dialogue*. 4th ed. New York: Routledge, 2002.

Friedman, R. Z. "Does the 'Death of God' Really Matter?" *International Philosophical Quarterly* 23.3 (1983) 321–32 .

Frierson, Patrick. "Kant and the End of Wonder." In *Philosophy Begins in Wonder: An Introduction to Early Modern Philosophy, Theology, and Science*, edited by Péter Losonczi, 285–309. Eugene, OR: Pickwick, 2010.

Gadamer, Hans-Georg. *Truth and Method*. 2nd ed. London: Continuum, 2006.

Galileo. "Letter to the Grand Duchess." In *Discoveries and Opinions of Galileo*, translated by Stillman Drake, 173–216. New York: Anchor, 1957.

Gandhi, Mohandas K. *Collected Works*. Vol. 30. New Delhi: Publications Division Government of India, 1999.

———. "Young India." September 25, 1915. In *Collected Works*, 29:190. New Delhi: Publications Division Government of India, 1999.

Garcia, Cheryl Crozier. "Brothers from Different Mothers—Confucius, Benedict, and Francis: The Historical Search for Humane Leadership." *Journal of Human Resource and Sustainability Studies* 1 (2013) 34–42.

Gelfert, Alex. "Hume on Curiosity." *British Journal for the History of Philosophy* 21.4 (2013) 711–32.

George, Robert P., ed. *Natural Law and Moral Inquiry*. Washington, DC: Georgetown University Press, 1998.

Gilio-Whitaker, Dina. *As Long as Grass Grows: The Indigenous Fight for Environmental Justice, from Colonization to Standing Rock*. Boston: Beacon, 2019.

Goetz, Jennifer L., and Emiliana Simon-Thomas. "The Landscape of Compassion: Definitions and Scientific Approaches." In *The Oxford Handbook of Compassion Science*, edited by Emma M. Seppälä et al., 3–15. Oxford: Oxford University Press, 2017.

Goldenberg, Suzanne. "Texas Congressman Cites Noah's Ark as Evidence against Climate Change." *Mother Jones*, April 12, 2013. http://www.motherjones.com/environment/2013/04/texas-congressman-cites-noahs-ark-evidence-against-climate-change.

Goodell, Jeff. *The Water Will Come: Rising Seas, Sinking Cities, and the Remaking of the Civilized World*. New York: Back Bay, 2018.

Goodenough, Ursula. "Is the Good Book a Good Guide in the Climate Change Debate?" *NPR*, November 18, 2010. http://www.npr.org/blogs/13.7/2010/11/18/131412508/is-the-good-book-a-good-guide-in-the-climate-change-debate.

Grisez, Germain. "The First Principle of Practical Reason: A Commentary on the *Summa Theologiae*." *Natural Law Forum* 10.1 (1965) 168–201.

———. "Natural Law, God, Religion, and Human Fulfillment." *American Journal of Jurisprudence* 46.1 (2001) 3–36.

Groody, Daniel G., and Gustavo A. Gutierrez. *The Preferential Option for the Poor beyond Theology*. Notre Dame: University of Notre Dame Press, 2013.

Grossman, Jonathan H. "The Absent Jew in Dickens: Narrators in *Oliver Twist*, *Our Mutual Friend*, and *A Christmas Carol*." *Dickens Studies Annual* 24 (1996) 37–57.

Gutiérrez, Gustavo. *A Theology of Liberation: History, Politics, and Salvation*. Rev. ed. Translated by Caridad Inda and John Eagleson. Maryknoll, NY: Orbis, 1988.

Hägglund, Martin. *This Life: Why Mortality Makes Us Free*. London: Profile, 2019.

Haight, Roger. *Faith and Evolution: A Grace-Filled Naturalism*. Maryknoll, NY: Orbis, 2019.

Hanh, Thich Nhat. *Living Buddha, Living Christ*. London: Rider, 1995.

Hannah-Jones, Nikole. "It Is Time for Reparations." *New York Times Magazine*, June 24, 2020. https://www.nytimes.com/interactive/2020/06/24/magazine/reparations-slavery.html.

Harris, Daniel I. "Compassion and Affirmation in Nietzsche." *Journal of Nietzsche Studies* 48.1 (2017) 17–28.

Harris, Sam. "An Atheist Manifesto." 2005. https://samharris.org/an-atheist-manifesto/.

———. *The End of Faith*. New York: Norton, 2005.

Harrison, Peter. "Curiosity, Forbidden Knowledge, and the Reformation of Natural Philosophy in Early Modern England." *Isis* 92.2 (2001) 265–90.

Hegel, Georg Wilhelm Friedrich. *Phenomenology of Spirit*. Oxford: Oxford University Press, 1977.

Heller, Erich. "Faust's Damnation: The Morality of Knowledge." *Chicago Review* 15.4 (1962) 1–26.

Herrmann, Andrew F. "Kierkegaard and Dialogue: The Communication of Capability." *Communication Theory* 18.1 (2008) 71–92. https://doi.org/10.1111/j.1468-2885.2007.00314.x.

Heschel, Abraham. *God in Search of Man*. New York: Farrar, Straus & Giroux, 1983.

———. "The Meaning of Observance." In *Understanding Jewish Theology*, edited by Jacob Neusner, 93–103. Binghamton, NY: Binghamton University Press, 2001.

Hidden, David L. W., III. "The Alleged Feudalism of Anselm's *Cur Deus Homo* and the Benedictine Concepts of Obedience, Honor, and Order." *Nova et Vetera*, English ed., 9.4 (2011) 1055–87.

Himes, Kenneth R., et al., eds. *Modern Catholic Social Teaching: Commentaries and Interpretations*. 2nd ed. Washington, DC: Georgetown University Press, 2018.

Hitchens, Christopher. *God Is Not Great*. New York: Twelve, 2007.

hooks, bell, and Cornel West. *Breaking Bread*. New York: Routledge, 2016.

Hopkins, Gerard Manley. "My Prayers Must Meet a Brazen Heaven." In *Gerard Manley Hopkins, Poetry and Prose*, 17. London: Orion, 2002.

Humanists International. "The Right to Apostasy in the World." https://humanists.international/get-involved/resources/the-right-to-apostasy-in-the-world/.

Humanists UK. "Non-Religious Continue to Face Severe Persecution in 70 Countries—New Report." *Politics*, November 13, 2019. https://www.politics.co.uk/opinion-former/press-release/2019/11/13/non-religious-continue-to-face-severe-persecution-in-70-countries-new-report/.

Hume, David. *Dialogues Concerning Natural Religion*. In *The Philosophical Works of David Hume*, 2:419–550. Edinburgh: Adam Black and William Tait, 1826.

———. *An Enquiry Concerning the Principles of Morals*. Indianapolis: Hackett, 1983.

———. *The Natural History of Religion*. London: A. and H. Bradlaugh Bonner, 1889. https://oll.libertyfund.org/titles/340#Hume.

———. *A Treatise of Human Nature*. Oxford: Oxford University Press, 1978.

Ifergan, Pini. *Hegel's Discovery of the Philosophy of Spirit*. New York: Palgrave MacMillan, 2014.

Ignatieff, Michael. *The Ordinary Virtues: Moral Order in a Divided World*. Cambridge: Harvard University Press, 2017.

Ignatius Loyola. *The Spiritual Exercises and Selected Works*. Translated by George E. Ganss. Mahwah, NJ: Paulist, 1991.

"Impacts of COVID-19 Disproportionately Affect Poor and Vulnerable: UN Chief." *UN News*, June 30, 2020. https://news.un.org/en/story/2020/06/1067502.

Islamic Relief Worldwide. "Muslims Must Take Action on Climate Crisis to Preserve Holy Pilgrimage." https://www.islamic-relief.org/muslims-must-take-action-on-climate-crisis-to-preserve-holy-pilgrimage/.

Ivereigh, Austen. *Wounded Shepherd: Pope Francis and His Struggle to Convert the Catholic Church*. New York: Picador, 2020.

Jaspers, Karl. *Origin and Goal of History*. London: Routledge, 2014.

Jenkins, Jack. "'Nones' Now as Big as Evangelicals, Catholics in the US." *Religion News Service*, March 21, 2019. https://religionnews.com/2019/03/21/nones-now-as-big-as-evangelicals-catholics-in-the-us/.

Jenkins, Philip. *The Lost History of Christianity: The Thousand-Year Golden Age of the Church in the Middle East, Africa, and Asia—And How It Died*. New York: Harper, 2009.

Johnson-Laird, P. N., and Keith Oatley. "Emotions, Music, and Literature." In *Handbook of Emotions*, edited by Michael Lewis et al., 102–13. 3rd ed. New York: Guilford Press, 2008.

Jones, William R. *Is God a White Racist?* Boston: Beacon, 1998.

Judah, Ben. *This Is London: Life and Death in the World City*. London: Picador, 2016.

Kamali, Mohammad Hashim. *The Middle Path of Moderation in Islam: The Qur'anic Principle of Wasatiyyah*. Oxford: Oxford University Press, 2015.

Kant, Immanuel. *The Critique of Practical Reason*. Translated by Thomas K. Abbott. London: Longmans, 1889.

———. *Critique of Pure Reason*. Translated by Norman Kemp Smith. New York: St. Martin's, 1965.

———. *Religion within the Limits of Reason Alone*. Translated by T. H. Greene and H. H. Hudson. New York: Harper Torchbooks, 1960.

———. "What Is Enlightenment?" In *Kant: Political Writings*, edited by H. S. Reiss, translated by H. B. Nisbett, 54–60. Cambridge: Cambridge University Press, 1991.

Kardong, Terrence G. *The Life of St. Benedict by Gregory the Great: Translation and Commentary*. Collegeville, MN: Liturgical, 2009.

Kenny, Anthony. *The Unknown God*. London: Continuum, 2004.

Kenny, Neil. *The Uses of Curiosity in Early Modern France and Germany*. Oxford: Oxford University Press, 2004.

Kierkegaard, Soren. *Fear and Trembling*. Translated by Howard and Edna Hong. Princeton, NJ: Princeton University Press, 1983.

King, Jason, and Julie Hanlon Rubio, eds. *Sex, Love, and Families: Catholic Perspectives*. Collegeville, MN: Liturgical, 2020.

King, Martin Luther, Jr. "Letter from Birmingham Jail." In *Why We Can't Wait*, 64–84. New York: Penguin/Signet Classic, 2000.

———. *Strength to Love*. Boston: Beacon, 1981. Ebook.

Knitter, Paul F. "Inter-Religious Dialogue and Social Action." In *The Wiley-Blackwell Companion to Inter-Religious Dialogue*, edited by Catherine Cornille, 133–48. Malden, MA: John Wiley, 2013.

Kogan, Michael S. *Opening the Covenant: A Jewish Theology of Christianity*. Oxford: Oxford University Press, 2008.

Kojève, Alexandre. *Introduction to the Study of Hegel*. New York: Basic, 1969.

Kolbert, Elisabeth. *The Sixth Extinction: An Unnatural History*. New York: Picador, 2015.

Korn, Eugene B., and John T. Pawlikowski, eds. *Two Faiths, One Covenant? Jewish and Christian Identity in the Presence of the Other*. Lanham, MD: Rowman & Littlefield, 2005.

Kovacs, George. "Atheism and the Ultimate Thou." *International Journal of the Philosophy of Religion* 5.1 (1974) 1–15.

Kraynak, Robert P. *Christian Faith and Modern Democracy*. Notre Dame, IN: University of Notre Dame Press, 2001.

Kroemer, James. "Vanquish the Haughty and Spare the Subjected: A Study of Bernard of Clairvaux's Position on Muslims and Jews." *Medieval Encounters* 18.1 (2012) 55–92.

Kugel, James L. *How to Read the Bible: A Guide to Scripture Then and Now*. New York: Free Press, 2007.

Kung, Hans, and Karl-Josef Kuschel, eds. *A Global Ethic: Declaration of the Parliament of the World's Religions*. Translated by John Bowden. London: SCM, 1993.

Kurtz, Paul. *The Courage to Become: The Virtues of Humanism*. Westport, CT: Praeger, 1997.

Lamb, Christina. *Our Bodies, Their Battlefield: What War Does to Women*. London: HarperCollins, 2020.

Lanchester, John. *The Wall: A Novel*. New York: Norton, 2019.

Lane, Dermot A. *Stepping Stones to Other Religions: A Christian Theology of Inter-Religious Dialogue*. Dublin: Veritas, 2011.

———. *Theology and Ecology in Dialogue: The Wisdom of Laudato Si'*. Dublin: Messenger, 2020.

Langer, Lawrence L. *Using and Abusing the Holocaust*. Bloomington: Indiana University Press, 2006.

Latinovic, Vladimir, et al., eds. *Catholicism Engaging Other Faiths: Vatican II and Its Impact*. London: Palgrave Macmillan, 2018.

Laytner, Anson. *Arguing with God: A Jewish Tradition*. Northvale: Jason Aronson, 1990.

Lear, Jonathan. *Radical Hope: Ethics in the Face of Cultural Devastation*. Cambridge: Harvard University Press, 2008.

Lennon, J. Michael. *Norman Mailer: A Double Life*. New York: Simon & Schuster, 2014.

Levi, Primo. *Survival in Auschwitz*. Translated by Stuart Woolf. New York: Touchstone, 1996.

Levinas, Emmanuel. *Ethics and Infinity: Conversations with Philippe Nemo*. Translated by Richard A. Cohen. Pittsburgh: Duquesne University Press, 2009.

Li, Chenyang. *The Confucian Philosophy of Harmony*. Abingdon, Oxfordshire: Routledge, 2014.

Liljeblad, Jonathan, and Bas Verschuuren, eds. *Indigenous Perspectives on Sacred Natural Sites: Culture, Governance and Conservation*. Abingdon, Oxfordshire: Routledge, 2019.

Lipka, Michael. "10 Facts about Atheists." *Pew Research Center*, December 6, 2019. https://www.pewresearch.org/fact-tank/2019/12/06/10-facts-about-atheists/.

Locke, John. "Letter Concerning Toleration." In *John Locke: Political Writings*, 390–435. Indianapolis, IN: Hackett, 2003.

Lundbom, Jack, et al., eds. *The Book of Jeremiah: Composition, Reception, Interpretation*. Leiden: Brill, 2018.

Luther, Martin. *Large and Small Catechism*. Translated by F. Bente and W. H. T. Dau. CreateSpace, 2014.

Lynch, Colum. "Can Pope Francis Get the Catholic Church's Mind off of Sex?" *Foreign Policy*, May 11, 2016. https://foreignpolicy.com/2015/05/11/can-pope-francis-get-the-catholic-churchs-mind-off-of-sex/.

MacIntyre, Alasdair. *After Virtue*. 2nd ed. Notre Dame, IN: Notre Dame University Press, 2003.

———. *Whose Justice? Which Rationality?* London: Duckworth, 1988.

Mahlamäki, Tiina. "Religion and Atheism from a Gender Perspective." *Approaching Religion* 2.1 (2012) 58–65.

Mailer, Norman. *The Naked and the Dead*. London: Penguin, 2018.

Maimonides. *The Book of Knowledge: From the Mishneh Torah of Maimonides*. Translated by H. M. Russell and Rabbi J. Weinberg. Brooklyn, NY: Ktav, 1983.

Mallet, Victor. *River of Life, River of Death: The Ganges and India's Future*. Oxford: Oxford University Press, 2017.

Manson, Neil C. "Epistemic Restraint and the Vice of Curiosity." *Philosophy* 87.340 (2012) 239–59.

Mardock, James D. "Of Daughters and Ducats: Our Mutual Friend and Dickens's Anti-Shylock." In *Borrowers and Lenders: The Journal of Shakespeare and Appropriation* 1.2 (2005) n.p. http://www.borrowers.uga.edu/781449/displayne.

Margolin, Ron. "The Implicit Secularism of Martin Buber's Thought." *Israel Studies* 13.3 (2008) 64–88.

Marsden, Lee. "The Golden Rule: Interfaith Peacemaking and the Charter for Compassion." *The Review of Faith & International Affairs* 16.3 (2018) 61–75.

Martín, Inés San. "Indigenous Leader Says 'Brother Francis' Risking His Life for the Amazon." *Crux*, September 17, 2019. https://cruxnow.com/amazon-synod/2019/09/indigenous-leader-says-brother-francis-risking-his-life-for-the-amazon/.

Martin, Michael. *Atheism: A Philosophical Justification*. Philadelphia: Temple University Press, 1990.

Matarasso, Pauline, trans. and ed. *The Cistercian World: Monastic Writings of the Twelfth Century*. London: Penguin, 1993.

McCarthy, Cormac. *The Road*. New York: Vintage, 2006.

McCarthy, Justin. "U.S. Confidence in Organized Religion Remains Low." *Gallup*, July 8, 2019. https://news.gallup.com/poll/259964/confidence-organized-religion-remains-low.aspx?g_source=link_NEWSV9&g_medium=NEWSFEED&g_campaign=item_&g_content=U.S.%2520Confidence%2520in%2520Organized%2520Religion%2520Remains%2520Low.

McClendon, John. *Black Christology and the Quest for Authenticity*. Lanham, MD: Rowman & Littlefield, 2019.

———. *Philosophy of Religion and the African American Experience: Conversations with My Christian Friends*. Leiden, NL: Brill, 2017.

McKibben, Bill. "A Very Grim Forecast." *New York Review of Books*, November 22, 2018. https://www.nybooks.com/articles/2018/11/22/global-warming-very-grim-forecast/.

McKim, Robert, ed. *Laudato Si' and the Environment: Pope Francis' Green Encyclical*. Abingdon, Oxon: Routledge, 2020.

Mehta, Hemant. "Why Do Seven States' Constitutions Still Say Atheists Can't Hold Public Office?" *Friendly Atheist*, December 7, 2014. https://friendlyatheist.patheos.com/2014/12/07/seven-states-constitutions-say-atheists-cant-hold-public-office-but-why-not-toss-out-those-unenforceable-laws/.

Melville, Herman. *Moby-Dick*. Herfordshire: Wordsworth, 2002.

Mencher, Rabbi Edythe Held. "Everything in Moderation . . . Except Moderation." *ReformJudaism.org*. https://reformjudaism.org/everything-moderationexcept-moderation.

Midgley, Mary. *Evolution as a Religion*. London: Routledge, 2002.

———. *The Myths We Live By*. New York: Routledge, 2011.

Miller, Christian. "Honesty." In *Moral Psychology*, vol. 5, *Virtue and Character*, edited by Walter Sinnott-Armstrong and Christian Miller, 237–73. Cambridge, MA: MIT Press, 2017.

Miller, Vincent J., ed. *The Theological and Ecological Vision of Laudato Si': Everything Is Connected*. London: Bloomsbury, 2017.

Milton, John. *Paradise Lost*. Edited by John Leonard. London: Penguin, 2003.

———. *Paradise Lost*. The John Milton Reading Room. Edited by Thomas H. Luxon. https://milton.host.dartmouth.edu/reading_room/pl/note/text.shtml.

Moltmann, Jürgen. *The Crucified God*. Translated by R. A. Wilson and John Bowden. Minneapolis: Fortress, 2015 .

Montaigne. *The Complete Essays of Montaigne*. Translated by Donald M. Frame. Stanford: Stanford University Press, 2016.

Mooallem, Jon. "'We Have Fires Everywhere': Escaping California's Deadliest Blaze." *New York Times Magazine*, July 31, 2018. https://www.nytimes.com/interactive/2019/07/31/magazine/paradise-camp-fire-california.html.

Moon, Jordona W., et al. "Religious People Are Trusted because They Are Viewed as Slow Life-History Strategists." *Psychological Science* 29.6 (2018) 947–60. doi:10.1177/0956797617753606.

More, Thomas. "Preface to the Vintage Spiritual Classics Edition." In *The Rule of St. Benedict*, by Benedict, edited by Timothy Fry, xv–xxv. New York: Vintage, 1998.

Morrison, John. *Cornel West*. Philadelphia: Chelsea, 2004.

Myers, Ched. *Binding the Strong Man: A Political Reading of Mark's Story of Jesus*. Anniversary ed. Maryknoll: Orbis, 2008.

Nathanson, Stephen. *An Eye for an Eye: The Immorality of Punishing by Death*. 2nd ed. Lanham, MD: Rowman & Littlefield, 2001.

Nayder, Lillian. *The Other Dickens: A Life of Catherine Hogarth*. Ithaca, NY: Cornell University Press, 2012.

Neusner, Jacob. *A Rabbi Talks with Jesus*. Rev. ed. Montreal: McGill-Queen's University Press, 2000.

Nielsen, Kai. *Atheism and Philosophy*. New York: Prometheus, 1985.

———. "An Examination of the Thomistic Theory of Natural Moral Law." *Natural Law Forum*, paper 39, 1959. http://scholarship.law.nd.edu/nd_naturallaw_forum/39.

Nietzsche, Friedrich. *The Anti-Christ*. In *The Twilight of the Idols and the Anti-Christ: or How to Philosophize with a Hammer*, translated by R. J. Hollingdale, 123–99. London: Penguin, 1990.

———. *Beyond Good and Evil*. Translated by Helen Zimmern. New York: MacMillan, 1907.

———. *The Gay Science*. Translated by Josefine Nauckhoff. Cambridge: Cambridge University Press, 2001.

———. *Thus Spoke Zarathustra: A Book for None and All*. Translated by Walter Kaufmann. New York: Penguin, 1978.

Nikulin, Dmitriĭ Vladimirovich. *On Dialogue*. Lanham, MD: Rowman & Littlefield, 2006.

Norenzayan, Ara. *Big Gods: How Religion Transformed Cooperation and Conflict*. Princeton: Princeton University Press, 2012.

"*Nostra Aetate*. Declaration on the Relation of the Church to Non-Christian Religions." October 28, 1965. https://www.vatican.va/archive/hist_councils/ii_vatican_council/documents/vat-ii_decl_19651028_nostra-aetate_en.html.

Nouwen, Henri J. M., et al. *Compassion: A Reflection on the Christian Life*. Rev. ed. London: Darton, Longman & Todd, 2016.

Nussbaum, Martha. *Upheavals of Thought: The Intelligence of Emotions*. Cambridge: Cambridge University Press, 2001.

O'Donovan, Joan Lockwood. "Rights, Law, and Political Community: A Theological and Historical Perspective." *Transformation* 20.1 (2003) 30–38.

O'Donovan, Oliver, and Joan Lockwood O'Donovan. *Bonds of Imperfection: Christian Politics, Past and Present*. Grand Rapids: Eerdmans, 2003.

O'Hara, Dennis, et al., eds. *Integral Ecology for a More Sustainable World: Dialogues with Laudato Si'*. Lexington: Lexington Books, 2019.

O'Neill, Kate. "The World Is Drowning in Rubbish." *Chatham House*, December 5, 2019. https://www.chathamhouse.org/publications/twt/world-drowning-rubbish.

Oppy, Graham. "Ontological Arguments." *Stanford Encyclopedia of Philosophy*, 2019. http://plato.stanford.edu/entries/ontological-arguments/.

Orange, Tommy. *There There*. New York: Vintage, 2018.

Orphan, Kenn. "As the World Burns, the Powerful Go on Holiday." *Counterpunch*, January 8, 2020. https://www.counterpunch.org/2020/01/08/as-the-world-burns-the-powerful-go-on-holiday/.

Otto, Rudolf. *The Idea of the Holy*. Oxford: Oxford University Press, 1923.

Overall, Christine. "Feminism and Atheism." In *The Cambridge Companion to Atheism*, edited by Michael Martin, 233–49. New York: Cambridge University Press, 2007.

Owen, Wilfred. "Dulce et Decorum Est." Poetry Foundation, https://www.poetryfoundation.org/poems/46560/dulce-et-decorum-est.

Ozment, Katherine. *Grace without God: The Search for Meaning, Purpose, and Belonging in a Secular Age*. New York: Harper Perennial, 2017.

Pappin, Gladden J. "Directing Philosophy: Aquinas, Studiousness, and Modern Curiosity." *Review* of *Metaphysics* 68.2 (2014) 313–46.

Pardue, Stephen T. *The Mind of Christ: Humility and the Intellect in Early Christian Theology*. London: Bloomsbury, 2013.

Patterson, William R. "The Problem of Evil and Liberal Theologies." *Essays in the Philosophy of Humanism* 24.2 (2016) 187–205. doi:10.1558/eph.31723.

Paul VI, Pope. *Dei Verbum*. November 18, 1965. https://www.vatican.va/archive/hist_councils/ii_vatican_council/documents/vat-ii_const_19651118_dei-verbum_en.html.

Penchansky, David. *Twilight of the Gods: Polytheism in the Hebrew Bible*. Louisville: Westminster John Knox, 2005.

Pennock, Robert T. *An Instinct for Truth: Curiosity and the Moral Character of Science*. Boston: MIT Press, 2019.

Peri, Alexis. *The War Within: Diaries from the Siege of Leningrad*. Cambridge: Harvard University Press, 2017.

Perry, Michael J. *The Idea of Human Rights: Four Inquiries*. New York: Oxford University Press, 1998.

Pew Research Center. "2. Young Adults around the World Are Less Religious by Several Measures." June 13, 2018. https://www.pewforum.org/2018/06/13/young-adults-around-the-world-are-less-religious-by-several-measures/.

———. "America's Changing Religious Landscape." May 15, 2015. https://www.pewforum.org/2015/05/12/americas-changing-religious-landscape/.

———. "Chapter 3: Demographic Profiles of Religious Groups." May 12, 2015. https://www.pewforum.org/2015/05/12/chapter-3-demographic-profiles-of-religious-groups/.

———. "The Gender Gap in Religion around the World." March 22, 2016. https://www.pewforum.org/2016/03/22/the-gender-gap-in-religion-around-the-world/.

———. "Generational Cohort." N.d. https://www.pewforum.org/religious-landscape-study/generational-cohort/.

Phan, Peter C. *Asian Christianities: History, Theology, Practice*. Maryknoll, NY: Orbis, 2018.

———. *Being Religious Interreligiously*. Maryknoll, NY: Orbis, 2004.

———. *The Joy of Religious Pluralism*. Maryknoll, NY: Orbis, 2017.

Phillips, Jonathan. "St Bernard of Clairvaux, the Low Countries and the Lisbon Letter of the Second Crusade." *The Journal of Ecclesiastical History* 48.3 (1997) 485–97.

Pinn, Anthony. *The End of God-Talk: An African American Humanist Theology.* Oxford: Oxford University Press, 2011.

———. *Writing God's Obituary: How a Good Methodist Became a Better Atheist.* New York: Prometheus, 2014.

Plantinga, Alvin. *God, Freedom, and Evil.* Grand Rapids: Eerdmans, 1977.

Plato. *Apology.* In *Plato in Twelve Volumes*, vol. 1, translated by Harold North Fowler, introduction by W. R. M. Lamb. Cambridge, MA: Harvard University Press, 1966. Electronic text with Greek original at: http://www.perseus.tufts.edu/hopper/text?doc=urn:cts:greekLit:tlg0059.tlg001.perseus-eng1.

———. *Euthyphro.* In *Plato in Twelve Volumes*, vol. 1. Cambridge, MA: Harvard University Press, 1966. Electronic text with Greek original at: http://www.perseus.tufts.edu/hopper/text?doc=Perseus%3Atext%3A1999.01.0170%3Atext%3DEuthyph.%3Asection%3D10a.

Pontes, Felicio, Jr. "Lessons for COP 26 from the Amazon Synod: Respect for Indigenous People Critical to Rainforest Preservation." *National Catholic Reporter*, December 26, 2019. https://www.ncronline.org/news/earthbeat/lessons-cop-26-amazon-synod.

Pontifical Council for Inter-Religious Dialogue. "Dialogue and Proclamation: Reflection and Orientations on Interreligious Dialogue and the Proclamation of the Gospel of Jesus Christ." http://www.vatican.va/roman_curia/pontifical_councils/interelg/documents/rc_pc_interelg_doc_19051991_dialogue-and-proclamatio_en.html.

Pope, Stephen L., and Charles Hefling, eds. *Sic et Non: Encountering Dominus Iesus.* Maryknoll, NY: Orbis, 2002.

"Pope Francis Apologizes to Indigenous Peoples for 'Grave Sins' of Colonialism." *Indian Country Today*, July 10, 2015. https://newsmaven.io/indiancountrytoday/archive/pope-francis-apologizes-to-indigenous-peoples-for-grave-sins-of-colonialism-tlGAXDXgwkCkvmn10DjT3Q.

Powell, Michael. *Canyon Dreams: A Basketball Season on the Navajo Nation.* New York: Blue Rider, 2019.

Pratt, Douglas. *The Church and Other Faiths: The World Council of Churches, the Vatican, and Interreligious Dialogue.* Bern: Peter Lang, 2010.

Putnam, Hilary. "Levinas and Judaism." In *The Cambridge Companion to Emmanuel Levinas*, edited by Simon Critchley and Robert Bernasconi, 33–62. Cambridge: Cambridge University Press, 2002.

Race, Alan, and Knitter, Paul, eds. *Perry Schmidt-Leukel's Fractal Interpretation of Religious Diversity.* Maryknoll, NY: Orbis, 2019.

Ralph, Laurence. *The Torture Letters: Reckoning with Police Violence.* Chicago: University of Chicago Press, 2020.

Raphael, Melissa. *The Female Face of God in Auschwitz: A Jewish Feminist Theology of the Holocaust.* London: Routledge, 2003.

Rawls, John. *Political Liberalism.* New York: Columbia University Press, 2003.

———. *A Theory of Justice.* Cambridge, MA: Harvard, 1971.

Ray, Darby Kathleen. "Anselm of Canterbury." In *Empire and the Christian Tradition: New Readings of Classical Theologians*, edited by Kwok Pui-lan et al., 123–38. Minneapolis: Fortress, 2007.

Recinella, Dale. *The Biblical Truth about America's Death Penalty.* Lebanon, NH: Northeastern University Press, 2004.

Regan, Ethna. *Theology and the Boundary Discourse of Human Rights.* Washington, DC: Georgetown University Press, 2010.

Rich, Nathaniel. *Losing Earth: A Recent History.* New York: Farrar, Straus & Giroux, 2019.

Richards, Michael. "Why the Age of Sexual Consent Continues to Be a Worldwide Challenge." *The Conversation*, April 4, 2018. https://theconversation.com/why-the-age-of-sexual-consent-continues-to-be-a-worldwide-challenge-94334.

Rieger, Joerg. *Christ and Empire: From Paul to Postcolonial Times.* Minneapolis: Fortress, 2007.

Right Wing Watch Staff. "The 'Green Dragon' Slayers: How the Religious Right and the Corporate Right Are Joining Forces to Fight Environmental Protection." *People for the American Way*, April 2011. http://www.pfaw.org/rww-in-focus/the-green-dragon-slayers-how-the-religious-right-and-the-corporate-right-are-joining-fo.

Roberts, Robert C., and Ryan West. "The Virtue of Honesty: A Conceptual Exploration." In *Integrity, Honesty, and Truth Seeking*, edited by Christian B. Miller and Ryan West, 97–126. Oxford: Oxford University Press, 2020.

Robinson, Kim Stanley. *New York 2140: A Novel.* New York: Orbit, 2018.

Robson, David. "The Underground Railroad to Save Atheists." *The Atlantic*, January 18, 2018. https://www.theatlantic.com/international/archive/2018/01/the-underground-railroad-to-save-atheists/550229/.

Roewe, Brian. "Five Years Ago, Pope Francis Asked Us to Care for Earth. Have We Listened?" *National Catholic Reporter*, May 24, 2020. https://www.ncronline.org/news/earthbeat/five-years-ago-pope-francis-asked-us-care-earth-have-we-listened.

Rorty, Richard. "Pragmatism as Anti-Authoritarianism." *Revue Internationale de Philosophie* 53.7 (1999) 7–20.

Rorty, Richard, and Gianni Vattimo. *The Future of Religion.* Edited by Santiago Zabalo. New York: Columbia University Press, 2005.

Rowlatt, Justin. "Dalai Lama: 'Compassion and Humanity Important during Coronavirus Pandemic.'" *BBC*, June 13, 2020. https://www.bbc.com/news/av/world-asia-53017668/dalai-lama-compassion-and-humanity-important-during-coronavirus-pandemic.

Royce, Josiah. *The Philosophy of Loyalty.* New York: MacMillan, 1916.

———. *The Problem of Christianity.* Vol. 2, *The Real World and the Christian Ideas.* New York: MacMillan, 1913.

Rush, Elizabeth. *Rising: Dispatches from the New American Shore.* Minneapolis: Milkweed, 2019.

Ryrie, Alec. *Unbelievers: An Emotional History of Doubt.* London: William Collins, 2019.

Sadler, Gregory. "Anselm and the Seven Levels of Humility." April 24, 2011. https://gbsadler.blogspot.com/2011/04/anselm-on-seven-levels-of-humility.html.

———. "Anselm of Canterbury 1033–1109." *Internet Encyclopedia of Philosophy.* http://www.iep.utm.edu/anselm/.

———. "More on Anselm and Humility." May 1, 2011. http://gbsadler.blogspot.ie/2011/05/more-on-anselm-and-humility.html.

———. "The Two Guardians of the Mountain of Humility." May 29, 2011. http://gbsadler.blogspot.ie/2011/06/two-guardians-of-mountain-of-humility.html.

Safina, Carl. *Becoming Wild: How Animal Cultures Raise Families, Create Beauty, and Achieve Peace*. New York: Henry Holt, 2020.

Salenson, Christian. *Christian de Cherge: A Theology of Hope*. Trappist, Kentucky: Cistercian, 2012.

Sallinger, J. D. *The Catcher in the Rye*. Toronto: Bantam, 1986.

Sarukkai, Sundar. "Science and the Ethics of Curiosity." *Current Science* 97.6 (2009) 756–67.

Scales, Len. "Central and Late Medieval Europe." In *The Oxford Handbook of Genocide Studies*, edited by Donald Bloxham and A. Dirk Moses, 280–303. Oxford: Oxford University Press, 2013.

Schneider, Laurel. *Beyond Monotheism: A Theology of Multiplicity*. London: Routledge, 2008.

Shanks, Andrew. *Faith in Honesty: The Essential Nature of Theology*. New York: Routledge, 2016.

Shaw, George Bernard. "Introduction to *Great Expectations*." In *Great Expectations*, by Charles Dickens, edited by Edgar Rosenberg, 631–41. New York: Norton, 1999.

Sherkat, Darren. *Changing Faith: The Dynamics and Consequences of American's Shifting Religious Identities*. New York: New York University Press, 2014.

Sieff, Kevin. "The World Is Drowning in Ever-Growing Mounds of Garbage." *The Washington Post*, November 21, 2017. https://www.washingtonpost.com/world/africa/the-world-is-drowning-in-ever-growing-mounds-of-garbage/2017/11/21/cf22e4bd-17a4-473c-89f8-873d48f968cd_story.html.

Singer, Peter. *Rethinking Life and Death*. New York: St. Martin's, 1994.

Skinner, Jordan. "Thought Is the Courage of Hopelessness: An Interview with Philosopher Giorgio Agamben." *Verso*, June 17, 2014. https://www.versobooks.com/blogs/1612-thought-is-the-courage-of-hopelessness-an-interview-with-philosopher-giorgio-agamben.

Smith, Adam. *The Theory of Moral Sentiments*. New York: Kelley, 1966.

Smith, Gary. *Radical Compassion: Finding Christ in the Heart of the Poor*. Chicago: Loyola, 2006.

Sobrino, Jon. *No Salvation Outside the Poor: Prophetic-Utopian Essays*. Maryknoll, NY: Orbis, 2008.

———. *Where Is God? Earthquake, Terrorism, Barbarity, and Hope*. Translated by Margaret D. Wilde. Maryknoll, NY: Orbis, 2004.

Spong, John Shelby. *A New Christianity for a New World*. New York: HarperCollins, 2001.

———. *The Sins of Scripture*. New York: HarperOne, 2006.

———. *Why Christianity Must Change or Die*. New York: HarperCollins, 1998.

Squires, Nick. "Conservative Catholics Accuse Pope Francis of Being Idolatrous over Indigenous Amazon Symbols." *The Independent*, November 12, 2019. https://www.telegraph.co.uk/news/2019/11/12/conservative-catholics-accuse-pope-francis-idolatrous-indigenous/.

Stedman, Chris. *Faitheist: How an Atheist Found Common Ground with the Religious*. Boston: Beacon, 2013.

Steffen, Lloyd. *Ethics and Experience*. Lanham, MD: Rowman & Littlefield, 2012.

Steinsaltz, Rabbi Adin. "Curious Jews." *The Times of Israel*, May 18, 2015. https://blogs.timesofisrael.com/curious-jews/.

Stiegman, Emero. "Bernard of Clairvaux, William of St. Thierry, the Victorines." In *The Medieval Theologians*, edited by G. R. Evans, 129–55. Oxford: Blackwell, 2001.

Sugirtharajah, R. S. *Jesus in Asia*. Cambridge: Harvard University Press, 2018.

Sweetser, Thomas P. *Can Francis Change the Church? How American Catholics Are Responding to His Leadership.* New York: Crossroads, 2019.

Swidler, Leonard. *The Age of Global Dialogue*. Eugene, OR: Pickwick, 2016.

———. "Deep-Dialogue/Critical-Thinking/Competitive-Cooperation: The Most Authentic Human Way to Be and Act." *Journal of Ecumenical Studies* 47.2 (2012) 143–51.

———. "The Dialogue Decalogue." *Journal of Ecumenical Studies* 15.3 (1978) 413–14.

———. "The Dialogue Decalogue: Ground Rules for Interreligious Dialogue." *Journal of Ecumenical Studies* 20.1 (1983) 1–4.

Teahan, Madeleine. "'There Is No Middle Way between Atheism and Catholicism,' Says Harvard Professor Who Has Converted." *Catholic Herald*, October 28, 2016. https://catholicherald.co.uk/news/2016/10/28/there-is-no-middle-way-between-atheism-and-catholicism-says-harvard-professor-who-is-converting/.

Teirstein, Zoya. "The Pope Might Make Destroying the Earth a Sin. Will Catholics Listen?" *Mother Jones*, November 26, 2019. https://www.motherjones.com/environment/2019/11/the-pope-might-make-destroying-the-earth-a-sin-will-catholics-listen/.

Telushkin, Joseph. *Hillel: If Not Now, When?* New York: Schocken, 2010.

Thatamanil, John. *Circling the Elephant: A Comparative Theology of Religions.* New York: Fordham University Press, 2020.

Thomas, R. S. *Selected Poems*. London, Penguin, 2004.

Tillich, Paul. *The Courage to Be*. 2nd ed. New Haven, CT: Yale University Press, 2000.

Tinker, George E. "Tink." *American Indian Liberation: A Theology of Sovereignty.* Maryknoll, NY: Orbis, 2008.

Tolkien, J. R. R. *The Lord of the Rings: The Two Towers*. London: HarperCollins, 2012.

Tolstoy, Leo. *A Confession*. Translated by David Patterson. New York: Norton, 1984.

United Nations. "United Nations Declaration on the Rights of Indigenous Peoples." September 13, 2007. https://www.un.org/development/desa/indigenouspeoples/wp-content/uploads/sites/19/2018/11/UNDRIP_E_web.pdf.

United States Conference of Catholic Bishops. "Encountering Christ in Harmony: A Pastoral Response to Our Asian and Pacific Island Brothers and Sisters." Washington, DC, 2018. http://www.usccb.org/issues-and-action/cultural-diversity/asian-pacific-islander/upload/asian-and-pacific-island-pastoral-response-encountering-christ-in-harmony-2018.pdf.

Vanhoozer, Kevin J. "Scripture and Tradition." In *The Cambridge Companion to Postmodern Theology*, edited by Kevin Vanhoozer, 149–69. Cambridge: Cambridge University Press, 2009.

Veldman, Robin Globus. *The Gospel of Climate Skepticism: Why Evangelical Christians Oppose Action on Climate Change.* Oakland: University of California Press, 2019.

Vivekenanda. *Swami Vivekenanda: A Contemporary Reader.* Abingdon: Routledge, 2015.

Vonnegut, Kurt. *Slaughterhouse Five*. New York: Vintage, 1991.

Wagner, Robert, and Andrew Briggs. *Penultimate Curiosity: How Science Swims in the Slipstream of Religion.* Oxford: Oxford University Press, 2016.

Wallace-Wells, David. *The Uninhabitable Earth: Life after Warming*. New York: Penguin, 2019.

Walsh, P. G. "The Rights and Wrongs of Curiosity (Plutarch to Augustine)." *Greece & Rome* 35.1 (1988) 73–85.

Watson, Peter. *The Age of Atheists: How We Have Sought to Live Since the Death of God*. New York: Simon & Schuster, 2014.

Watts, Jonathan. "Amazonian Chief Raoni Metuktire: 'Bolsonaro Has Been the Worst for Us.'" *The Guardian*, January 2, 2020. https://www.theguardian.com/world/2020/jan/02/amazonian-chief-raoni-metuktire-bolsonaro-has-been-the-worst-for-us.

West, Cornel. "Cornel West: Truth." In *Examined Life: Excursion with Contemporary Thinkers*, edited by Astra Taylor, 1–24. New York: Free Press, 2009.

Wiesel, Elie. *And the Sea Is Never Full. Memoirs 1969—*. Translated by Marion Wiesel. New York: Knopf, 2010.

———. *Legends of Our Time*. Translated by Marion Wiesel. New York: Schocken, 1982.

———. *Wise Men and Their Tales: Portraits of Biblical, Talmudic, and Hasidic Masters*. New York: Schocken, 2005.

Wilkerson, Isabel. *Caste: The Origins of Our Discontents*. New York: Random House, 2020.

Wilson, Alan T. "Honesty as a Virtue." *Metaphilosophy* 49.3 (2018) 262–80.

Wilson, A. N. *The Mystery of Charles Dickens*. New York: HarperCollins, 2020.

Wilson, E. O. *On Human Nature*. Cambridge, MA: Harvard University Press, 2004.

Witherup, Ronald D. *The Word of God at Vatican II: Exploring Dei Verbum*. Collegeville, MN: Liturgical, 2014.

Wolterstorff, Nicholas. *Justice: Rights and Wrongs*. Princeton: Princeton University Press, 2008.

Wooden, Cindy. "Indigenous Vow to Stand with Pope Francis, with Each Other." *Crux*, October 18, 2019. https://cruxnow.com/amazon-synod/2019/10/indigenous-vow-to-stand-with-pope-francis-with-each-other/.

Wordsworth, William. "Ode [Intimations of Immortality]." In *Wordsworth's Poetry and Prose*, edited by Nicholas Halmi, 432–39. Norton Critical Editions. New York: Norton, 2014.

"The World Is Drowning in Plastic." *El Universal*, November 11, 2018. https://www.eluniversal.com.mx/english/world-plastic.

Wright, Robert. *The Evolution of God*. New York: Little Brown, 2009.

Yee, Vivian. "Yemen Aid Falls Short, Threatening Food and Health Programs." *New York Times*, June 2, 2020. https://www.nytimes.com/2020/06/02/world/middleeast/yemen-saudi-united-nations-aid.html?searchResultPosition=2.

Zuckerman, Phil. *Faith No More: Why People Reject Religion*. Oxford: Oxford University Press, 2015.

Zuckerman, Phil, and John Shook, eds. *The Oxford Handbook of Secularism*. Oxford: Oxford University Press, 2017.

Index

Lightning Source UK Ltd.
Milton Keynes UK
UKHW011433161021
392324UK00001B/48

9 781725 275294